China-Gulf Oil Cooperation Under the Belt and Road Initiative

Tingting Zhang · Dehua Wang

Editors

China-Gulf Oil Cooperation Under the Belt and Road Initiative

上海交通大學出版社
SHANGHAI JIAO TONG UNIVERSITY PRESS

Springer

Editors
Tingting Zhang
International Energy Research Center
(IERC)
Shanghai Jiao Tong University
Shanghai, China

Dehua Wang
Shanghai Municipal Center for
International Studies
Shanghai, China

Institute of Information Science
Shanghai Academy of Social Sciences
Shanghai, China

ISBN 978-981-15-9282-9   ISBN 978-981-15-9283-6   (eBook)
https://doi.org/10.1007/978-981-15-9283-6

Jointly published with Shanghai Jiao Tong University Press
The print edition is not for sale in China Mainland. Customers from China Mainland please order the print book from: Shanghai Jiao Tong University Press.

This Springer imprint is published by the registered company Springer Nature Singapore Pte Ltd.
The registered company address is: 152 Beach Road, #21-01/04 Gateway East, Singapore 189721, Singapore

Foreword

Energy security is a major strategic issue related to sustainable economic development, long-term national security and people's well-being. Energy resources, especially oil and gas resources, are strategic resources, economic resources, diplomatic resources and military resources. Facing the new situation and new challenges in the international energy market, how to promote China's energy revolution, adjust its energy development strategy, and ensure the security of China's oil and gas supply is a major issue that must be taken seriously.

At present, the world is facing a wave of the energy revolution. In the era of diversified new energy, the value potential of various energy forms, namely the capital attributes, is gradually being recognized. The pace of energy capitalization and financialization is continuously accelerating, which makes the energy security issues in China more complex and urgent. From a domestic perspective, China's resource endowment of "rich coal, poor oil, and poor gas" makes energy a strategic shortcoming and faces greater security risks: the first one is the short-term emergency risks mainly due to China's shortage of oil and gas strategic reserves; the second is the long-term supply risk that the energy import dependence is becoming more and more serious; the third is the regional balance risks, where energy production centers and load centers are far apart. From the perspective of the international crude oil situation, the certainty and uncertainty of the global crude oil situation coexist. The certainty is that the overall global oil resource volume is still increasing. The uncertainty is the increase in the probability of the sudden occurrence of uncertain events like crude oil "black swan" events, which stimulates large fluctuations in oil prices and the unpredictable change in the international crude oil market. According to relevant data, China's net imports of crude oil in 2019 exceeded the 500 million ton mark for the first time, and the external dependence of crude oil and oil products broke through 70%. Against the backdrop of a difficult balance between supply and demand in the world oil market, the increased trade friction between China and the United States, Europe and other major economies, and the increased geopolitical risks, ensuring a stable supply of crude oil is crucial to China's energy security and economic development.

The Belt and Road Initiative (BRI) is a new concept of deepening international cooperation proposed by Chinese president Xi Jinping in 2013. Energy cooperation has become an important part of China's opening up to the outside world. It is of great significance in safeguarding national security, ensuring a stable supply of energy, improving China's discourse power in the energy market, and helping China's energy companies to "go out". The Belt and Road Initiative covers important oil and gas producing countries such as Russia, Kazakhstan, Turkmenistan, Azerbaijan, Saudi Arabia, and Iran, as well as important oil and gas consuming countries such as China, India, Japan, and South Korea, whose oil and gas production and consumption occupy an important position in the world. Among them, the Gulf Cooperation Council (GCC), including Saudi Arabia, the UAE, Kuwait, Qatar, Oman, and Bahrain, is an important oil supply region along the Belt and Road. In 2019, the proven crude oil reserves in the region reached 496.29 billion barrels, accounting for 30.8% of the world's proven reserves; in 2018, the daily crude oil production in the region reached 17.726 million barrels, accounting for 23.4% of global crude oil production. Benefited from the abundant oil resources and production capacity, the GCC has shown a strong export capacity. Since 2000, China's crude oil imports from the GCC have consistently maintained around 30% of its total imports. In recent years, while some developed countries such as the United States are gradually realizing a strategic shift in energy supply from oil in the Middle East to domestic energy and energy in other countries, China, however, has continued to maintained its dependence on oil in the Gulf region, which is not only a realistic consideration of the energy demand based on its own economic development and energy demand, but also the realization of the Belt and Road version, and the satisfaction of the needs of in-depth cooperation and docking with countries in the Gulf countries.

As is known to all, the energy issue is global, strategic, and extensive. It is the focus of the international politics, economy, defense, diplomacy, and climate change games. No country can solve it alone. The Strategic Petroleum Reserve (SPR) is a long-term and arduous task serving national energy security. The SPR in China started late. Since the first national oil reserve base, Zhenhai National Oil Reserve Base, was completed and delivered in October 2006, the curtain of the national oil reserve has really opened. Up to the present, more than 10 years have passed, and nine major national oil reserve bases have been established. However, the current reserve scale and capacity are still far from the national oil reserve safety standard set by the International Energy Agency, and there is an urgent need to further improve China's oil emergency reserve system. Because only by persistently carrying out the reserve work can we achieve the Chinese proverb "When there is food in the hand, there is no panic in the heart".

In this context, in order for China and the Gulf countries to reach a new level of oil cooperation and maintain healthy development, we must also break through the existing cooperation methods and cooperation content and seek new and more stable growth points for cooperation. In recent years, the International Energy Research Center of Shanghai Jiao Tong University has been paying attention to the energy cooperation between China and the GCC countries under BRI. This book summarizes the previous research results related to this topic, sorts out the oil resources, production and consumption situation along the Belt and Road and the GCC countries, discusses the current status of oil cooperation between China and the GCC countries, and explores the potential of oil cooperation between China and the GCC. It analyzes the opportunities and challenges of China's oil reserves, and points out that the establishment of a joint oil stockpiling could be a new way to deepen and consolidate the oil cooperation relationship between China and the GCC. It is hoped that the research results in this book can not only provide decision-making reference for China's energy development, but also provide reference for professionals and ordinary readers.

Zhen Huang
Academician of Chinese Academy
of Engineering; Vice President of Shanghai Jiao
Tong University
Shanghai, China

Preface

Against the backdrop of weak global economic recovery and bottlenecks in domestic economic growth, China has proposed the initiative of jointly building the "Silk Road Economic Belt" and the "21st Century Maritime Silk Road" (the Belt and Road Initiative), aimed at strengthening regional cooperation and seeking economic development. The Belt and Road runs through nearly 70 countries and regions in Asia, Africa, and Europe, with a population of about 4.4 billion. Among them, the Gulf Cooperation Council (GCC) at the intersection of the Belt and Road route is considered to be one of the important strategic fulcrum points along the Belt and Road. For a long time, the GCC countries (or the Gulf) has occupied an important position in China's energy import structure. About one third of China's oil imports come from the GCC countries. In addition, one third of LNG consumed by China is also imported from the GCC countries. However, the current international energy pattern shows the rapid development of non-traditional energy sources, the "titling westward" of energy production centers and the "titling eastward" of energy consumption centers, coupled with changes in the content and prospects of international energy cooperation, which have given the potential impact for on China and the GCC countries' energy cooperation under the new international energy landscape.

While some developed countries, led by the United States, are gradually realizing a strategic shift in energy supply from the Gulf to domestic energy and other countries' energy, China continues to expand and maintain its dependence on oil from the Gulf, which is not only based on the practical considerations about its own economic development and demand for energy, but also to achieve the Belt and Road vision and the need for in-depth cooperation and docking with the GCC countries. In this context, in order for China and the GCC countries to reach a new level of oil cooperation and maintain healthy and orderly development, it is necessary to break through existing cooperation ways and content and seek new and more stable points of cooperation growth.

With the support of the International Energy Research Center (IERC) of Shanghai Jiao Tong University, this book focuses on the issues of bilateral energy cooperation between China and the Gulf, sorts out the petroleum resources, production and consumption of the countries within the Belt and Road route and the Gulf, and summarizes the characteristics of China's oil transportation and the current status of its oil reserves. The current status of oil cooperation, cooperation risks, and prospects for cooperation between China and the Gulf countries are discussed. This book can be read by academics related to energy issues and anyone interested in energy issues or energy geopolitical issues.

The book is organized as follows: Chap. 1 is the background; Chap. 2 reviews the oil resources and production and consumption of countries along the Belt and Road and in the GCC countries; Chap. 3 analyzes the current status of oil cooperation between China and the GCC countries; Chap. 4 introduces the development status of China's energy transportation corridors and the countermeasures to improve the safety of China's offshore energy transportation corridors; Chap. 5 introduces the experience of national oil reserves in several developed countries and the current status of China's oil reserves; Chap. 6 discusses the current situation and opportunities for oil exporters in Middle East to establish joint oil stockpiling with importers in Northeast Asia; Chap. 7 analyzes the geopolitical risks of oil cooperation between China and the Gulf countries; Chap. 8 makes a conclusion and answers how China can strengthen energy cooperation with the Gulf countries in the context of the Belt and Road Initiative. Chapters 1, 2, 3, and 5 of this book was written by Tingting Zhang, Chaps. 4, 7 and 8 was written by Dehua Wang.

We have many institutions and people to thank for the creation and production of this book.

First, we must thank our friends Tilak K Doshi and Sammy Six; who devoted Chap. 6 for this book. Our thanks must go to Strategic Planning Analyst Jie Shen from Saudi Aramco, and Mr. Keneeth White from King Abdullah Petroleum Studies and Research Center.

During the research of this book, the research team held several seminars and exchanges in Shanghai, Beijing and other places, and conducted in-depth exchanges and discussions with experts and scholars related research institutions, enterprises, universities and government departments. In the process of preparing this book, the authors received strong support from Academician Zhen Huang, vice president of Shanghai Jiao Tong University and the director of the IERC. The authors would like to extend their sincere thanks to Weidong Chen, Yang Jin, Lei Wu, Haibin Wang, Xi Wang, Lijun Yu, Jianzhong Zhuang, Yuehua Shi, Lihua Zhu, Ting You, Can Yang, Dan Du, Lizhen Yao and Yaxuan Xue for their contribution to various part of this book. All remaining errors are the author's sole responsibility.

Shanghai, China   Tingting Zhang
April 2020   Dehua Wang

Contents

About the Editors

Dr. Tingting Zhang is currently an Assistant Research Professor of Power Machinery and Engineering at School of Mechanical Engineering, Shanghai Jiao Tong University (SJTU), Shanghai, China. She is also a Research Associate of Energy Geopolitics in International Energy Research Center at SJTU. Dr. Zhang received her BA in Light Chemical Engineering and MA in Pulp & Paper Making Engineering at Guangxi University before she obtained her doctorate in Power Machinery and Engineering at SJTU in 2014. Her fields of research interests include energy system assessment, low-carbon energy transformation, and energy geopolitics. Since her Ph.D., she has participated in a number of research projects as the main participator. She joined a collaborative project with KAPSARC and submitted a paper "Analysis of Cooperation Potential on Low-Carbon Energy Between GCC and NEA" to "Energy Relations and Policy Making in Asia' (ISBN 978-981-10-1093-4). She currently hosts the National Natural Science Foundation of China (Grant No. 71904122). She has published nearly 30 per-reviewed journal articles and newspaper comments on topics related to energy security and energy geopolitics, and has authored and edited two books as well.

Prof. Dehua Wang is Director and Professor, Institute of South and Central Asia Studies, Shanghai Municipal Center for International Studies; Senior Fellow, Center for International Energy Research Center, Shanghai Jiao Tong University. Advisor to China Association for South-Asia Studies; Ex-Senior Fellow, Center for National Strategic Studies, SJTU, Ex-Vice Presidents, of Shanghai Institute for International Strategic Studies and Institute of Information Science, Shanghai Academy of Social Sciences (SASS). Professor Wang mainly focusses on South Asia and energy security studies while he is an author of more than 20 books: such as 1. *Rise of the Asian Giants: Dragon-Elephant Tango*; 2. *Rising China in the Age of Oil-Price Peak*; 3. *A Study of New Silk Roads, New Dreams and Energy Channels*; 4. *China-Gulf Cooperation in China's Petroleum Stockpiling Under the "Belt and Road" Initiative*, etc.

Acronyms

AIIB	Asian Infrastructure Investment Bank
ANER	Agency for National Resources and Energy
APEC	Asia-Pacific Economic Cooperation
ASEAN	Association of Southeast Asian Nations
B&R	The Belt and Road
BCIM-EC	Bangladesh–China–India–Myanmar Economic Corridor
BEIS	Department for Business, Energy & Industrial Strategy
BRI	The Belt and Road Initiative
CAPP	Canadian Association of Petroleum Producers
CEFC China	CEFC China Energy Company Limited
CIS	Commonwealth of Independent States
CNPC	China National Petroleum Corporation
COR	Commercial Oil Reserve
CPC	The Communist Party of China
CPEC	China-Pakistan Economic Corridor
CPSSP	Professional Committee for Strategic Oil Stocks
CS	Compressor station
CSO	Compulsory stockholding obligation
DE	Energy Directorate
DECC	Department of Energy and Climate Change
DOE	Department of Energy
EBV	Erdölbevorratungsverband
EEC	European Economic Community
EIA	U.S. Energy Information Administration
EIU	The Economist Intelligence Unit
EPCA	Energy Policy and Conservation Act
EU	European Union
FTA	Free Trade Area
GATT	General Agreement on Tariffs and Trade
GCC	Gulf Cooperation Council
HREC	Himalaya Rim Economic Corridor
IEA	International Energy Agency

JNOC	Japan National Oil Corporation
JOGMEC	Japan Oil, Gas and Metals National Corporation
KL	Kiloliters
LP	Liquid petroleum
Mboe	Million barrels of oil equivalent
METI	Ministry of Economy, Trade and Industry
MITI	Ministry of International Trade and Industry
MMbbl	Million barrels
Mt	Million tonnes
Mtoe	Million tonnes of oil equivalent
MW	Mega-watts
NATO	North Atlantic Treaty Organization
NBSC	National Bureau of Statistics of China
NEHHOR	Northeast Home Heating Oil Reserve
NESO	National emergency strategy organization
OECD	Organization for Economic Co-operation and Development
OPEC	Organization of the Petroleum Exporting Countries
OPR	Office of Petroleum Reserves
PAD	Petroleum Administration for Defense
PSA	Petroleum Stockholding Act
S. & Cent. America	Central and South America
SAARC	South Asian Association for Regional Cooperation
SADC	Southern African Development Community
SAGESS	Société anonyme de gestion des stocks de sécurité
SEZs	Special Economic Zones
SPR	Strategic Petroleum Reserve
TAP	Trans Adriatic Pipeline
UAE	United Arab Emirates
WTO	World Trade Organization
WW	World War
WWII	World War II

Chapter 1
Introduction

Tingting Zhang

At present, the world economic recovery process is slow, showing the characteristics of low-speed growth, low interest rates and low inflation, as well as the imbalance of income and expenditure, the unbalance of the rich and the poor and the phased imbalance of the global economic coordination mechanism. The economic development of all countries in the world is deeply linked due to the economic globalization. Similarly, economic globalization has also highlighted the international tendency of energy security issues. Some scholars have defined energy security in terms of availability, affordability, cleanliness and sustainability. As the world's largest energy consumer, China faces severe challenges in its energy security under the new situation. The Gulf states are one of the most important oil supply regions in the world, and its energy security issues also have unique regional characteristics. In view of this, discussing the issue of energy cooperation between China and the Gulf states under the new situation is not only conducive to enhancing the energy security of both sides, but also promoting economic cooperation between the two sides and achieving a win–win result.

1.1 Global Energy Situation

The global energy landscape has changed dramatically over the past few decades. Benefited from technological advances and the rapid development of unconventional energy sources, unconventional energy sources represented by shale gas, tight oil, oil sands, and deep-sea oil are quietly rewriting the global energy landscape. "Multi-polarization" and "Westward tilt to the east" are the characteristics of the current global energy pattern. "Multi-polarization" refers to multiple "centers" of global

T. Zhang (✉)
International Energy Research Center, Shanghai Jiao Tong University, Shanghai, China
e-mail: zhangtingting@sjtu.edu.cn

© Shanghai Jiao Tong University Press 2021
T. Zhang and D. Wang (eds.), *China-Gulf Oil Cooperation Under the Belt and Road Initiative*, https://doi.org/10.1007/978-981-15-9283-6_1

energy supply and consumption. "Westward tilt to the east" refers to the global energy production center from the "west tilt" in the Middle East to the western hemisphere, and the energy consumption center is tilting east to emerging economies represented by China and India. The contrasting patterns in energy demand and production lead to significant shifts in global energy trade flows.

In terms of energy supply, global energy supply has broken the dominance of the Middle East in the past and started to "tilt" towards the western hemisphere. The Second Industrial Revolution brought oil to the world and made the Gulf of Mexico a hub for global oil production at the time. With the discovery of oil in the Middle East in the middle of the twentieth century, the oil supply center gradually shifted to the Persian Gulf, making it the "heartland" of world's oil production. After the Cold War, the scope of oil supply in the Persian Gulf region further expanded, forming a giant "inner crescent oil storage zone" composed of North Africa via the Persian Gulf and the Caspian Ring to Russia's Siberia. The region has stored nearly three-quarters of the world's oil and 40% of natural gas, making it an important hub of global energy supply. However, breakthroughs in oil and gas exploration and development technologies in recent years have unlocked the potential for unconventional energy development in Americas. A new energy axis has emerged, connecting Canada, the United States, Venezuela, and Brazil in order from north to south, reshaping the world's energy landscape. The core oil production status of the Persian Gulf region is being challenged, and global oil production is showing a "tilt to the west" trend. The world's oil and gas production show a "migration to the west" trend. The American countries such as the United States, Canada, Brazil, and Venezuela are gradually replacing Russia, Central Asia, and the Middle Ea.st as hot spots for global oil and gas development and supply. It is predicted that the rapid growth of U.S. tight oil and shale gas would lead to a significant increase in net energy exports from the Americas, such that by 2040 the Americas are a material source of energy exports to the rest of the world [1].

From the view of energy consumption, major global energy demand centers have shifted eastward, given the rapid rise of emerging economies in Asia. Statistics show that the OECD's primary energy consumption as a percentage of total global energy consumption has fallen from 68.8% in 1973 to 40.9% in 2018 [2]. It is predicted that OECD will account one-third of energy demand by 2040, with the non-OECD accounting for over two-thirds of demand [1]. Much of the increase in energy demand is concentrated in developing Asia, where rising prosperity and improving living standards support increasing energy consumption per head. China is one of major contributor to the increase of global energy consumption. With rapidly rising population and a major switch away from the traditional use of biomass, Africa emerges as a major source of global growth for oil, natural gas and renewables [3]. However, Africa's energy consumption remains small relative to its size: in 2040 Africa accounts for almost a quarter of the world's population, but only 6% of energy demand [1]. China remains the largest market for energy: roughly double the size of India in 2040 [1].

From the point of energy structure view, the trend of green and low-carbon energy has become a global consensus since twenty-first century. Driven by global greenhouse gas emissions and the need for green and clean development, green, low-carbon, and clean energy are rapidly developing globally. The basic energy transformation trend in various countries is to realize the transformation from a fossil energy-based energy source to a clean and low-carbon energy-based sustainable energy system. Natural gas and non-fossil energy have become the main directions of world energy development. BP's statistic shows that the share of natural gas and renewables consumption of the world's total in 2018 is 23.9% and 10.9%, respectively [2]. It also predicted that renewables would overtake coal as the largest source of global power by 2040 [1]. Another institution, International Energy Agency (IEA), pointed out that the power mix is being re-shaped by the rise of renewables and natural gas and forecasted that renewables account for nearly half of total electricity generation in 2040 [3].

1.2 Energy Situation in China

With the development of the global economy, China's GDP has also maintained a medium and high-speed growth rate since the reform and opening up, and energy production and consumption have also continued to increase, and the growth rate has remained above the world average growth rate. According to statistics, China's primary energy consumption reached 3,273.5 million tonnes of oil equivalent (Mtoe) in 2018, accounting for 23.6% of the world's total primary energy consumption [2]. From the perspective of energy consumption structure, coal still occupies a dominant position in China with a share of 59.0% in 2018, followed by oil at the share of 18.9%, natural gas at the percentage of 7.8%, and non-fossil energy with a share of 14.3% [4]. It is predicted that China's share of global energy demand will drop to 22.5% in 2040, which will still be the main driving force for the growth of global energy demand. China's energy consumption structure will also continue to evolve, and the dominant position of coal will decline from 59% in 2018 to 35% by 2040—largely offset by increasing shares of renewables and natural gas [1].

Admittedly, China's request to energy demand will be increase in the next 20 years, however, its domestic fossil production capacity is limited by resource endowment and environmental protection requirements. Hence, China's energy demand will inevitably depend on foreign energy markets. Data from National Bureau of Statistics of China (NBSC) show that China was a net energy exporter in 1978, and the total domestic energy production was higher than the total energy consumption [4]. However, China's foreign dependence on energy consumption in 2018 was increased to 18.8%, of which crude oil reached 69% and natural gas reached 42.7% [4]. China imported 464.5 million tons of crude oil and 81.9 million tons of petroleum products in 2018. Crude oil is mainly imported from the Middle East (43.8%), West Africa (15.5%), Russia (15.4%), and Central and South America (13.3%); petroleum products are mainly imported from the Asia–Pacific (55.6%) and the Middle East (24.6%)

[2]. Unpredictable risks are existed for China's import of crude and petroleum products from these regions. For instance, there are unstable regional security factors like political upheaval, terrorism and piracy treats in some region, and long-distance marine oil transportation will also be affected by these unsafe factors, which will impact China's energy security to a certain extent.

Facing the current and future energy situation, Chinese government has proposed to promote energy revolution in the area of energy consumption, energy supply, energy technology and energy system, and pointed out the need to strengthen international cooperation in all aspects to achieve energy security under open conditions. Among them, the establishment of a certain scale of Strategic Petroleum Reserves (SPR) is one of the important ways for China to cope with the interruption of energy supply and improve energy security. Compared with foreign countries, China started its SPR late, and it was not until 2001 that it formally decided to establish SPR. After nearly 20 years of development, China's SPR construction has made some progress, but there are still some problems. For example, there is still a gap compared to the 90-day safety line recommended by the IEA. For another example, China's SPR are dominated by government funding and have high costs. Therefore, it is urgent for China to optimize the structure of oil reserves, improve the status of commercial oil reserves, and further encourage private capital to participate in expanding the scale of national oil reserves.

1.2.1 The Proposal of the Book

As described that changes in the international environment have brought new challenges to China's energy security, while China has not substantially participated in global energy governance. At the domestic level, China is also facing the dual pressures of energy consumption growth and energy transition. In 2013, Chinese President Xi Jinping raised the Belt and Road Initiative (BRI) when visiting Kazakhstan and Indonesia. Since 2013, the Belt and Road Initiative, with policy coordination, connectivity of infrastructure, unimpeded trade, financial integration and closer people-to-people ties as its main goals, has advanced in solid steps. Significant progress has been made, including a number of landmark early results [5]. Participating countries have obtained tangible benefits, and their appreciation of and participation in the initiative is growing.

Energy cooperation is one the important items within BRI. On 16 May, 2017, "*Vision and Actions on Energy Cooperation in Jointly Building Silk Road Economic Belt and 21st-Century Maritime Silk Road*" was enacted by Chinese government which officially interpreted the energy cooperation principles, cooperation priorities and China's action and vison under BRI [6]. It is reported that BRI "seeks to foster energy cooperation in order to jointly build up an open, inclusive, and beneficial community of shared interests, responsibility and destiny". During the past 6 years, significant achievements have been made regarding energy cooperation under BRI. China has signed a great number of cooperation framework agreements and MoUs with other Belt and Road (B&R) countries, and has carried out extensive cooperation in the fields of electricity, oil and gas, nuclear power, new energy, and coal. It works with relevant countries to ensure the safe operation of oil and gas pipeline networks and optimize the configuration of energy resources between countries and regions [5]. The China-Russia crude oil pipeline and the China-Central Asia natural gas pipeline have maintained stable operation. Certain sections of the eastern route of the China-Russia natural gas pipeline entered service in December 2019 [7] and the entire eastern route will be completed and enter service in 2024. In addition, China-Myanmar oil and gas pipelines have been completed [5].

The Middle East, represented by the Gulf Cooperation Council (GCC), has been China's main energy supply source for a long time. China and the GCC countries have maintained close trade links. About one third of China's oil and one third of LNG are imported from GCC countries each year. The energy relationship between China and the GCC countries is one of the most important energy relationships around the world, and the two sides form an interdependent relationship of mutual benefit. The GCC is located at the intersection of the Belt and Road route and is considered as an important strategic fulcrum on the B&R route. Since BRI was proposed, GCC countries have also actively responded to the initiative. Under the general trend of the transformation of the international energy structure to non-traditional energy sources and the transfer of energy production and consumption centers, the energy cooperation between China and the GCC countries will also be affected by the changes in the new international energy structure, with a changing cooperation contents, ways, and prospect. From a development perspective, China's oil and other energy imports will continue to grow in the future. With the decline in European energy consumption, the "energy independent' of United States, the interdependence degree between China and GCC countries will be further strengthened. Therefore, the main goal of this book is to investigate how to stabilize and deepen the oil trade relationship between GCC countries and China in the context of BRI both from a global energy development perspective and a geopolitical perspective.

References

1. BP. 2019. *BP energy outlook*, 2019th ed. London: BP.
2. BP. 2019. *BP Statistical Review of World Energy 2019*. London: BP.
3. IEA. 2019. *World energy outlook 2019*. Paris: International Energy Agency.
4. NBSC. 2019. *China Statistical Yearbook 2019*. Beijing: China Statistics Press.
5. The Belt and Road Initiative Progress, Contributions and Prospects. 2019. https://www.yidaiyilu.gov.cn/info/iList.jsp?cat_id=10006&cur_page=1. Accessed 22 April 2019.
6. Vision and Actions on Energy Cooperation in Jointly Building Silk Road Economic Belt and 21st-Century Maritime Silk Road. 2017. https://eng.yidaiyilu.gov.cn/zchj/qwfb/13754.htm. Accessed 16 May 2017.
7. The Northern Section of the Sino-Russian East natural Gas Pipeline will be put into Use. December 1, 2019. 2019. https://www.yidaiyilu.gov.cn/xwzx/gnxw/106425.htm. Accessed 16 October 2019.

Chapter 2
The Belt and Road Petroleum Map and the Challenge of China's Energy Cooperation with B&R Countries

Tingting Zhang

As an important resource, oil occupies a special position in modern industry and the modern life of mankind. The oil-led energy system is the material basis for the survival and development of human society and the source of power for global economic activities. As the degree of economic globalization deepens when entering the twenty-first century, energy demand around the world continues to rise and energy peaks are increasingly cracked, further highlighting the contribution of energy to social development. The Belt and Road Initiative has received wide attention since its introduction, not only because of its potential development space, but also because of its abundant energy resources along the route. The focus of this chapter will be on the status of oil resources in countries along the Belt and Road, especially the status of oil resources in the GCC countries.

2.1 Global Oil Distribution

There are abundant oil resources on the earth, but the geographical and national distribution of these resources is very uneven. The world has both oil-rich areas and scarce oil resources; there are both oil-rich countries and countries with scarce oil resources. Plus, the level of development and utilization of petroleum resources is not balanced. This has led to the geographical and national imbalances in the distribution of global oil reserves, oil production, and oil consumption, which in turn has triggered a distinctive oil trade flow.

T. Zhang (✉)
International Energy Research Center, Shanghai Jiao Tong University, Shanghai, China
e-mail: zhangtingting@sjtu.edu.cn

© Shanghai Jiao Tong University Press 2021
T. Zhang and D. Wang (eds.), *China-Gulf Oil Cooperation Under the Belt and Road Initiative*, https://doi.org/10.1007/978-981-15-9283-6_2

2.1.1   Global Oil Reserve

Due to geological structure, the distribution of crude oil is extremely uneven in general: about three-quarters of the oil resources are concentrated in the eastern hemisphere, and the western hemisphere is one-fourth. From the northern and southern hemispheres, oil resources are mainly concentrated in the northern hemisphere. In general, petroleum resources are mainly concentrated in the north latitudes of 20–40° and 50–70°. Figure 2.1 shows the proved crude oil reserves of top 15 countries around the world in 2018 [1]. It's obviously that Venezuela holds the highest proved crude oil reserve with an amount of 303.3 billion barrels. Saudi Arabia has the second largest proven crude oil reserves with an amount of 297.7 billion barrels. Then followed by Canada, Iran, Iraq, Russia, Kuwait, United Arab Emirates (UAE), US, Libya, Nigeria, Kazakhstan, China, Qatar, and Brazil. The total amount of proven crude oil reserves for the 15 countries are 1618.8 billion barrels, accounting for 93.6% the world's proved crude oil reserves [1].

From the perspective of regional distribution, crude oil resources are mainly distributed in the Middle East and the America Continent (shown in Table 2.1 [1]).

2.1.1.1   North America

North America has abundant crude oil reserves. The proved crude oil reserves increased from 126.9 billion barrels in 1995 to 236.7 billion barrels in 2018 with a globe share of 13.7%. The countries with the richest proven crude oil reserves of North American are Canada, followed by the United States and Mexico. According to BP Statistical Review of World Energy 2019, Canada holds 167.8 billion barrels

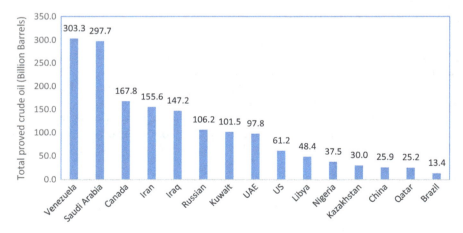

Fig. 2.1   Top 15 countries in global crude oil proved reserves in the year of 2018. *Data source* BP Statistical Review of World Energy 2019

Table 2.1 Distribution of global proven crude oil reserves

Regions	Proved crude oil reserves/billion barrels				Global share/%			
	1995	2005	2015	2018	1995	2005	2015	2018
North America	126.9	223.6	227.5	236.7	11.3	16.2	13.5	13.7
S. & Cent. America	83.7	103.3	324.1	325.1	7.4	7.5	19.2	18.8
Europe	20.0	17.7	13.9	14.3	1.8	1.3	0.8	0.8
CIS	121.1	121.8	140.8	144.7	10.8	8.8	8.4	8.4
Middle East	663.3	755.5	802.9	836.1	59.0	54.9	47.7	48.3
Africa	72.0	111.3	126.3	125.3	6.4	8.1	7.5	7.2
Asia Pacific	37.9	43.4	48.8	47.6	3.4	3.2	2.9	2.8

Data source BP Statistical Review of World Energy 2019

of proved crude oil with 9.7% of worlds' total, while US has 61.2 billion barrels of proved crude oil with 3.5% of worlds' total. Crude oil in Canada is mainly distributed in the provinces of Alberta, Saskatchewan and Manitoba in the west, while the crude oil in US are primarily located on the Gulf Coast, the Gulf Coast of California, and Alaska. Among them, Texas and Oklahoma are the most famous oil producing areas.

2.1.1.2   S. & Cent. America

S. & Cent. America (Central and South America) has always been one of the world's major oil producers and exporters. It has become one of the regions with the fastest growth rate in world crude oil reserves and oil production benefitted from the discovery of heavy oil in recent years. The total amount of proved crude oil in S. & Cent. America has a quickly increase from 83.7 billion barrels in 1995 to 325.1 billion barrels in 2018. In 1995, The global share of proven crude oil for S. & Cent. America was only 7.5% in 1995, however, the share in 2018 was increased to 18.8%. This depends to a large extent on the discovery of a large amount of heavy oil in Venezuela. Since the proven reserves of crude oil in Venezuela in 2016 have surpassed Saudi Arabia, it has been the country with the largest oil reserves in the world. In addition to Venezuela, Brazil and Ecuador are countries with abundant crude oil reserves in the region. The proven reserves in 2018 were 13.4 and 2.8 billion barrels respectively, ranking 15 and 29 respectively [1]. Venezuela's crude oil resources are mainly distributed in the western Maracaibo Lake region, the eastern Anso Ateji region, the Monagas region, the central Barinas and the Apure region. Brazil's crude oil is mainly distributed in the southeastern seas of Campos and Santos. Ecuador's crude oil is mainly distributed in the eastern Amazon Basin, the western peninsula of Guayas, and the Guayaquil Bay area.

2.1.1.3   Europe

The proved crude oil reserves in Europe is the lowest in the world. Since 1995, European proved crude oil has fallen by 28.4%. It holds 14.3 billion barrels in 2018, accounting 0.8% of world's total proved crude oil reserves. Norway is the country with the highest proven oil reserves in Europe, accounting for 60% of the region's total reserves. United Kingdom has 2.5 billion barrels of proven crude oil with a share of 17.5% of European total reserves.

2.1.1.4   Commonwealth of Independent States (CIS)

Among the CIS countries, Russia, Kazakhstan and Azerbaijan have the richest oil resources. Turkmenistan and Uzbekistan have a small amount of oil resources. The total proved crude oil reserves of CIS in 1995 was 121.2 billion barrels, while it increased to 144.7 billion barrels in 2018. Russia is the country with the highest proven crude oil reserves in CIS. In 2018, Russia has proven reserves of about 106.2 billion barrels, ranking sixth in the world [1]. Kazakhstan in Central Asia is the second-largest country in terms of crude oil reserves in the region. The proven reserves are 30 billion barrels, ranking 12th in the world [1]. Russia's oil resources are mainly distributed in the West Siberian region, accounting for 54% of Russia's total resources. In addition, Volga-Ural, Eastern Siberia and the Far East are also rich in oil reserves. The Barents Sea, the Kara Sea and the Sea of Okhotsk are also rich in oil resources. Kazakhstan's oil resources are mainly distributed in the Caspian Sea, Mangshrak, North Uschurt, South Turgay and Chuhe-Saresu Basin.

2.1.1.5   Middle East

Known as the "world oil depot", the Middle East Persian Gulf region is located at the hub of Europe, Asia and Africa, and has very rich crude oil resources. According to BP statistics, as shown in Table 2.1, the oil reserves in the region have occupied half of the world's total. Although the ratio of reserves from 1995 to 2018 to total global reserves fell from 59.0% to 48.3%, the total amount of proven reserves in the region is still increasing. Among the top ten in the world's crude oil reserves, the Middle East countries accounted for five seats, namely Saudi Arabia, Iran, Iraq, Kuwait and the United Arab Emirates. Among them, Saudi Arabia's proven oil reserves in 2018 were 297.7 billion barrels, ranking second in the world. Iran's proven crude oil reserves are 155.6 billion barrels, ranking fourth in the world. Iraq's proven crude oil reserves are 147.2 billion barrels, ranking fifth in the world. The proven reserves of Kuwait and UAE are 101.5 and 97.8 billion barrels respectively, ranking eighth and ninth in the world. In addition, countries such as Qatar, Oman and Yemen also have abundant oil resources.

2.1.1.6 Others

The proven crude oil of Africa in 2018 was 125.3 billion barrels, equivalent to 7.2% world's total crude oil reserves. Africa's crude oil is mainly distributed in the Gulf of Guinea region of West Africa and North Africa. Libya, Nigeria, Algeria, Angola, Sudan, Egypt, Uganda, Gabon, Congo and Chad are among the top 10 countries in terms of proven reserves in Africa. Among them, Libya has proven crude oil reserves of 48.4 billion barrels in 2018, ranking tenth in the world [1]. Nigeria has proven crude oil reserves of 37.5 billion barrels, ranking 11th in the world [1]. Asia Pacific holds a total proven crude oil of 47.6 billion barrels equal to 2.8% of world's total reserves. China has the highest proved crude oil reserve in Asia Pacific.

2.1.2 Global Oil Production

In 2018, the top 15 countries in terms of oil production were United States, Saudi Arabia, Russia, Canada, Iran, Iraq, UAE, China, Kuwait, Brazil, Mexico, Nigeria, Kazakhstan, Qatar, and Norway, respectively (shown in Fig. 2.2 [1]). The total daily oil production of these countries were 76.8 million barrels accounting for 81.1% of world's total.

From the perspective of oil production distribution, as shown in Table 2.2 [1], the major oil producing areas of the world are mainly concentrated in the Middle East and North America.

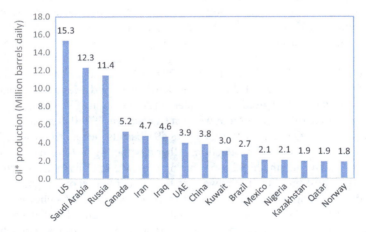

Fig. 2.2 Top 15 countries in global crude oil production in the year of 2018. *Data source* BP Statistical Review of World Energy 2019. * Oil here includes crude oil, shale oil, oil sands, condensates, and NGLs

Table 2.2 Distribution of global crude oil production

Regions	Crude oil production/Thousand barrels per day				Global share/%			
	1995	2005	2015	2018	1995	2005	2015	2018
North America	13778.5	13707.3	19747.6	22587.4	20.3	16.8	21.6	23.8
S. & Cent. America	5779.0	7337.4	7758.6	6536.7	8.5	9.0	8.5	6.9
Europe	6641.8	5818.3	3587.5	3523.1	9.8	7.1	3.9	3.7
CIS	7168.5	11690.0	13909.3	14482.9	10.6	14.3	15.2	15.3
Middle East	20150.4	25476.8	30012.3	31762.4	29.7	31.1	32.8	33.5
Africa	7050.2	9777.4	8132.6	8192.9	10.4	12.0	8.9	8.6
Asia Pacific	7269.1	7986.0	8398.9	7633.0	10.7	9.8	9.2	8.1

Data source BP Statistical Review of World Energy 2019

2.1.2.1 North America

North America is one of the main oil producing areas around the world. As shown in Table 2.2, in 1995 and 2005, the daily oil production in the region was maintained at 13 million barrels. In 2015, the daily oil production surged to 19.748 million barrels, and it further increased to 22.587 million barrels in 2018. The oil production of United States ranking first in the world accounted for 67.8% of the region's total oil production, and Canada accounting for 23.1% of the region's total.

Oil sands and crude oil are the two primary types of oil production in Canada. Oil sands production in Canada was 1,063,644 barrels with a daily output of 2,914 barrels in 2018. The oil sands resources are situated almost entirely in Alberta and can be delineated by the Athabasca, Cold Lake and Peace River deposits [2]. In this constrained environment, oil sands production, which can be recovered either by mining or in situ projects, is forecast to grow by 1.34 million b/d, reaching 4.25 million b/d by 2035 from 2.91 million in 2018 [2]. Canadian crude oil is mainly produced in the provinces of Alberta, Saskatchewan and Manitoba in the west. According to statistics released by the Canadian Association of Petroleum Producers (CAPP) [3], crude oil production in western Canada was 379.049 million barrels in 2018, with an average daily output of 1,308,491 barrels, accounting for 92.94% of the total Canadian crude oil production. Alberta is the highest-producing province in Western Canada and the highest-producing province in Canada. Saskatchewan is the second-highest province in the western region and the second-highest province in Canada. The combined production from Alberta and Saskatchewan in 2018 accounted for 95% of the total of conventional crude oil produced in Western Canada. East coast offshore is the main producer of crude oil in eastern Canada. The main crude oil production fields in Alberta include Judy Creek field with a daily output of 1.113 million barrels, Pembina field with a daily output of 49,393 barrels, Provost field with a daily output of 40,624 barrels, and Valhalla field with a daily output of 15,846 barrels in 2018 [3]. Crude oil fields in Viewfield North, Weyburn, Dodsland, and Celtic with daily crude oil output of 35,087 barrels, 25, 813 barrels, 21,054 barrels, and 10, 316 barrels in 2018, respectively, are the main fields for crude oil production in Saskatchewan. Canada's crude oil refining capacity in 2018 was 1,877,736 barrels per day, and the refinery utilization rate was 81% [3]. It is reported that Canadian crude oil production is expected to increase by 1.27 million b/d by 2035, with a 1.44% annual increase [2]. Canada's crude oil refineries are concentrated in the Alberta, Ontario and Quebec regions. Most of the crude oil produced in western Canada flows to refineries across the United States.

According to U.S. Energy Information Administration (EIA) statistics [4], the United States produced 4,011,521 thousand barrels of crude oil in 2018, of which Petroleum Administration for Defense (PAD) District 1 produced 20,160 thousand barrels, PAD District 2 was 741,560 thousand barrels, and PAD District 3 was 2,576,232 thousand. Barrels, PAD District 4 is 324,464 thousand barrels, PAD District 5 is 349,105 thousand barrels. It is obviously that PAD District 3 holds the largest crude oil production, followed by PAD District 2, PAD District 5 and PAD District 4. As listed in Table 2.3 [4], North Dakota has the largest crude oil output in PAD District 2, with a share of 62.2% of PAD District 2's total and 11.5% of U.S. total. Texas is the largest crude oil producing state in PAD District 3 with a share of 62.5% of PAD District 3's total and 40.1% of U.S. total. The offshore crude oil production in PAD District 3 takes the share of 24.9% of PAD District 3's total and 16.0% of U.S. total. The primary crude oil producing state in PAD District 4 and PAD District 5 are Colorado and Alaska, respectively. As of January 1, 2019, the United States currently operates a total of 132 petroleum refineries with a total operating refining capacity of 18,692,335 barrels per day. Among them, PAD District 1 has 8 refineries with a refining capacity of 1,224,000 barrels per day, PAD District 2 has 25 refineries, with a refining capacity of 4,075,515 barrels per day, and PAD District 3 has 56 refineries with a refining capacity of 9,840,599 barrels per day, PAD District 4 has 16 refineries with a refining capacity of 677,150 barrels per day, and PAD District 5 has 27 refineries with a refining capacity of 2,875,071 barrels per day [5]. It can be seen that the most important production capacity in the United States is located in PAD District 2 and 3 of the United States. The combined capacity of the two districts accounts for 74.4% of the total capacity of the United States. The capacity of PAD District 3 accounts for 52.6% of the total capacity of the U.S.

2.1.2.2 S. & Cent. America

Oil production in Central and South America is relatively low as shown in Table 2.2. In 1995, the daily oil production in the region was 5.779 million barrels, accounting for 8.5% of the world's total. In 2005, the daily output increased to 7.337 million barrels, accounting for 9.0% of the global total. In 2015, the daily output of oil increased to 7.759 million barrels, while the global share has fallen to 8.5%. In 2018, the daily oil production decreased to 6.537 million barrels accounting for a global share of 6.9%. Brazil is the country with the highest daily oil production in Central and South America. The daily output in 2018 was 2.683 million barrels, accounting for 2.8% of the world's total. Venezuela with the daily output of 1.514 million barrels

Table 2.3 U.S. production of crude oil by PAD District and state, 2018

PAD District	State	Total/Thousand barrels	Daily average/Thousand barrels
PAD District 1	Florida	1,839	5
	New York	221	1
	Pennsylvania	6,478	18
	Virginia	5	0
	West Virginia	11,618	32
PAD District 2	Illinois	8,420	23
	Indiana	1,684	5
	Kansas	34,714	95
	Kentucky	2,265	6
	Michigan	5,408	15
	Missouri	90	0
	Nebraska	2,056	6
	North Dakota	461,531	1,264
	Ohio	23,224	64
	Oklahoma	200,685	550
	South Dakota	1,273	3
	Tennessee	210	1
PAD District 3	Alabama	5,884	16
	Arkansas	5,018	14
	Louisiana	48,841	134
	Mississippi	16,953	46
	New Mexico	248,958	682
	Texas	1,609,075	4,408
	Federal Offshore PAD District 3	641,503	1,758
PAD District 4	Colorado	177,817	487
	Idaho	88	0
	Montana	21,540	59
	Utah	37,063	102
	Wyoming	87,955	241
PAD District 5	Alaska	174,800	479
	Arizona	11	0
	California	169,166	463
	Nevada	255	1
	Federal Offshore PAD District 5	4,874	13

Data source EIA database (https://www.eia.gov)

in 2018 is the second largest oil producing country in S. & Cent. America. Colombia is the third largest oil producer in the region, with a daily output of 866,101 barrels in 2018, accounting for 0.9% of the world's total. Argentina, Peru and other countries also have a certain amount of oil production.

2.1.2.3   Europe

Europe is the region with the least oil output shown in Table 2.2. It had a daily oil output of 6,641.8 thousand barrels with a global share of 9.8% in 1995. However, the oil production in this region declined year by year, and fell to 3,523.1 thousand barrels with a global share of 3.7% in 2018. European's oil production was dominated by Norway which had a daily output of 1,844 thousand barrels in 2018. United Kingdom contributed 1,085 thousand barrels per day in 2018 ranking second in the region.

2.1.2.4   CIS

It can be seen that CIS has considerable oil output. In 1995, the oil output was 7,168.5 thousand barrels per day, and then continued to increase to 14,482.9 thousand barrels per day. Meanwhile, its global share increased from 10.6% in 1995 to 15.3% in 2018. With a daily output of 11,438 thousand barrels, Russia is the highest oil producing country in CIS, accounting for 12.1% of world's total oil production. Kazakhstan is the second largest oil producing country in CIS with a daily output of 1, 927 thousand barrels. Azerbaijan holding a daily output of 795 thousand barrels rank third in CIS. Turkmenistan is the fourth largest oil producing country in CIS.

2.1.2.5   Middle East

The Middle East has been the focus of oil production for many years. According to statistics [1], the oil production in the Middle East in 1965 was 8.387 million barrels per day. By the oil crisis of the 1970s, the oil production in the region once reached a daily output of 22.53 million barrels, and was maintained over 10 million barrels per day for many years. In 1995, the oil production in the Middle East increased to over 20 million barrels, and has been maintained until recently. In 2015, the daily output of oil exceeded 30 million barrels. In 2018, the region's daily output reached 31.762 million barrels, accounting for 33.5% of the global total. Saudi Arabia is the region's largest oil-producing country and one of the top three global oil producers in the world except the United States and Russia. The second largest oil producer in the region is Iran with a daily output of 4.715 million barrels, accounting for 5.0% of the world's total. The third largest oil producer in the region is Iraq with a daily oil production of 4.614 million barrels in 2018, accounting for 4.9% of the world's total. The fourth largest oil-producing country is the United Arab Emirates. Its daily output in 2018 was 3.942 million barrels, accounting for 4.2% of the world's total.

The fifth largest oil producer is Kuwait with a daily output in 2018 of 3.049 million barrels, accounting for 3.2% of the global total. The sixth largest oil producer in the Middle East is Qatar with a daily output of 1.879 million barrels in 2018 accounting for 2.0% of the world's total. In addition, countries such as Oman also have a certain amount of oil production.

2.1.2.6   Others

African oil production has changed slightly over the past two decades shown in Table 2.2. The oil production of Africa in 2018 was 8,192.8 thousand barrels with a global share of 8.6%. Nigeria has the largest oil output in Africa, followed by Angola, Algeria, Libya, Egypt and Republic of Congo. The total oil output of the six countries account for 86.7% of Africa's total oil production in 2018. Oil production in the Asia-Pacific region has also fluctuated over the past two decades. Its oil production in 2018 was 7,633 thousand barrels. However, its global share decreased from 10.7% in 1995 to 8.1% in 2018. China with a daily oil output of 3,798 thousand barrels dominated the oil production in Asia Pacific. India has considerable oil production, as well as Indonesia.

2.1.3   Global Oil Consumption

As the economy develops, the consumption of oil also increases. According to BP statistics [1], the global total oil consumption increased from 70.466 million barrels per day in 1995 to 99.843 million barrels per day, with an growth rate of 1.5% each year. Table 2.4 summarizes the daily consumption of oil in different regions in the world. It can be seen that the center of global oil consumption is mainly

Table 2.4   Distribution of global crude oil consumption

Regions	Crude oil production/Thousand barrels per day				Global share/%			
	1995	2005	2015	2018	1995	2005	2015	2018
North America	21,295.6	25,109.9	23,871.5	24,714.3	30.2	29.7	25.1	24.8
S. & Cent. America	4,460.9	5,308.3	7,001.0	6,795.5	6.3	6.3	7.4	6.8
Europe	15,863.1	16,867.3	14,713.2	15,275.9	22.5	19.9	15.5	15.3
CIS	3,864.6	3,353.9	3,955.3	4,098.7	5.5	4.0	4.2	4.1
Middle East	4,600.6	6,452.0	9,098.8	9,135.9	6.5	7.6	9.6	9.2
Africa	2,193.1	2,901.5	3,856.7	3,959.4	3.1	3.4	4.1	4.0
Asia Pacific	18,188.2	24,586.6	32,551.2	35,863.3	25.8	29.1	34.2	35.9

Data source BP Statistical Review of World Energy 2019

concentrated in the Asia-Pacific region and North America, and the oil consumption in the Asia-Pacific region exceeds one-third of the world's total.

2.1.3.1 North America

North America is one of the major consumers around the world. In 1995, the daily oil consumption in the region was 21,295.6 thousand barrels, accounting for 30.2% of the world's total. In 2005, the daily consumption increased to 25,109.9 thousand barrels, accounting for 29.7% of the world's total. The oil consumption in North America fell to 23,871.5 thousand barrels per day, which accounted for 25.1% of the world's total. In 2018, the oil consumption in this region rebounded to 24,713.3 thousand barrels per day with a global share of 24.8%. The United States is the largest oil-consuming country in the region and the world's largest oil consumer as well. The daily consumption of the United States in 2018 accounts for 20.5% of the world. In the same year, the daily oil consumption in Canada and Mexico accounted for 2.5% and 1.8% of the world, respectively.

2.1.3.2 S. & Cent. America

Oil consumption in the Central and South America is relatively small. In 1995, the region's oil consumption was 4.461 million barrels per day, accounting for 6.3% of the world's total. In 2005, the daily oil consumption was 5.308 million barrels per day, accounting for 6.3% of the world's total. The daily consumption of oil in 2018 was 6.796 million barrels per day, which equals to 7.2% of the global total. Brazil is the country with the largest oil consumption in the region, with a global share of 3.1% in 2018. This is followed by Argentina and Venezuela, where oil consumption accounts for 0.6% and 0.4% of global total, respectively. These three countries consumed 60.8% of the total oil consumption in the region.

2.1.3.3 Europe

Europe is the third largest oil consumer in the world. Between 1995 and 2018, the total oil consumption in Europe showed small fluctuations. In 2005, the total daily consumption of oil in the region increased from 15.863 million barrels in 1995 to 16.867 million barrels. In 2015, the total oil consumption fell to 14.713 million barrels, and in 2018 it rebounded slightly to 15.276 million barrels. However, its global share of crude oil consumption fell from 22.5% in 1995 to 15.3% in 2018. Germany is the country with the largest oil consumption in the region, followed by the United Kingdom, France, Spain, Italy and Turkey. The total oil consumption of these countries accounted for 59.8% of the region's total.

2.1.3.4   Asia Pacific

The Asia Pacific region is the world's largest region in terms of oil consumption. Between 1995 and 2018, the total oil consumption in the Asia Pacific region nearly doubled, from 18.188 million barrels in 1995–35.863 million barrels in 2018, with an average annual growth rate of 3.0%. In 2018, the total oil consumption in the Asia Pacific region accounted for 35.9% of the world's total. China is the largest contributor according to oil consumption in the region. In 2018, China's total oil consumption was 13.515 million barrels per day, accounting for 37.7% of the total oil consumption in the region. India is the second largest oil consumer in the region, with a daily consumption of 5.156 million barrels in 2018, accounting for 14.4% of the region's total. Japan is the third largest oil consumer in the region, with a daily oil consumption of 3.854 million barrels in 2018, accounting for 10.7% of the region's total oil consumption. South Korea's oil consumption in 2018 was 2.793 million barrels, accounting for 7.8% of the region's total. These four countries account for 70.6% of the total oil consumption in the Asia-Pacific region.

2.1.3.5   Others

Oil consumption in other regions is relatively small. In the Middle East, the total oil consumption in 2018 accounted for 9.2% of the world's total. Saudi Arabia is the largest oil consumer in the region, followed by Iran, which has a combined share of 61.3% of the region's total oil consumption. In 2018, CIS and Africa accounted for only 4.1% and 4.0% of the world's total oil consumption.

2.1.4   Global Oil Movement

According to the data from BP Statistical Review of World Energy [1], the regions for world's crude oil export are mainly concentrated in the Middle East, CIS, North Africa, and North America.

2.1.4.1   Middle East

The Middle East is the region with the largest export volume of crude oil in the world. Although the proportion of crude oil exported from the Middle East in the world's crude oil export trade has declined in recent years, its export volume still accounts for more than one-third of the world's crude oil trade. In 2018, the export volume of the Middle East was 989.3 Million tonnes (Mt), accounting for 43.7% of the world's total crude oil exports. Therefore, crude oil exports in the Middle East play an important role in determining the world trade map. From the recent direction of crude oil exports in the Middle East, the Asian region is the most important market.

The amount of crude oil exported to China in 2018 is 203.2 Mt, accounting for 20.5% of the total exports in the Middle East; the amount of crude oil exported to India is 146.8 Mt, accounting for 14.8% of the total exports in the Middle East; the amount of crude oil exported to Japan is 131.0 Mt, accounting for 13.2% of the total exports of the Middle East; the amount of crude oil exported to Singapore is 40.1 Mt, accounting for 4.1% of the total exports of the Middle East. With Australia and other countries combined, the volume of crude oil exported from the Middle East to Asia accounts for 75.0% of its total exports. In addition to the Asian market, crude oil in the Middle East is also exported to the United States, Europe and Africa. In 2018, the proportion of exports to these places accounted for 7.4, 12.5 and 1.7% of their total exports, respectively.

2.1.4.2   Russia

Russia is an important oil exporter around the world. In 2018, Russia exported a total of 275.9 Mt of crude oil and 173.1 Mt of oil products. Its crude oil exports accounted for 12.2% of the world's total crude oil trade, and exported oil products accounted for 14.0% of the world's total oil products trade. Russia's crude oil are mainly exported to Europe. In 2018, crude oil exports to Europe accounted for 55.6% of its total exports. Russia's second largest crude oil export partner is China. In 2018, it exported 71.6 Mt of crude oil to China, accounting for 26.0% of its total crude oil exports. The third largest exporter of Russian crude oil is Japan with a share of 2.5% of Russian total crude oil export. Similar to crude oil, Russian oil products are also primarily exported to Europe. In 2018, it exported 112.5 Mt of refined oil to Europe.

2.1.4.3   West Africa

West Africa is one of the important regions for the crude oil export market. In 2018, the West African region exported 219.9 Mt of crude oil, accounting for 9.7% of the total global crude oil trade. The refined oil products only exported 7.5 Mt, accounting for 0.6% of the total trade in refined oil products worldwide. The distribution of crude oil exported from West Africa is more extensive. The region with the most exports is China, accounting for 32.7% of the total exports in West Africa; followed by Europe with a share of 28.7%; the third largest exporter is India, accounting for 12.6% of West Africa's total crude export; the proportion of exports to the United States is 7.6%, the proportion to Central and South America is 4.3%. In addition, some crude oil in West Africa is also exported to Australia and Japan.

2.1.4.4   S. & Cent. America

Central and South America is also an important oil exporter. In 2018, Central and South America exported 156.7 Mt of crude oil, accounting for 6.9% of the total global crude oil trade, and exporting 28.6 Mt of petroleum products, accounting for 2.3% of the total global trade in petroleum products. From the perspective of export flows, crude oil in Central and South America is mainly exported to China, the United States, India and Europe. The proportion of crude oil exported to these four regions in 2018 was 39.6, 36.3, 14.6 and 6.5% of the total exports, respectively. In addition, about 1.2% of crude oil in S. & Cent. America is exported to Japan.

2.1.4.5   North America

In recent years, with the adjustment of the global oil situation, the oil export in North America has also increased. In 2018, the region's crude oil exports totaled 345.9 Mt, accounting for 15.3% of the total global crude oil trade, meanwhile, North America had an export of oil products reaching up to 290.7 Mt, accounting for 23.5% of the total oil trade worldwide. From the perspective of crude oil export, most of the crude oil in North America is supplied to the United States, with a ratio of 62.8%. Secondly, about 5.4% of crude oil is exported to Canada, 13.2% of crude oil is exported to Europe, and 4.1% of crude oil is exported to India. In addition, a small amount of crude oil is exported to Central and South America, Japan, Singapore and other countries. Among the regions, Canada is the largest crude oil exporter, accounting for 8.4% of total global trade. In 2018, Canada exported 190.9 Mt crude oil, of which about 96.3% was exported to the United States; Mexico exported 33.1 Mt in 2018, of which 53.7% of crude oil was also exported to the United States. US crude oil exports grew rapidly, from 24.4 Mt in 2016 to 93.2 Mt in 2018. US crude oil is mainly exported to Europe, Canada, China and India. The Asia Pacific region is the largest market for US crude oil exports. The United States is also the country with the largest export volume of petroleum products. In 2018, it exported 251.6 Mt of petroleum products, accounting for 20.3% of the total trade in petroleum products. US petroleum products are mainly exported to Central and South America, Mexico, Canada and Europe.

2.1.4.6   Others

In addition to the above five regions, North Africa and the other CIS countries excluding Russia also export certain amount of crude oil. In 2018, North Africa exported 95.6 Mt of crude oil, accounting for 4.2% of the total global crude oil trade. The remaining CIS countries except Russia exported 85.9 Mt of crude oil in 2018, accounting for 3.8% of the total global crude oil trade.

In general, the global oil trade has formed a situation of multi-polar coexistence in the Middle East, North America, Russia and other CIS countries, as well as Central and South America.

2.2 Oil Situation Within Belt and Road

The Belt and Road covers countries in Asia, Africa, Europe, Oceania, North America, and South America. Since the BRI was proposed in 2013, many countries around the world have actively responded to and participated in the Belt and Road construction. As of the end of October 2019, there were nearly 140 participating countries who have already signed cooperation agreement with China [6]. According to statistics [7, 8], the total population of these participating countries in 2018 is about 3.317 billion, accounting for 43.7% of the world's total, while the gross national product has reached 19,719.588 billion current US dollars with a global share of 23.0%. The vast majority of countries along the Belt and Road are emerging economies and developing countries, and are generally in a period of rising economic development.

To further describe the oil profile along the Belt and Road, here we selected several countries from the total 140 countries along the Belt and Road that closely bonded to oil-related issues to further describe the oil profile along the Belt and Road in combination with the data availability and the statistics accessibility.

2.2.1 Crude Oil Proven Reserve Within Belt and Road

According to EIA data [9], about 77 countries out of the 140 countries involved in the B&R have a certain amount of proved crude oil reserve. The selected countries holding crude oil reserve are listed in Table 2.5.

Table 2.5 Selected countries holding crude oil reserve involved in the Belt and Road

Region	Counting	Selected countries
Asia	9	Thailand, Indonesia, Philippines, Malaysia, Myanmar, Viet Nam, Brunei, Pakistan, Bangladesh
Africa	21	Sudan, South Africa, Cote d'Ivoire, Cameroon, Cameroon, Ghana, Gabon, Mauritania, Angola, Ethiopia, Nigeria, Chad, Congo-Brazzaville, Algeria, Uganda, Morocco, Tunisia, Libya, Egypt, Equatorial Guinea, Benin, Niger
Eurasian	11	Azerbaijan, Georgia, Kazakhstan, Kyrgyzstan, Tajikistan, Uzbekistan, Belarus, Russia, Lithuania, Latvia, Turkmenistan
Middle East	12	United Arab Emirates, Kuwait, Qatar, Oman, Saudi Arabia, Bahrain, Iran, Iraq, Yemen, Syria, Jordan, Israel
Europe	13	Austria, Greece, Poland, Serbia, Czech Republic, Bulgaria, Slovakia, Albania, Croatia, Hungary, Romania, Italy, Turkey
Oceania	2	New Zealand, Papua New Guinea
South America	6	Chile, Bolivia, Venezuela, Suriname, Ecuador, Peru
North America	3	Trinidad and Tobago, Barbados, Cuba

Data source EIA database (https://www.eia.gov)

Table 2.6 Distribution of crude oil proven reserves involved in the Belt and Road

Region	Proved crude oil reserves/billion barrels				Global share of proven crude oil reserve/%			
	1997	2005	2015	2019	1997	2005	2015	2019
Asia	11.76	10.78	14.04	13.24	1.2	0.8	0.8	0.8
Africa	68.29	100.61	126.33	123.71	6.7	7.9	7.6	7.7
Europe	1.23	1.19	1.13	1.68	0.1	0.1	0.1	0.1
Eurasian	57.40	77.84	118.89	118.89	5.6	6.1	7.2	7.4
Middle East	677.00	729.34	803.12	804.62	66.3	57.1	48.6	49.9
Oceania	0.40	0.29	0.25	0.22	0.0	0.0	0.0	0.0
South America	68.37	83.51	308.37	312.75	6.7	6.5	18.7	19.4
North America	0.70	1.74	0.85	0.37	0.1	0.1	0.1	0.0
Total	885.15	1005.30	1372.98	1375.48	86.6	78.7	83.1	85.4

Data source EIA database (https://www.eia.gov)

It is reported that the selected countries above has abundant proved crude oil reserves. These countries are divided into 8 groups based on geographic location. The proved crude oil reserves of each region are shown in Table 2.6 [9]. According to statistics, the total proved crude oil reserves of these countries involve in the Belt and Road increased from 885 billion barrels in 1997 to 1,375 billion barrels in 2019 with a global of 85.4%. In terms of distribution, there are six of the top 20 basins known to have the most recoverable oil reserves in the Belt and Road, including the Arabian Basin, the Zagros Basin, the Western Siberian Basin, and Volga. Ural, the Pre-Caspian Basin and the South Caspian Basin [10].

The Middle East is the region with the most abundant oil resources along the Belt and Road. The data in Table 2.6 shows that the proven reserves of crude oil in the Middle East increased from 677 billion barrels in 1997 to 804.62 billion barrels in 2019. In 1997, the proven reserves of crude oil accounted for 66.3% of the world's total, while in 2018 the share declined to 49.9% of the world's total. Similar to Sect. 2.2.1, crude oil reserves in the Middle East are mainly distributed in Saudi Arabia, Iran, Iraq, Kuwait, and the United Arab Emirates.

South America is the second largest area of proved crude oil resources along the Belt and Road (see Table 2.6). In 1997, the region's proven oil reserves were 68.37 billion barrels. In 2015, the proven reserves of crude oil in the region soared to 308.37 billion barrels, and in 2019 it further increased to 312.75 billion barrels. The global share of proved crude oil reserves in South America increased from 6.7% in 1997 to 19.4% in 2019. The increase in crude oil reserves in South America is due to the discovery of heavy oil in Venezuela from 2011. Proved crude oil of Venezuelan in 2019 has reached up to 302.81 billion barrels, making it the world's largest countries based on crude oil resource.

Africa and the Eurasian region are also important oil resource areas along the Belt and Road. Africa's proven crude oil reserves have increased from 68.29 billion barrels in 1997 to 123.71 billion barrels in 2019. Proven crude oil reserves in the Eurasian region increased from 57.4 billion barrels in 1997 to 118.89 billion barrels in 2019. In 2019, the proven reserves of African crude oil accounted for 7.7% of the world's total, and the Eurasian region accounted for 7.4% of the world's total. Africa's crude oil resources are mainly distributed in Libya, Nigeria, Algeria and Angola. Crude oil in the Eurasian region is mainly distributed in Russia, Kazakhstan and Azerbaijan.

Selected countries in Asia show in Table 2.5 has a certain amount of crude oil resources. As illustrated in Table 2.6, the proved crude oil reserves in Asia is 13.24 billion barrels with a global share of 0.8% in 2019. Likewise, selected countries in Europe involved in the Belt and Road hold 0.1% of world' total proved crude oil reserves in 2019. Selected countries in South America and North America have very limited crude oil resources.

2.2.2 Oil Production Within Belt and Road

Data shows that more than 90 countries out of the 140 countries involved in the B&R have the ability to produce oil [9]. The selected countries producing oil and oil products are listed in Table 2.7.

Table 2.7 Selected countries related to oil producing involved in the Belt and Road

Region	Counting	Selected countries
Asia	13	South Korea, Mongolia, Thailand, Indonesia, Philippines, Singapore, Timor-Leste, Malaysia, Myanmar, Viet Nam, Brunei, Pakistan, Bangladesh
Africa	23	Sudan, South Africa, Cote d'Ivoire, Cameroon, South Sudan, Ghana, Zambia, Mozambique, Gabon, Angola, Ethiopia, Kenya, Nigeria, Chad, Congo-Brazzaville, Zimbabwe, Algeria, Morocco, Tunisia, Libya, Egypt, Equatorial Guinea, Niger
Eurasian	13	Azerbaijan, Georgia, Kazakhstan, Kyrgyzstan, Tajikistan, Uzbekistan, Ukraine, Belarus, Estonia, Russia, Lithuania, Latvia, Turkmenistan
Middle East	12	United Arab Emirates, Kuwait, Qatar, Oman, Saudi Arabia, Bahrain, Iran, Iraq, Yemen, Syria, Jordan, Israel
Europe	17	Austria, Greece, Poland, Serbia, Czech Republic, Bulgaria, Slovakia, Albania, Croatia, Bosnia and Herzegovina, Slovenia, Hungary, Macedonia, Romania, Portugal, Italy, Turkey
Oceania	2	New Zealand, Papua New Guinea
South America	7	Chile, Bolivia, Uruguay, Venezuela, Suriname, Ecuador, Peru
North America	6	Costa Rica, Panama, Trinidad and Tobago, Barbados, Cuba, Jamaica

Data source EIA database (https://www.eia.gov)

Table 2.8 Distribution of petroleum production involved in the Belt and Road

Region	Daily petroleum production/Thousand barrels per day				Global share of petroleum production/%			
	1997	2005	2015	2018	1997	2005	2015	2018
Asia	2,792.2	3,039.0	2,957.3	2,884.1	4.0	3.6	3.0	2.9
Africa	7,287.8	10,086.4	8,638.4	8,573.6	10.4	11.8	8.9	8.5
Europe	445.5	474.4	540.8	488.4	0.6	0.6	0.6	0.5
Eurasian	7,142.2	11,766.2	14,133.6	14,622.2	10.2	13.8	14.6	14.5
Middle East	20,420.5	26,091.8	29,345.9	31,267.8	29.0	30.7	30.2	31.0
Oceania	148.0	68.1	108.0	78.2	0.2	0.1	0.1	0.1
South America	3,577.1	3,599.8	3,395.7	2,311.6	5.1	4.2	3.5	2.3
North America	163.1	229.5	161.6	141.4	0.2	0.3	0.2	0.1
Total	41,976.4	55,355.1	59,281.3	60,367.2	59.7	65.0	61.0	59.9

Data source EIA database (https://www.eia.gov)

The daily petroleum production for the selected countries which are catalogued into 8 groups are listed in Table 2.8 [9]. It can be seen that the 93 countries involved in the Belt and Road has a total petroleum producing capacity of 41,976.4 thousand barrels per day in 1997 with a global share of 59.7%. In 2018, the total petroleum production capacity was increased to 60,367.2 thousand barrels per day, and still accounted for 59.9% of the world's total.

As shown in Table 2.8, the Middle East is the region with the largest oil production along the Belt and Road. In 1995, its daily oil production was 20,420.5 thousand barres, and in 2018 it increased to 31,267.8 thousand barrels, with the proportion of the world's total petroleum production increased from 29% to 31%. It is obvious that Saudi Arabia is the country with the highest daily oil production in the Middle East and also the country with the highest oil production in the Belt and Road region. Followed by Iran, Iraq, United Arab Emirates, Kuwait, Qatar and Oman. These seven countries accounted for 51.5% of the total oil production along the Belt and Road.

The Eurasian region is another important oil producing region along the Belt and Road as listed in Table 2.8. The daily oil production in the region doubled from 7,142.2 thousand barrels in 1995 to 14,622.2 thousand barrels in 2018, and the daily oil production in 2018 accounted for 14.5% of the world's total. Undoubtedly, Russia is the country with the highest oil production in Eurasian and the second largest country in terms of oil production along the Belt and Road. The daily oil production of Russia in 2018 accounts for 78.0% of the total oil production in Eurasian. Kazakhstan and Azerbaijan also have considerable oil production.

Africa is the third largest oil procuring region along the Belt and Road (see in Table 2.8). It has a total petroleum producing capacity of 2,884.1 thousand barrels per day in 2018, and holds 8.5% of the world's total petroleum production. The selected countries in Asia and South America has relative lower oil producing capacity, with the amount of 2,884.1 thousand barrels per day and 2,311.6 thousand barrels per day, respectively. The selected countries in Europe, Oceania, and North America has limited petroleum production.

2.2.3   Oil Consumption Within the Belt and Road

Similar to Sect. 2.2.1 and 2.2.2, the countries that has closely tie with oil consumption involved in the Belt and Road are summarized in Table 2.9 [9]. Almost every country is inseparable from the consumption of oil.

The daily petroleum consumption for the countries show in Table 2.9 was also grouped into 8 regions and illustrated in Table 2.10 [9]. Since there are no available data related to oil consumption in 2018 for each country, the data of the year 2016 is used here to represent the latest one. It can be seen that the countries involved in

Table 2.9   Selected countries related to oil consumption involved in the Belt and Road

Region	Counting	Selected countries
Asia	20	South Korea, Afghanistan, Mongolia, Thailand, Indonesia, Philippines, Singapore, Timor-Leste, Malaysia, Myanmar, Cambodia, Viet Nam, Laos, Brunei, Pakistan, Sri Lanka, Bangladesh, Nepal, Maldives, Bhutan
Africa	44	Sudan, South Africa, Senegal, Sierra Leone, Cote d'Ivoire, Somalia, Cameroon, South Sudan, Seychelles, Guinea, Ghana, Zambia, Mozambique, Gabon, Namibia, Mauritania, Angola, Djibouti, Ethiopia, Kenya, Nigeria, Chad, Congo, Zimbabwe, Algeria, Tanzania, Burundi, Cape Verde, Uganda, Gambia, Togo, Rwanda, Morocco, Madagascar, Tunisia, Libya, Egypt, Equatorial Guinea, Liberia, Lesotho, Comoros, Benin, Mali, Niger
Eurasian	15	Azerbaijan, Georgia, Armenia, Kazakhstan, Kyrgyzstan, Tajikistan, Uzbekistan, Ukraine, Belarus, Estonia, Russia, Lithuania, Latvia, Moldova, Turkmenistan
Middle East	14	United Arab Emirates, Kuwait, Qatar, Oman, Lebanon, Saudi Arabia, Bahrain, Iran, Iraq, Yemen, Syria, Jordan, Israel, Palestinian Territories
Europe	21	Cyprus, Austria, Greece, Poland, Serbia, Czech Republic, Bulgaria, Slovakia, Albania, Croatia, Bosnia and Herzegovina, Montenegro, Slovenia, Hungary, Macedonia, Romania, Malta, Portugal, Italy, Luxembourg, Turkey
Oceania	9	New Zealand, Papua New Guinea, Samoa, Niue, Fiji, Cook Islands, Tonga, Vanuatu, Solomon islands
South America	8	Chile, Guyana, Bolivia, Uruguay, Venezuela, Suriname, Ecuador, Peru
North America	11	Costa Rica, Panama, El Salvador, Dominican Republic, Trinidad and Tobago, Antigua and Barbuda, Dominica, Grenada, Barbados, Cuba, Jamaica

Data source EIA database (https://www.eia.gov)

Table 2.10 Distribution of oil consumption involved in the Belt and Road

Region	Daily oil consumption/Thousand barrels per day				Global share of proven crude oil reserve/%			
	1997	2005	2015	2016	1997	2005	2015	2016
Asia	5,251.3	7,145.7	9,150.9	9,619.9	7.5	8.4	9.5	9.9
Africa	2,196.5	2,894.8	4,029.9	4,124.2	3.1	3.4	4.2	4.3
Europe	4,186.1	4,463.0	3,748.0	3,768.7	6.0	5.3	3.9	3.9
Eurasian	4,404.6	3,966.5	4,773.4	4,877.4	6.3	4.7	5.0	5.0
Middle East	4,148.3	6,010.0	8,695.8	8,362.2	5.9	7.1	9.1	8.6
Oceania	154.3	204.8	233.1	240.7	0.2	0.2	0.2	0.2
South America	1,005.9	1,388.7	1,697.2	1,625.0	1.4	1.6	1.8	1.7
North America	500.6	594.3	671.1	678.3	0.7	0.7	0.7	0.7
Total	21,847.5	26,667.9	32,999.5	33,296.4	31.1	31.4	34.4	34.3

Data source EIA database (https://www.eia.gov)

the Belt and Road consumed about one-third of the world's total petroleum, from an amount of 21,847.5 thousand barrels per day in 1995 to 32,999.5 thousand barrels per day in 2016. The selected countries in Asia has the highest daily oil consumption, followed by the Middle East, Eurasian, Africa, and Europe.

Comparing the oil production and consumption in the above-mentioned countries involved in the Belt and Road region, it is obviously that the local oil production in most areas cannot meet domestic oil consumption and needs to be imported from abroad. As shown in Table 2.11, except for the four regions including the Middle East, Eurasian, Africa and South America, which are net oil exporting regions, the other four regions are net oil importing regions. For example, the Asia imported

Table 2.11 The difference between oil production and oil consumption for the regions involved in B&R

Region	The difference between oil production and consumption/Thousand barrels per day			
	1997	2005	2015	2016
Asia	2,459.0	4,106.7	6,193.5	6,581.8
Africa	−5,091.3	−7,191.5	−4,608.5	−3,966.7
Europe	3,740.7	3,988.7	3,207.3	3,276.1
Eurasian	−2,737.6	−7,799.7	−9,360.2	−9,382.4
Middle East	−16,272.2	−20,081.8	−20,650.1	−22,753.0
Oceania	6.3	136.7	125.2	140.7
South America	−2,571.2	−2,211.1	−1,698.5	−1,529.4
North America	337.4	364.8	509.5	527.2

Data source EIA database (https://www.eia.gov)

6,581.8 thousand barrels of oil per day in 2016, accounting for 68.4% of its total oil consumption. In 2016, Europe imported 3,276.1 thousand barrels of oil per day, accounting for 86.9% of its total oil consumption, while the North American imported 527.2 thousand barrels of oil per day, accounting for 77.7% of its total oil consumption. Oceania imported 140.7 thousand barrels per day of oil in 2016, accounting for 58.5% of its total oil consumption. It can be seen that the Belt and Road region made up of the selected countries shown in Table 2.9 imports about 10,525.9 thousand barrels per day of foreign oil, accounting for 31.6% of the total oil consumption in the region.

2.3 International Energy Cooperation Between China and B&R Countries

By the end of October 2019, China had signed 197 cooperation documents with the 137 countries and 30 international organizations to build the BRI [6], among which energy cooperation is one of important topic.

2.3.1 Oil Imports of China from B&R Countries

China has very close tie with countries along the Belt and Road in terms of oil cooperation. Data of UNCTADSTAT released by United Nations Conferences on Trade and Development shows that about 76 countries out of the total 143 countries involved in B&R export petroleum to China in 2018 (listed in Table 2.12) [11].

Statistics of UNCTADSTAT [11] show that China spent 291 billion U.S. dollars in 2018 to import petroleum from the whole world, of which over 87% were imported from the B&R countries shown in Table 2.12. From the perspective of the distribution of the countries along the Belt and Road, China imported the most oil from the Middle East, accounting for 47.36%, followed by Africa and Eurasian, accounting for 19.82% and 16.74%, and Asia ranked fourth, with the share of 12.51%. China spends 3.43% of its oil imports from South America, with only a small amount of oil imports from Europe and North America (as shown in Fig. 2.3).

In Africa, Angola is the largest customer of Chinese oil imports. In 2018, the cost of China's oil imports from Angola was 26.75 billion U.S. dollars. Congo-Brazzaville is China's second largest oil importer in Africa, and the cost of oil imported from the country in 2018 was US 6.6 billion U.S. dollars. Libya ranks third, and China's oil imports from the country in 2018 were 5.05 billion U.S. dollars. The fourth and fifth are Gabon and Ghana, with imports of 2.25 billion and 2.01 billion U.S. dollars, respectively. South Sudan is sixth, Equatorial Guinea is seventh, Egypt is eighth, Algeria is ninth, and Nigeria is tenth. The above ten countries account for 96.8% of China's oil imports in Africa in 2018.

Table 2.12 List of countries involved in B&R that China imported petroleum from in 2018

Region	Counting	Selected countries
Asia	11	South Korea, Mongolia, Thailand, Indonesia, Philippines, Singapore, Malaysia, Myanmar, Viet Nam, Brunei, Pakistan
Africa	22	Sudan, South Africa, Senegal, Cote d'Ivoire, Cameroon, South Sudan, Guinea, Ghana, Gabon, Angola, Ethiopia, Nigeria, Chad, Congo, Algeria, Uganda, Madagascar, Libya, Egypt, Equatorial Guinea, Liberia, Niger
Eurasian	9	Azerbaijan, Kazakhstan, Uzbekistan, Ukraine, Estonia, Russia, Lithuania, Latvia, Turkmenistan
Middle East	10	United Arab Emirates, Kuwait, Qatar, Oman, Saudi Arabia, Bahrain, Iran, Iraq, Yemen, Israel
Europe	16	Austria, Greece, Poland, Czech Republic, Bulgaria, Slovakia, Albania, Croatia, Slovenia, Hungary, Romania, Malta, Portugal, Italy, Luxembourg, Turkey
Oceania	2	New Zealand, Papua New Guinea
South America	5	Chile, Bolivia, Venezuela, Ecuador, Peru
North America	1	Panama

Data source UNCTADSTAT (https://unctadstat.unctad.org/wds/ReportFolders/reportFolders.aspx?
sCS_ChosenLang=en)

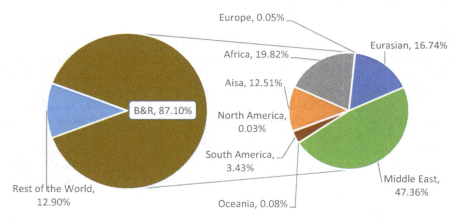

Fig. 2.3 Share of China's petroleum imports from B&R in 2018. *Data source* UNCTADSTAT (https://unctadstat.unctad.org/wds/ReportFolders/reportFolders.aspx?sCS_ChosenLang=en). (*Note* petroleum here includes petroleum, petroleum products and related materials)

Among the selected countries involve in B&R in East and South Asia, China imported the most oil from South Korea in 2018, reaching 9.55 billion U.S. dollars, followed by Malaysia from which China imported oil at 6.58 billion U.S. dollars. Singapore ranked third, and China's oil imports from the country was 4.70 billion U.S. dollars. Indonesia ranked fourth, and China's petroleum import value was 4.23

billion U.S. dollars. Vietnam ranked fifth. China imported 3.55 billion U.S. dollars from Vietnam. The above 5 countries account for 60.1% of China's total oil imports from Asia in 2018. Thailand, Mongolia, the Philippines, Brunei, and Pakistan are in the bottom five.

The Middle East is China's main region for oil imports along the Belt and Road. Saudi Arabia is China's largest source of oil imports. In 2018, China imported 36.07 billion U.S. dollars in oil from Saudi Arabia. The No. 2 player in the region is Iraq. In 2018, China imported 24.13 billion U.S. dollars in oil from Iraq. The third is Oman. In 2018, China imported 18.82 billion U.S. dollars in oil from Oman. The fourth is Iran. China spent $ 17.01 billion U.S. dollars to buy oil from Iran in 2018. Fifth is Kuwait, where China purchased 13.40 billion U.S. dollars of oil from Kuwait. The sixth is the United Arab Emirates, where China spent 9.14 billion U.S. dollars to buy oil from. These six countries accounted for 98.8% of China's total oil imports from the Middle East in 2018. Qatar, Yemen, Bahrain and Israel ranked seventh, eighth, ninth and tenth, respectively.

In Eurasia, Russia is China's largest petroleum supplier. In 2018, China's oil imports from Russia reached 39.72 billion U.S. dollars, accounting for 93.6% of China's total oil imports in Eurasia. Kazakhstan is China's second largest oil supplier in the region. In 2018, China purchased 2.28 billion dollars of oil in the Kazakhstan, accounting for 5.4% of China's total oil imports from Eurasia in 2018. In addition, China also imports oil from Azerbaijan, Turkmenistan, Lithuania, Ukraine, Uzbekistan, Estonia and Latvia.

In South America, Venezuela is China's major oil supplier. China purchased 7.47 billion U.S. dollars of oil from Venezuela in 2018. This is followed by Ecuador, where China imported 1.02 billion U.S. dollars in oil from the country in 2018. China's oil imports from these two countries account for 97.7% of the total imports from South America.

China imports relatively little oil from Europe, Oceania and North America. From the perspective of the countries selected by the Belt and Road Initiative, China's oil imports from Europe include Italy, Greece, Malta, Poland, Romania, and Albania. Oceania's oil imports mainly come from Papua New Guinea and New Zealand, and North America is mainly Chile.

2.3.2 Typical Oil Cooperation Projects of Chinese Company Toward B&R Countries

Since BRI was launched in 2013, China's international oil and gas cooperation has developed rapidly. In 2018, China's oil and gas business expanded to dozens of countries around the world, managing and operating over 100 oil and gas cooperation projects [12]. The three state oil companies, namely PetroChina, Sinopec and CNOOC, still dominate the international oil and gas cooperation in China, and private oil and gas companies have stepped up their foreign cooperation. CNPC's overseas exploration activities were centered on large-scale, high-quality and readily producible reserves, leading to achievements in a number of key zones. These activities resulted in total overseas equity crude production of 75.35 million tons of oil equivalent with a newly added equity recoverable reserves of 18.03 million tons of crude oil in 2018 [13]. Sinopec hold a total overseas equity crude production of 39.58 million barrels in 2018 [14]. By the end of 2018, there were tens of oil cooperation projects in China along the Belt and Road. Some of the main projects are briefly described below.

2.3.2.1 Central Asia-Russia

The main target for CNPC in central Asia-Russia is to build a core oil and gas cooperation zone under the Belt and Road Initiative. On June 20, 2018, the Engineering Construction Training Center of Daqing Oilfield of CNPC signed a technical cooperation agreement with the Russian Welding Society (NAKS) [15]. The signing of this cooperation agreement has a positive and far-reaching impact on upgrading China's petroleum welding technology level, promoting Daqing Oilfield's participation in Russian engineering construction, and further enhancing the internationalization of China's petroleum welding technology.

On November 25, 2018, Gubkin Branch of Zhongman Petroleum and Natural Gas Group Corp. Ltd. (ZPEC) signed a two-year contract for the drilling of 14 horizontal production wells with a contract value of 200 million yuan with YARGEO, a subsidiary of Novartek Group, Russia's largest independent natural gas producer [16]. The signing of this contract marks a major step forward for ZPEC in the Russian drilling integrated services market.

2.3.2.2 Middle East

CNPC's target in the Middle East is to build a high-end cooperation zone that gives full play to the company's comprehensive and integrated advantage [13]. The offshore Bu Haseer Oilfield in Abu Dhabi, UAE became operational one year after its construction. The newly-signed Abu Dhabi Offshore Project started to produce oil [13]. The Halfaya Oilfield Phase III (CPF3) project became operational, bringing a 200,000 bbl/d addition to processing capacity and boosting the field's total annual capacity to 20 million tons; a power station and water injection pipelines were put into operation at the Rumaila Oilfield, with other upgrades and ramp-ups proceeding as planned [13].

In April 2019, the first set of 1-series atmospheric distillation unit (U01) and system tube bridge (U74) of the Kuwait Azul refinery, which was jointly contracted by Techicas Reunidas (TR), Sinopec Engineering (Group) Co., LTD. (SEG) and Hanwha, were successfully intermediated accepted [17]. This is one of Sinopec's overseas projects involved in contract construction. The Kuwait Azul refinery project is a national key construction project under BRI, and is also an example of the win-win development of Sinopec and the countries along the Belt and Road. In addition, on July 4, 2018, Kuwait Branch of Sinopec Oilfield Service Corporation signed a contract for 20 rigs with Kuwait National Petroleum Company (KNPC) with a contract period of "5 + 1" years [18]. This contract will help Kuwait achieve its goal of producing 4 million barrels of crude oil per day by 2020.

On July 22, 2019, Abu Dhabi National Oil Company (ADNOC) signed a Strategic Framework Agreement with China National Offshore Oil Corporation (CNOOC) to explore new opportunities for collaboration in both the upstream and downstream sectors as well as in LNG [19]. ADNOC and CNOOC have also agreed to share knowledge, best practices and latest proven technologies in the area of ultra-sour gas development with the aim of improving operational efficiency in sour gas processing and treatment; delivering efficiency, performance and reliability for sour gas drilling operations; and improving field and reservoir development plans. In the downstream space, ADNOC and CNOOC have agreed to analyze the potential of certain mutually beneficial business opportunities, including the potential collaboration in new integrated refining and petrochemical assets in China; cooperation in CNOOC's existing refining assets; as well as a broader partnership and joint-investment across the refining and petrochemical value chain.

On 25 November, 2019, Abu Dhabi National Oil Company (ADNOC) signed a broad Framework Agreement with China's Rongsheng Petrochemical Co. Ltd. (Rongsheng) to explore domestic and international growth opportunities which will support the delivery of its 2030 smart growth strategy [20]. The agreement will see both companies explore opportunities in the sale of refined products from ADNOC to Rongsheng, downstream investment opportunities in both China and the United Arab Emirates, and the supply and delivery of liquified natural gas (LNG) to Rongsheng.

2.3.2.3   Africa

In Sudan and South Sudan, CNPC International Nile exceeded production targets for the year, by strengthening oilfield management, improving well stimulation measures and increasing profit-generating output. The company managed to put the Block 1/2/4 in South Sudan back into production with a daily capacity of 22,000 barrels [13]. The Raphia FPF and second Daniela CPF facilities for the Chad Project Phase 2.2 became operational [13].

In April 2018, Sinopec Shanghai Petrochemical Company Limited (SPC) cooperated with Sinopec Chemical Commercial Holding Company Limited to realize the transit export of refined oil products through Chenshan port. On August 11, the 80,000-ton foreign product oil ship berthed at Chenshan port, loaded with about 30,000 tons of SPC diesel, sailed to Quanzhou, Fujian where assembled diesel, and then headed to Richard Bay Port, South Africa. As of August 20, 2018, SPC has delivered more than 110,000 tons of diesel with the help of Chenshan port [21].

2.3.2.4 Others

In Kazakhstan, the Shymkent Refinery renovation project Phase II was completed and went on stream [13]. As one of Kazakhstan's top three refineries, the Shymkent Refinery is jointly operated by CNPC and KazMunaiGas. Started in 2014, the renovation project comprises of two phases: Phase I was made operational at the end of June 2017; Phase II went on stream in September 2018. The revamping efforts have turned the Shymkent Refinery into a state-of-the-art, eco-friendly refinery with significantly improved processing capabilities. In particular, the light oil yield has increased from 56% to 80% and oil products are compliant with the Euro IV and Euro V standards as well as the local regulations for clean fuels, playing an important role in promoting eco-friendliness and securing oil products supply [13].

On 1 March, 2018, Sinopec Jiujiang Company's overseas project team successfully completed a single test of 13 large units of 5 sets of the Atyrau oil deep processing project in Kazakhstan, laying a solid foundation for the joint test run of the unit [22].

CNOOC has made five new world-class discoveries in the Stabroek block in Guyana. CNOOC Limited holds 25% interest. It is reported that the first oil of Liza Phase I will be planned in 2020, with peak production of 120,000 boe/day. The Final Investment Decision (FID) of Liza Phase II is expected to be approved in 1H 2019. The collective discoveries by the end of 2018 has established the potential for producing over 750,000 boe/day. The whole project in Guyana has competitive development costs [23].

On 5 September, 2018, COSL INDO and PERTAMINA held a block expiration handing over ceremony at the offshore operation support base of the SES block, which marked the successful completion of CNOOC's first overseas project [24]. During the operation of CNOOC, the SES block produced a total of 338 million barrels of oil and gas equivalents, of which 312 million barrels of crude oil were produced, and the cumulative export of natural gas exceeded 4.36 billion cubic meters. It has achieved economic value and made important contributions to local economic and social development.

On 8 January, 2018, under the witness of the chairman of both Hengli Group and Sinochem Group, Hengli Co., Ltd. and Sinochem Oil signed an agreement to establish a trade joint venture in Singapore, and agreed to use their respective Singapore companies as the main body in accordance with Hengli. 80%, Sinochem 20% joint venture to set up a trading company, responsible for the import and purchase of crude oil by Hengli Refining, export sales of refined oil and petrochemicals, and international third-party re-exports of crude oil and refined oil [25]. It is predicted that the scale of the joint venture company will reach more than 30 million tons per year. On June 12, 2018, Hengli Oilchem was officially established in Singapore and then became a private oil customer of Saudi Aramco Asia in the Chinese market.

2.3.3   Challenges of Energy Cooperation Under the BRI

As stated in Sect. 2.3.2, a series of oil cooperation achievements have been made by Chinese oil companies with countries along the Belt and Road route, however, there are still various challenges for Chinese oil companies conducting international oil cooperation. These challenges primarily include geopolitical risk, national sovereignty risk, local legal risk and local natural environment risk [26].

2.3.3.1   Geographic Risk

Geopolitical risks are mainly reflected in the constraints of regional powers. The Belt and Road Initiative, as an extensive and diversified cooperation platform, will provide China with better opportunities for cooperation with the countries involved in the BRI. However, with the further development of the world's multi-polarization and the rapid rise of China, it is inconsistent with the expectations of some major power in Western countries and attempts to interfere with China's development at different levels, which poses a serious challenge to the construction and development of the BRI and increases difficulties for China to direct invest in countries and regions along the B&R route.

Regional instability is also a major challenge for energy cooperation along the Belt and Road. Although majority of countries along the Belt and Road route have shown positive willingness, the grim regional situation and problems still exist. For example, the Ukrainian crisis, the Islamic State issue, the Somali's pirate issue, the Palestinian-Israeli conflict, the Iranian nuclear issue, the Afghanistan and Libya issues, etc. are difficult to resolve in a short period of time, and will be long-term regional problems. These unstable factors may disrupt the continuity of oil and gas cooperation policies, and bring many adverse effects on the proposed projects or projects under construction and the legal rights of foreign investors.

2.3.3.2   National Sovereignty Risk

The Belt and Road Initiative is an international arrangement, but energy projects often serve national policies. It can be seen from the experience of trans-European energy network construction that conflicts of interest within and among countries often exist. For example, the offshore wind power connection in the Baltic and North Sea projects face significant social challenges due to passing through densely populated areas. In addition, the short-term/long-term and partial/overall policy priorities of international cooperation are different. Tariffs and other regulations are usually focused on short-term costs and benefits, while it is entirely possible for a country to make decisions contrary to its short-term interests in order to promote the long-term development of a region. For example, Russian natural gas is the EU's most economical choice, but the EU still spares no efforts to promote the diversification of energy sources so as to ensure long-term security. In addition, the feasibility studies and building license procedures for cross-border energy projects take a long time to complete, which can lead to delays or even cancellations. Such problems cannot be avoided in "Belt and Road" energy cooperation [27].

2.3.3.3 Legal Risk

BRI oil cooperation involves large number of countries, large amounts of money, and a long industrial chain. However, the legal system in China's existing multilateral cooperation framework is still inadequate. Therefore, the promotion and protection of the current B&R energy cooperation projects mainly depend on a range of bilateral agreements between China and its neighboring countries, plus political medication and diplomacy. Due to the differences in the specific content and soundness of the laws and regulations of many countries, and some countries often modify the corresponding legal provisions, this brings certain legal risks to oil cooperation under the BRI as well. Formulating a robust legal framework is always a huge work. China has tried to gradually establish institutions such as the Asian Infrastructure Investment Bank (AIIB) to eliminate barriers that exist cross-border cooperation. However, with the increase in the number and complexity of cross-border energy cooperation projects under the BRI, China urgently needs to establish a more comprehensive multilateral legal framework with countries along the Belt and Road route to manage potential disputes and risks.

2.3.3.4 Financial Risk

In the financial field, there are three main factors affecting the B&R oil cooperation: (1) A number of different countries are involved in the BRI, and these countries have not formed a unified international settlement currency. Once the international economy fluctuates, the exchange rates of the countries in the region may also fluctuate to a large extent, which may cause financial risks such as changing financing environments, rising capital costs, and exchange losses. (2) The financial strength and business environment of the countries along the B&R route affect the final implementation of energy investment projects such as petroleum cooperation projects. It is reported that less than 40% of the countries along the B&R route have relatively high financial strength, which affects energy cooperation with related countries to a certain extent. (3) The project returns are slow due to the large scale and long cycle of energy cooperation projects, which brings risks to project financing. Simple government support may be difficult to meet project financing needs. That's why the PPP mode, in which the government provides a political commitment for project promotion while the private sector is responsible for construction, operation and maintenance, was widely encouraged under BRI [27]. Although the PPP model can transfer financing risks to the social capital side, significant uncertainties still exists for private capital's continued investment as they face the political, economic, and social risks when investing the cross-border energy cooperation projects. The project profitability and investment environment are the two key factors for private capital to make investment decisions.

2.3.3.5 Environmental Risk

Due to the impact of climate change, most countries around the world have payed much attention on environmental protection of energy cooperation projects. When carrying out oil cooperation with countries along the Belt and Road route, we must pay attention not only to the substantial impact of energy projects on the local natural environment, but also to local environmental protection policies such as carbon emissions, to ensure that the project meets the requirements of environmental protection and sustainable development.

References

1. BP. 2019. *BP Statistical Review of World Energy* 2019. London: BP.
2. CAPP. 2019. *2019 Crude Oil Forcast, Markets and Transportation.* Canada: Canadian Association of Petroleum Producers.
3. CAPP's Statistical Handbook. 2019. Canadian association of petroleum producers. https://www.capp.ca/publications-and-statistics/statistics/statistical-handbook. Accessed 2019-11-18.
4. EIA. 2019. *Petroleum Supply Annual*, vol. 1. Washington, DC: U.S. Energy Information Administration.
5. EIA. 2019. *Refinery Capacity Report Washington.* DC: U.S. Energy Information Administration.
6. The list of countries that have signed a BRI cooperation document with China. 2019. https://www.yidaiyilu.gov.cn/gbjg/gbgk/77073.htm. Accessed 2019-04-12.
7. The World Bank data. 2019. The World Bank. https://data.worldbank.org/indicator/NY.GDP.MKTP.CD. Accessed 2019-11-08.
8. World macroeconomic database. 2019. EPS China Data. http://olap.epsnet.com.cn/auth/platform.html?sid=DF9F62FF6D05206513B38A7121E99AB0. Accessed 2019-11-23.
9. International Energy Statistics. 2019. U.S. Energy Information Administration. https://www.eia.gov/beta/international/data/browser/. Accessed 2019-11-25.
10. Li, Fubin, Guoping Bai, Zhixin Wang, Chunfeng Yan, Weihong Wang, Minghui Yuan, Yu Bai, Wenbo Li, and Qian Wang. 2015. The oil and gas resources potential and prospects for cooperation of "One Belt And One Road". *China Mining Magazine* 10: 1–3 + 26. (in Chinese).
11. UNCTADstat database. 2019. https://unctadstat.unctad.org/wds/ReportFolders/reportFolders.aspx?sCS_ChosenLang=en. Accessed 2019-12-18.
12. Wang, Zhigang, Qingzhe Jiang, Xiucheng Dong, and Chaohong Gao. 2019. *Blue Book of China Oil & Gas Industry Development Analysis and Prospect Report.* Beijing: China Petrochemical Press.
13. CNPC. 2019. *2018 Annual Report.* Beijing: China National Petroleum Corporation.
14. SINOPEC. 2019. *2019 Annual Report.* Beijing: Sinopec.
15. Daqing Oilfield of CNPC signed an agreement with Russia. 2018. http://dqyt.cnpc.com.cn/dq/gsdt/201807/12fb2a8853eb4fa4808666f0c3919e79.shtml. Accessed 2018-07-03.
16. Novatek project opens a new chapter for ZPEC in Russian market. 2018. http://www.zpec.com/cn/news/detail/?id=1771. Accessed 2018-11-27.

17. Kuwaiti Azur refinery's first set has been delivered. 2019. http://www.segroup.cn/segroup/news/com_news/20190415/news_20190415_552390686625.shtml. Accessed 2019-04-09.
18. Sinopec Oilfield Service Corporation signed a 7 billion Yuan contract with KNPC. 2018. http://www.sohu.com/a/239067731_323087. Accessed 2018-07-03.
19. Mohamed bin Zayed and Xi Jinping. 2019. Witness Signing of ADNOC and CNOOC Strategic Framework Agreement. https://www.adnoc.ae/en/news-and-media/press-releases/2019/mohamed-bin-zayed-and-xi-jinping-witness-signing-of-adnoc-and-cnooc-strategic-framework-agreement. Accessed 2019-07-22.
20. ADNOC Signs Framework Agreement with China's Rongsheng Petrochemical to Explore Domestic and International Growth Opportunities. 2019. https://www.adnoc.ae/en/news-and-media/press-releases/2019/adnoc-signs-framework-agreement-with-chinas-rongsheng>. Accessed 2019-11-12.
21. SPC's petroleum produt is shipped to South Africa for the first time. 2018. http://oil.in-en.com/html/oil-2844776.shtml. Accessed 2018-08-20.
22. Oil deep processing project of Kazakhstan refinery operated by Sinopec Jiujiang Company successfully started. 2018. http://energy.cngold.org/c/2018-07-10/c5844491.html. Accessed 2018-11-23.
23. CNOOC. 2019. *2018 Annual Results*. Beijing: CNOOC Limited.
24. CNOOC's first overseas project completed. 2019. http://www.sasac.gov.cn/n2588025/n2588124/c9592750/content.html. Accessed 2018-09-18.
25. Hengli Oilchem officially operates in Singapore. 2018. http://www.shzywchina.com/index.php?s=/jysh38shzyw/news/info/id/1137.html. Accessed 2018-06-14.
26. Yang, T., Z. Li, and J. Qin. 2019. AHP- fuzzy comprehensive evaluation of the safety risk in power investment project along "the Belt and Road". In *E3S Web of Conferences*.
27. Yu, Jiahao, and Junzhe Shen. 2019. Energy cooperation and risk prevention under the "Belt and Road" Initiative. *China Oil & Gas* 26(02): 42–47 + 88–91.

Chapter 3
Energy Cooperation Between China and the GCC Countries Under the BRI

Tingting Zhang

In view of the rich oil resources of the GCC countries and the special geographical location along the Belt and Road route, the energy cooperation between China and the GCC countries should be deepened under the Belt and Road framework. To this end, this chapter will first sort out the current status of oil resources in the GCC countries, then analyze the status and prospects of oil trade between China and the GCC countries, and finally propose corresponding countermeasures on the basis of discussing the risks of energy cooperation between the two sides.

3.1 An Overview of the GCC

The GCC, also known as the Cooperation Council for the Arab States of the Gulf, is an organization of six oil-exporting countries of the Persian Gulf. It was formed on May 25, 1981 in the United Arab Emirates by the heads of the six Arab countries of the Gulf to foster economic, scientific, and business cooperation. GCC headquartered in Riyadh, the capital of Saudi Arabia. In 1984 the group formed a military arm called the Peninsular Shield Force to respond to military aggression against members. As of October 2019, the members were Bahrain, Kuwait, Oman, Qatar, Saudi Arabia, and the United Arab Emirates. These Middle East countries share the common faith of Islam and Arabian culture. They also share an economic interest distinct from their OPEC (Organization of the Petroleum Exporting Countries) membership. These countries seek to diversify their growing economies away from oil [1].

From the geographical point of view, the six countries of the Gulf are in the east and west hemispheres. The north is bordered by Iraq and Jordan, the south is adjacent to Yemen and the Arabian Sea, the east is the Arabian Gulf, and the west is the Red

T. Zhang (✉)
International Energy Research Center, Shanghai Jiao Tong University, Shanghai, China
e-mail: zhangtingting@sjtu.edu.cn

© Shanghai Jiao Tong University Press 2021
T. Zhang and D. Wang (eds.), *China-Gulf Oil Cooperation Under the Belt and Road Initiative*, https://doi.org/10.1007/978-981-15-9283-6_3

Table 3.1 The economy and population of the six Gulf countries in 2018

Countries	GDP and population				GDP per capital/($US per capital)
	GDP/million dollars	Population/thousand	GDP share/%	Population share/%	
Saudi Arabia	782,483	33,700	47.5	59.5	23,219
UAE	414,179	9631	25.1	17.0	43,005
Qatar	192,009	2782	11.7	4.9	69,026
Bahrain	37,746	1569	2.3	2.8	24,051
Kuwait	141,678	4137	8.6	7.3	34,244
Oman	79,295	4829	4.8	8.5	16,419

Data source The World Bank data (https://data.worldbank.org.cn/)

Sea. It has a very important strategic location. Most of the six countries in the Gulf are deserts, which have a tropical desert climate. The total area of the six countries is 2.66 million square kilometers. In 2018, the population was about 56.649 million, and the GDP was about 1647.391 billion U.S. dollars [2]. The main resources were oil and natural gas.

Saudi Arabia is the country with the highest GDP and the largest population in the six countries (as shown in Table 3.1 [2]). Saudi Arabia's GDP in 2018 accounted for 47.5% of the total GDP of six Gulf countries, and the proportion of the population in the six countries was 59.5%. The second largest country in the GCC is the United Arab Emirates. In 2018, its GDP and population accounted for 25.1 and 17.0% of the total of the six countries. Qatar is the third largest country in the region with the highest GDP per capital of $69,026, followed by Kuwait and Oman. Bahrain is the smallest one with a population of 1569 thousand and GDP per capital of 24,051 U.S. dollars.

The unique natural conditions and resource conditions of the six GCC countries have led to the formation of a single oil economic structure in the region. The oil industry is the pillar industry of the six countries. The oil production value accounts for about 35% of its GDP, and oil revenue accounts for 75% of its fiscal revenue. The rich energy reserves have made the six Gulf States one of the world's most important energy sources, and this has brought a huge oil dollar income. In general, the six countries' overseas investments are mainly in stocks, real estate, government bonds, bank deposits, etc., and they are less invested in production and construction projects. The economy of the Gulf countries is greatly affected by the changes of crude oil prices in the international market. In order to change the single-type economic structure and reduce dependence on crude oil exports, the GCC countries have invested heavily in infrastructure construction, developing irrigated agriculture, and improving the investment environment. In order to attract foreign investment, and encourage the development of processing industries and services such as finance, insurance and tourism, some progress has been made in diversifying economic sources recently.

It is reported that the export volume of crude oil in the six GCC countries exceeds 13 million barrels per day. The GCC's oil resources play an important role in the Belt and Road oil map. Some scholars have divided the New Silk Road into five sections: East Asia, Central Asia, West Asia, Central and Eastern Europe, and Western Europe [3]. The West Asia section, represented by the GCC, is at the intersection of the Belt and Road and is one of the important strategic fulcrums along the Belt and Road. On the one hand, China's Belt and Road Initiative is in line with the GCC economic integration process. China is pleased to see the GCC integration process continue to develop in depth and hopes to promote the China-GCC Free Trade Area (FTA) negotiations as soon as possible. Meanwhile, China also strive to reach an agreement on the negotiation of trade in goods at an early date. At the same time, it will create conditions for starting negotiations in various fields such as service trade, economic and technological cooperation, and investment. On the other hand, the GCC countries have strong economic strength and relatively mature markets. In the face of international economic recovery and transformation, there are also ambitious development plans, which will become the key areas for the promotion of BRI and will be the earliest area achieving effectiveness [4].

3.2 Oil Situation in the GCC Countries

Benefited from natural resources, the Gulf countries have abundant oil resources and play a very important role in the international energy system.

3.2.1 Oil Resource Endowment

Table 3.2 lists the proved crude oil reserves in the GCC countries [5, 6]. In 1995, the total amount of proven crude oil reserves in the GCC countries was 464.54 billion barrels, accounting for 70.4% of total proved crude oil reserves in the middle east, and 46.4% of that in the world. In 2005, the total amount of proved crude oil reserves in the GCC countries increased to 482.04 billion barrels, accounting for 66.1% of total proven crude oil reserves in the middle east, and 37.7% of that in the world. In 2019, the total amount of proven crude oil reserves increased to 496.29 billion barrels, however, the share of proven crude oil reserves to the middle east declined to 61.7%, and the share of the proven crude oil reserves to the world dropped to 30.8%. As shown in Sect. 2.1.1, oil around the world has been detected and proved own to the technology progress. Nevertheless, the proven crude oil reserves in the GCC countries increase very slowly over the past ten years.

Table 3.2 Proven crude oil reserves in the GCC countries

Countries	Proved crude oil reserves/billion barrels			The percentage of proved crude oil reserves to the Middle East total/%			The percentage of proved crude oil reserves to the world total/%		
	1995[a]	2005[a]	2019[b]	1995[a]	2005[a]	2019[b]	1995[a]	2005[a]	2019[b]
Bahrain	0.21	0.12	0.11	0.03	0.02	0.01	0.02	0.01	0.01
Kuwait	96.50	101.50	101.50	14.6	13.9	12.6	9.6	7.9	6.30
Oman	4.83	5.51	5.37	0.7	0.8	0.7	0.5	0.4	0.3
Qatar	3.70	15.21	25.24	0.6	2.1	3.1	0.4	1.2	1.6
Saudi Arabia	261.20	261.90	266.26	39.6	35.9	33.1	26.1	20.5	16.5
United Arab Emirates	98.10	97.80	97.80	14.9	13.4	12.1	9.8	7.6	6.1
Total	464.54	482.04	496.29	70.4	66.1	61.7	46.4	37.7	30.8

Notes [a]The data are sourced from EPS CHINA DATA (https://www.epschinadata.com/)
[b]The data are sourced from EIA database (www.eia.gov)

3.2.1.1   Bahrain

Bahrain is the country with the lowest amount of oil reserve among the GCC countries. In 1995, Bahrain had 210 million barrels of proven crude oil reserve, which only accounted for 0.03% of the total proven reserves in the Middle East, and 0.01% of world's proven reserves. Since 2005, the proven crude oil reserve in Bahrain has decreased to 120 million barrels, and the percentages of proven crude oil reserve to the Middle East and the world have been dropped to 0.02% and 0.01% respectively. Its proven crude oil in 2019 was further dropped to 110 million barrels. It can be seen that Bahrain has relative limited crude oil resource owing to the very small area of the territory.

3.2.1.2   Kuwait

Kuwait, as one of the countries with abundant oil reserves, its crude oil reserve ranks second in the GCC countries. As shown in Table 3.2, the proven crude oil reserve for Kuwait in 1995 was 96.50 billion barrels, accounting for 14.6% of total proven crude oil reserves in the Middle East, and 9.6% of that in the world. In 2005, the proven crude oil reserve in Kuwait increased to 101.50 billion barrels, the percentage of oil reserve to the Middle East and the world dropped to 13.9% and 7.9%, respectively. In 2019, the proven crude oil reserve for Kuwait is as same as that in 2005. However, the percentage of proven crude oil reserve to the Middle East and the world declined to 12.6% and 6.3% respectively.

3.2.1.3   Oman

Oman is also a country with relative few crude oil reserves among the six GCC countries. In 1995, Oman had about 4.83 billion barrels of proven crude oil reserve. In 2005, its proven crude oil reserve increased to 5.51 billion barrels. In 2019, the proven crude oil reserve in Oman dropped to 5.37 billion barrels. The percentage of proven crude oil reserve to the Middle East for Kuwait is stable around 7–8% during the period 1995–2019. Same as Bahrain, the percentage of proven crude oil reserve to the world declined from 0.5% in 1995 and 0.3% in 2019.

3.2.1.4   Qatar

Qatar is the fourth-largest country in terms of proven crude oil reserves in the six GCC countries. Statistics show that Qatar's proven crude oil reserve in 1995 was only 3.7 billion barrels, accounting for 0.6% of the Middle East and 0.4% of global proven crude oil reserves. In 2005, the proven crude oil reserve in Qatar quickly increased to 15.21 barrels, and the share of proven crude oil reserve to the Middle East rose to 2.1%, accounting for 1.2% of the world's total. In 2019, Qatar's proven crude oil reserve further increased to 25.24 billion barrels, accounting for 3.1% of the Middle East, and 1.6% of the world. Qatar is a country with the fastest-growing speed of proven oil reserves in the Middle East.

3.2.1.5   Saudi Arabia

Saudi Arabia is the country with the richest crude oil reserves among the GCC countries, and also one of the countries with largest crude oil reserves in the world. In 1995, the proven crude oil reserve in Saudi Arabia was 261.20 billion barrels, accounting for 39.6% of total proven crude oil reserves in the Middle East and 26.1% of that in the world. So far, the crude oil reserves in Saudi Arabia have grown slowly from 261.90 billion barrels in 2005 to 266.26 billion barrels in 2019. At the same time, its share of proven crude oil to the Middle East and the world dropped from 35.9% in 2005 to 33.1% in 2019, and 20.5% in 2005 and 16.5% in 2019, respectively.

3.2.1.6   UAE

The UAE is the third-largest country according to the proven crude oil reserves among the six GCC countries. In 1995, its proven crude oil reserve was 98.10 billion barrels. Since 2005, this value slightly dropped to 97.80 billion barrels. In 1995, the percentages of proven oil reserve for the UAE to the Middle East and the world were 14.9% and 9.8% respectively. However, the share to the Middle East and the world declined from 13.4% in 2005 to 12.1% in 2019, and 7.6% in 2005 to 6.1% in 2019, respectively.

3.2.2   Crude Oil Production

It is well known that oil has been a pillar of the economy for the GCC countries. Their crude oil plays a very important role in the world's oil market as well. Table 3.3 shows the crude oil production tendencies for the six GCC countries [7]. In 1995, the GCC countries had the cumulative crude oil production of 13,561.3 thousand barrels per day, accounting to 71.9% of the Middle East total, and 22.4% of the world total. In 2005, the cumulative crude oil production for the GCC countries increased to 15,971.9 thousand barrels per day, accounting for 70.3% of the Middle East total, and 22.3% of world total. In 2018, the cumulative crude oil production for the six GCC countries has been further raised to 17,726.1 thousand barrels per day. However, the share of crude oil production to the Middle East decreased to 68.9%, while the share to the world's total slightly increased to 23.4%.

Table 3.3 The crude oil production in the GCC countries

Countries	The daily crude oil production/(thousand barrels/day)			The percentage of crude oil production to the Middle East total/%			The percentage of crude oil production to the world total/%		
	1995	2005	2018	1995	2005	2018	1995	2005	2018
Bahrain	145.4	186.5	193.2	0.8	0.8	0.8	0.2	0.3	0.3
Kuwait	2006.6	2573.4	2736.6	10.6	11.3	10.6	3.3	3.6	3.6
Oman	848.1	714.8	870.0	4.5	3.1	3.4	1.4	1.0	1.1
Qatar	389.8	765.9	600.6	2.1	3.4	2.3	0.6	1.1	0.8
Saudi Arabia	8023.4	9353.3	10,317.3	42.6	41.2	40.1	13.3	13.1	13.6
United Arab Emirates	2148.0	2378.0	3008.3	11.4	10.5	11.7	3.6	3.3	4.0
Total	13,561.3	15,971.9	17,726.1	71.9	70.3	68.9	22.4	22.3	23.4

Data source OPEC Annual Statistical Bulletin 2019 (https://asb.opec.org/)

3.2.2.1 Bahrain

Bahrain's oil production is the lowest one among the six GCC countries. Statistics show that in 1995, Bahrain's daily oil production was 145.4 thousand barrels, accounting for 0.8% of the total oil production in the Middle East, and 0.2% of the total global oil production. In 2005, Bahrain's daily oil production increased to 186.5 thousand barrels, accounting for 0.8% of the Middle East and 0.3% of the world total. In 2018, Bahrain's daily oil production increased to 193.2 thousand barrels, still accounting for 0.8% of the Middle East total and 0.3% of the world total.

3.2.2.2 Kuwait

Kuwait's daily crude oil production ranks third among the six Gulf states. In 1995, Kuwait's crude oil production was 2006.6 thousand barrels per day, accounting for 10.6% of the total crude oil production in the Middle East and 3.3% of the world's total crude oil production. In 2005, Kuwait's daily crude oil production increased to 2573.4 thousand barrels, accounting for 11.3% of the Middle East total, and 3.6% of the world total. In 2018, Kuwait's daily crude oil output further increased to 2736.6 thousand barrels. However, the percentage of crude oil production to the Middle East for Kuwait dropped to 10.6%, while the percentage of crude oil output to the world total was still 3.6%.

3.2.2.3 Oman

Oman is the fourth-largest crude oil producer in the six Gulf countries. In 1995, Oman's daily crude oil production was 848.1 thousand barrels, accounting for 4.5% of the Middle East total and 1.4% of the global total. In 2005, Oman's crude oil production fell to 714.8 thousand barrels per day, and the percentage of crude oil production to the Middle East and to the world total also fell to 3.1% and 1.0% respectively. In 2018, Oman increased crude oil production to 870.0 thousand barrels per day, and the share of crude oil production to the Middle East total and to the world total increased to 3.4% and 1.1%, respectively.

3.2.2.4 Qatar

Qatar is the fifth-ranking country in terms of crude oil production in the six Gulf States and also one of the fastest growing crude oil producers. As shown in Table 3.3, Qatar's daily crude oil production in 1995 was 389.8 thousand barrels, accounting for 2.1% of the total daily crude oil production in the Middle East and 0.6% of the world's total crude oil production. In 2005, Qatar's daily crude oil output was doubled to 765.9 thousand barrels, accounting for 3.4% of the Middle East total, and 1.1% of the world total. In 2018, Qatar's crude oil production decreased, with daily production falling to 600.6 barrels, accounting for 2.3% of the Middle East total and a global share of 0.8%.

3.2.2.5   Saudi Arabia

The crude oil resource in Saudi Arabia is very abundant. Its crude oil output is the highest among the six GCC countries, and it is also one of the three countries with a daily output of more than 10 million barrels. In 1995, Saudi Arabia's crude oil production was 8023.4 thousand barrels per day, accounting for 42.6% of the Middle East total and 13.3% of world total. In 2005, Saudi Arabia's crude oil production further increased to 9353.3 thousand barrels per day, accounting for 41.2% of the Middle East total, and 13.1% of the global total. In 2018, Saudi Arabia's crude oil production further raised to 10,317.3 thousand barrels per day. The percentage of crude oil production to the Middle East total dropped to 40.1%, while the percentage to the world total was rebounded to 13.6%. According to statistics released by OPEC [7], Russia's daily crude oil production is higher than Saudi Arabia for a long time in the past. But since 1992, Saudi Arabia's daily crude oil output surpassed Russia, becoming the country with the highest crude oil production in the world. After 2002, the daily output of Russia's crude oil surpassed that of Saudi Arabia. The daily output of the two countries have been comparable in the following years. Since 2006, Russia's daily crude oil production has surpassed Saudi Arabia's and has remained almost to this day. In 2015 and 2016 alone, Saudi Arabia's crude oil output was slightly higher than Russia's. In 2018, the daily crude oil output of United States surpassed Russia and Saudi Arabia making United States the world's highest crude oil producer. Saudi Arabia's daily output of crude oil ranks third in the world.

3.2.2.6   United Arab Emirates

The UAE is the third-largest crude oil producer among the six GCC countries. According to statistics, in 1995, the UAE's daily crude oil production was 2148.0 thousand barrels, accounting for 11.4% of the daily crude oil production in the Middle East and 3.6% of the global crude oil production per day. In 2005, UAE's daily crude oil production increased to 2378 thousand barrels, accounting for 10.5% of the daily crude oil production to the Middle East total and 3.3% of the world total. In 2018, the UAE's crude oil production further increased to 3008.3 thousand barrels per day, accounting for 11.7% of the Middle East total and 4.0% of the world total respectively.

Table 3.4 The oil consumption in the GCC countries

Countries	The oil consumption/(thousand barrels/day)			The percentage of oil consumption to the Middle East total/%			The percentage of oil consumption to the world total/%		
	1995	2005	2017	1995	2005	2017	1995	2005	2017
Bahrain	21.1	56.3	64.4	0.51	0.94	0.75	0.03	0.07	0.07
Kuwait	172.8	332.1	447.3	4.2	5.5	5.2	0.2	0.4	0.5
Oman	41.9	80.3	170.0	1.0	1.3	2.0	0.1	0.1	0.2
Qatar	34.5	96.0	293.8	0.8	1.6	3.4	0.0	0.1	0.3
Saudi Arabia	1254.4	1936.5	3328.0	30.2	32.2	38.6	1.8	2.3	3.4
United Arab Emirates	315.8	524.6	905.1	7.6	8.7	10.5	0.5	0.6	0.9
Total	1840.5	3025.8	5208.6	44.4	50.3	60.5	2.6	3.6	5.3

Data source U.S. Energy Information Administration (https://www.eia.gov/)

3.2.3 Oil Consumption

Table 3.4 shows the oil consumption in the six GCC countries [5]. In 1995, the total oil consumption for the six GCC countries was 1840.5 thousand barrels per day, accounting for 44.4% of the Middle East total and 2.6% of the world total. In 2005, the total oil consumption increased to 3025.8 thousand barrels per day, accounting for 50.3% of the Middle East total and 3.6% of the world's total oil consumption. In 2017, the oil consumption of the six GCC countries further rose to 5208.6 thousand barrels per day, accounting to 58.8% of that in the Middle East and 5.3% of world total. Although the six GCC countries share relative less oil consumption than other developed or developing countries, oil consumption in GCC countries has grown rapidly in recent years.

3.2.3.1 Bahrain

As the smallest countries of the six GCC states, Bahrain's oil consumption is also the lowest one in the region. According to statistics, in 1995, the oil consumption in Bahrain was only 21.1 thousand barrels per day, accounting for 0.51% of the total oil consumption in the Middle East and 0.03% of the total world oil consumption. In 2005, Bahrain's oil consumption increased to 56.3 thousand barrels per day, and the proportion of oil consumption to the Middle East and to the world total increased to 0.94% and 0.07% respectively. In 2015, Bahrain's oil consumption further increased to 64.4 thousand barrels per day, accounting for 0.75% of the Middle East total, and 0.07% of the world total.

3.2.3.2 Kuwait

Kuwait is the third-largest country in terms of oil consumption in the six GCC States. In 1995, Kuwait's daily oil consumption was 172.8 thousand barrels, accounting for 4.2% of the total oil consumption in the Middle East and 0.2% of the total world oil consumption. In 2005, Kuwait's daily oil consumption nearly doubled to 332.1 thousand barrels. The percentage of the oil consumption to the middle east increased to 5.5%, while the percentage to the world total increased to 0.4% as well. In 2017, the oil consumption in Kuwait further rose to 447.3 thousand barrels per day, accounting to 5.2% of the oil consumption in the Middle East and 0.5% of that in the world.

3.2.3.3 Oman

Oman is the fifth-largest country in terms of oil consumption in the six GCC countries. In 1995, Oman's daily oil consumption was 41.9 thousand barrels per day, accounting for 1.0% of the daily oil consumption in the Middle East and 0.06% of the total world oil consumption. In 2005, Oman's daily oil consumption increased to 80.3 thousand barrels, accounting for 1.3% of the Middle East total and 0.10% of the world total. In 2017, Oman's oil consumption increased sharply to 170.0 thousand barrels per day, accounting for 2.0% of the total daily consumption in the Middle East and 0.17% of the total world oil consumption.

3.2.3.4   Qatar

Qatar's oil consumption ranks fourth among the six GCC States, but it is the fastest growing oil consumption country. According to statistics, in 1995, Qatar's daily oil consumption was only 34.5 thousand barrels, accounting for 0.8% of the Middle East's oil consumption and 0.05% of world oil consumption. In 2005, Qatar's daily oil consumption increased to 96.0 thousand barrels, accounting for 1.6% of the Middle East total and 0.11% of the world total. In 2017, Qatar's oil consumption increased sharply, with daily consumption reaching 293.8 thousand barrels, accounting for 3.4% of the total oil consumption in the Middle East and 0.30% of that in the world.

3.2.3.5   Saudi Arabia

In addition to being the country with the largest oil reserves and the highest crude oil output in the six GCC states, Saudi Arabia is also the country with the largest oil consumption in the region. According to statistics, in 1995, Saudi Arabia's daily oil consumption was 1254.4 thousand barrels, accounting for 30.2% of the total oil consumption in the Middle East and 1.8% of the total oil consumption in the world. In 2005, Saudi Arabia's daily oil consumption increased to 1936.5 thousand barrels, in 2017, the daily oil consumption further increased to 3228.0 thousand barrels. The percentage of oil consumption to the Middle East total increased from 32.2% in 2005 to 38.6% in 2017, while the percentage of oil consumption to the world total increased from 2.3% in 2005 to 3.4% in 2017.

3.2.3.6   The United Arab Emirates

The UAE is the second-largest country in terms of oil consumption in the six GCC States. In 1995, the daily consumption of oil in the UAE was 315.8 thousand barrels, accounting for 7.6% of total oil consumption in the Middle East and 0.5% of the world. In 2005, the daily consumption of oil in the UAE increased to 524.6 thousand barrels, accounting for 8.7% of the daily oil consumption in the Middle East and 0.6% of the global oil consumption. In 2017, the daily consumption of oil in the UAE further increased to 905.1 thousand barrels, accounting for 8.7% of the total daily consumption of oil in the Middle East and 0.9% of that in the world.

3.3   Oil Trade Situation Between China and the GCC Countries

The Middle East, represented by the GCC, is rich in oil and gas resources and has always been the axis of geopolitical oil supply. The crude oil trade between China and the GCC began in the early 1990s. In 1996, China became a net importer of crude oil. The initial stage of import of crude oil from the GCC countries was also the stage of rapid growth of China's crude oil consumption and imports. The GCC countries headed by Saudi Arabia served as the character of the main supplier for China's imported crude oil.

3.3.1   The Characteristics of Crude Oil Trade Between China and the GCC Countries

3.3.1.1   Persistent Growing of China's Crude Oil Import from the GCC Countries

The GCC countries has been one of China's major crude oil import sources for many years. Among the top ten countries of China's crude oil imports, the countries in the GCC account for about one-third. Table 3.5 lists the trends of China's crude oil import

Table 3.5   The amount and cost of China's crude oil import from the GCC countries

Year	Amount/Mt	Cost/billion dollars	Year	Amount/Mt	Cost/billion dollars
1992	3.48	0.51	2006	43.24	19.97
1993	4.88	0.68	2007	47.58	23.42
1994	3.58	0.44	2008	62.30	45.36
1995	4.36	0.58	2009	64.59	28.63
1996	5.89	0.84	2010	76.18	43.49
1997	9.67	1.45	2011	85.41	60.76
1998	8.40	1.00	2012	93.71	76.74
1999	7.85	1.00	2013	99.12	78.04
2000	23.85	4.96	2014	102.04	76.56
2001	21.35	3.89	2015	109.87	45.68
2002	20.96	3.80	2016	115.07	35.56
2003	26.79	5.73	2017	/	44.51
2004	36.33	9.66	2018	/	75.76
2005	37.57	14.01			

Data source EPS China Data, https://olap.epsnet.com.cn/; UNCTADSTAT database, https://unctad stat.unctad.org/EN/

from the GCC countries since 1992 [8]. As can be seen from the table, in 1992, China imported about 3.48 Mt of crude oil from the GCC countries spending 507 million US dollars. In 1995, crude oil imported from the GCC increased to 4.36 Mt, and imported crude oil cost US$ 577 million. After 2000, the crude oil imported from the GCC countries increased significantly, from 7.85 Mt in 1999 to 23.85 Mt in 2000, and the cost of imported crude oil reached US$ 4.964 billion. After entering the twenty-first century, China's crude oil imports from the GCC have increased sharply year by year. With the increase in oil prices, the corresponding cost of imported crude oil has also increased significantly. In 2005, crude oil imported from the GCC countries was 37.57 Mt, costing $9.664 billion. In 2010, crude oil imported from the GCC increased to 76.18 Mt, costing up to 43.49 billion US dollars. In 2013, due to the rise of crude oil prices, China's cost of importing crude oil from the GCC soared to US$ 78.044 billion, the highest point in history. In 2016, the amount of crude oil imported by China from the GCC countries increased to 115.07 Mt. Due to the decrease of crude oil prices in recent years, the cost of imported crude oil dropped to 35.565 billion US dollars. With the gradual recovery of oil prices in the past two years, China's cost of importing crude oil from the GCC countries has also increased from 44.51 billion U.S. dollars in 2017 to 75.76 billion U.S. dollars in 2018.

Figure 3.1 shows the trend of China's crude oil imports from the GCC countries. In the past 27 years, China's crude oil imports from the GCC countries have been on the rise, with five peaks during the period. In 1992, the proportion of crude oil imported from the GCC countries accounted for 9.1% of China's total crude oil imports, and the proportion of funds spent on imported crude oil to China's total crude oil imports was 11.3%. The first peak node was in 1993. The percentage of crude oil imported from

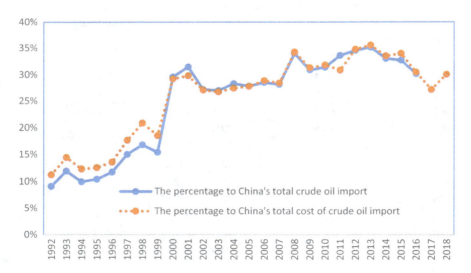

Fig. 3.1 The share of Crude oil import for China from the GCC countries. *Data source* EPS China Data, https://olap.epsnet.com.cn/; UNCTADSTAT database, https://unctadstat.unctad.org/EN/

the GCC countries to total imports rose to 11.9%, and the corresponding investment accounted for 14.4%. The second peak node was in 1998. The proportion of crude oil imported from the GCC countries to China's total crude oil imports increased to 16.8%, and the proportion of corresponding investment funds increased to 20.9%. The third peak node was in 2001. In this year, the percentage of China's imports of crude oil from the GCC countries increased to 31.5%, and the corresponding investment accounted for 29.8%. The fourth peak node is in 2008. China's imports of crude oil from the GCC countries accounted for 34.0% of the total imported crude oil, and the proportion of imported crude oil invested in total capital investment was 34.3%. The fifth peak node was in 2013. The amount of crude oil imported from the GCC countries accounted for 35.2% of the total crude oil imports, and the percentage of capital investment to total capital investment reached the historical maximum of 35.5%. In 2016, China's imports of crude oil from the GCC countries accounted for 30.2% of China's total crude oil imports, and the corresponding capital investment accounted for 30.5% of total capital investment. The share of cost on Chinese crude oil import from GCC countries in 2017 was dropped to 27.2%, and redound to 30.1% in 2018.

The reasons for the above-mentioned changes are mainly as follows. First, before the year of 2000, more than one-third of China's crude oil imports were mainly from the Asia-Pacific region [9]. At that time, the crude oil trade between China and the GCC countries has only just started, and it is gradually moving toward a deeper cooperative relationship. Second, after 2000, in order to reduce the risk of crude oil imports, China began to implement a diversified strategy of crude oil import sources, which means that China's crude oil imports are gradually maturing. However, due to China has been controlling the proportion of crude oil consumed in the energy structure, and as well as the increase of crude oil exports in other regions worldwide, the amount of crude oil imports for China from the GCC countries has also declined. Third, in recent years, the success of shale oil & gas revolution in US, the global oil market completion from Russia, and the discovery of large amounts of oil sand and heavy oil in Canada and Venezuela have made the Middle East face fierce completion in the global oil market. In order to maintain its market share, the GCC countries began to look eastward and actively seek cooperation with the Asian market. Therefore, the share of GCC oil in the Chinese crude oil market has increased.

3.3.1.2 Crude Oil Trade Links Between the Six GCC Countries and China

Figure 3.2 shows the crude oil trade between China and the six GCC countries. Data show that Oman was the first country in the GCC countries to build crude oil trade link with China. In 1992, Saudi Arabia and United Arab Emirates have also made crude oil trade link with China. However, the amount of crude oil imported from Oman still accounted for nearly 90% of the total crude oil imported from the GCC countries. This situation lasted until 1997 when Saudi Arabia has become the fastest growing country in the GCC that China imported crude oil from. The share

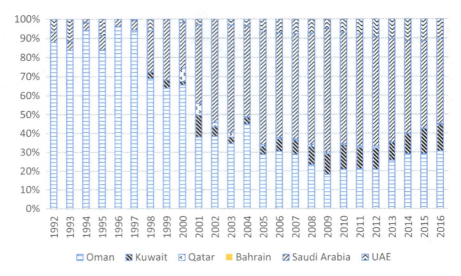

Fig. 3.2 The percentage of crude oil import from the six GCC countries. *Data source* EPS China Data, https://olap.epsnet.com.cn/; UNCTADSTAT database, https://unctadstat.unctad.org/EN/

of crude oil imported from Saudi Arabia among the six GCC countries increased from 5.4% in 1992 to 44.3% in 2016, while the share of oil imported from Oman decreased from 87.9% in 1992 to 30.5% in 2016. Overall, Saudi Arabia's position as a source of China's crude oil imports has risen rapidly, while Oman has declined but still occupies an important position. In recent years, China's crude oil imports from the United Arab Emirates and Kuwait are also rising. Especially after 2006, the proportion of crude oil from these two countries increased significantly. In 2016, China's crude oil imports from the United Arab Emirates and Kuwait accounted for 10.6% and 14.2% of the total imports from the six GCC countries, respectively. China imports less crude oil from Qatar, which accounted for 6.7% of the total imports from the GCC countries in 2000, and has been on a downward trend since then, with only 0.4% of the total imports in the six GCC countries in 2016. Bahrain and China have less trade in crude oil. Apart from Bahrain, other members of the GCC are all China's important source of crude oil imports. Saudi Arabia is China's largest crude oil trading partner in the GCC, followed by Oman, Kuwait and the United Arab Emirates. The oil trade relationship between China and Saudi Arabia determines the pattern of China's crude oil imports in the GCC region.

3.3.2   Factors Affecting China's Crude Oil Import from the GCC

3.3.2.1   Internal Factor: China's Growing Demand for Crude Oil Imports

Crude oil plays a very important role in the global energy structure. According to the world oil consumption data, the world oil consumption increased from 1525.8 Mt in 1965 to 4529.3 Mt in 2018, with an annual average growth rate of 2.1%. In the same period, the oil consumption for China increased from 11 to 628 Mt, with an average annual growth rate of 7.9%. China's total oil consumption in 2018 accounted for 13.9% of the total global oil consumption, which is the second largest oil consumer after the United States of America [10]. Nevertheless, China's oil production is far behind the domestic oil consumption rate which resulting in heavy demand-supply gap year by year (as shown in Table 3.6 [10]). Consequently, a large amount of oil needs to be imported from many foreign countries.

In 1990, China produced more crude oil than it consumed, and oil supplies were in surplus. In 1995, there was a gap of 10.6 Mt of crude oil production and consumption, and 36.7 million tons of crude oil was imported. In 2000, the demand-supply gap for China's crude oil was 62.0 Mt, and about 97.5 Mt of crude oil was imported. In 2005, China's crude oil supply and demand gap expanded to 144.1 Mt, and the amounts of crude oil import were nearly doubled to 171.6 Mt. In 2010, China's crude oil demand-supply gap was further increased to 238 Mt, and imports of crude oil reached a new high of 294.4 Mt. In 2015, China produced 214.6 Mt of crude oil, consumed 559.7 Mt, and the demand-supply gap reached 345.2 Mt. In 2018, China's total crude oil production dropped to 189.1 Mt, however, the total crude oil consumption was further increased to 628.0 Mt resulting the increasing demand-supply gap to 438.9 Mt. From 1990 to 2018, the average annual growth rates of China's crude oil production and consumption were 1.1% and 6.3%, respectively, while the average growth rate of the demand-supply gap was 11.0%. At the same time, the average growth rate of crude oil import for China was up to 16.1%. According

Table 3.6 Petroleum balance sheet for China

Unit/Mt	1990	1995	2000	2005	2010	2015	2018	Annual growth rate (%)
Production	138.3	150.1	163.0	181.4	203.0	214.6	189.1	1.1
Consumption	114.9	160.6	225.0	325.5	441.0	559.7	628.0	6.3
Demand-supply gap	23.5	−10.6	−62.0	−144.1	−238.0	−345.2	−438.9	11.0
Import	7.6	36.7	97.5	171.6	294.4	335.8	464.5	15.8

Source National Bureau of Statistics of China (https://www.stats.gov.cn/english/Statisticaldata/Ann ualData/)

to statistics, China's crude oil dependence on foreign countries approached 70% in 2018 [11]. The rising dependence on crude oil forces China to seek stable sources of oil imports. Although China has been trying to diversify its import channels, the Middle East has been the most important source of crude oil, accounting for 43.8% of China's total crude oil imports in 2018 [10].

3.3.2.2 External Factor: Penetration of the GCC's Crude Oil in the International Oil Market

GCC countries are well known for their abundant oil resources. As illustrated in Sect. 3.1.1, the six GCC countries hold a total proven crude oil reserves of 496.29 billion barrels at the end of 2019, which account for 61.7% of the Middle East total proven crude oil reserves and 30.8% of world's total proved crude oil reserves [5]. Saudi Arabia has a very outstanding performance in terms of crude oil reserves. Because of such advantages in crude oil reserves, GCC countries have strong crude oil export capabilities. The crude oil export of the GCC countries play a very important role in the international crude oil market.

As shown in Table 3.7 [7], in 1995, the GCC countries exported an average of 10,515 thousand barrels of crude oil per day, accounting for 31.8% of the world's total crude oil exports. In 2000, the GCC countries exported 10,822 thousand barrels of crude oil per day, accounting for 27.9% of the world's total. In 2005, the export of crude oil from the GCC countries increased significantly to 12,489 thousand barrels per day, accounting for 29.1% of the total global crude oil export. In 2010, the daily export of the GCC's crude oil dropped to 11,514 thousand barrels per day, accounting for 27.9% of the total global crude oil export. In 2018, the daily crude oil export of GCC countries reached 13,161 thousand barrels per day, accounting for 28.7% of the world's total. During the past two decades from 1995 to 2018, the crude oil export amount of GCC countries increased by 25.2%, with an average annual growth rate of 1.0%. Over the same period, the global crude oil exports increased by 38.3%, with an average annual growth rate of 1.4%.

Among the six GCC countries, Saudi Arabia is the largest crude oil exporter. In 2018, the daily export amount of Saudi's crude oil was 7372 barrels, accounting to 56.0% of the six GCC countries' total crude oil export amount and 16.1% of the world total. UAE and Kuwait are the second and the third largest crude oil exporters among the six GCC countries, with daily crude oil export amount of 2297 barrels and 2050 barrels, respectively in 2018. Crude oil exports from Oman, Qatar and Bahrain ranked fourth, fifth and sixth respectively. It is worth noting that Bahrain mainly exported oil products instead of crude oil before the year of 2008. Bahrain exported 2090 barrels per day of crude oil in 2009, and there were no records of crude oil exports in the years after 2010. Until 2013, Bahrain began to export crude oil, and the daily crude oil export volume increased from 714.3 barrels in 2013 to 160.0 thousand barrels in 2018, accounting to 40.2% of Bahrain's daily crude oil and petroleum products exports [7].

Table 3.7 Crude oil export in the GCC countries

Countries	Crude oil export/(1000 barrels/day)					The percentage of crude oil export to the world total/%				
	1995	2000	2005	2010	2018	1995	2000	2005	2010	2018
Oman	780	905	757	749	806	2.4	2.3	1.8	1.8	1.8
UAE	1925	1815	2195	2104	2297	5.8	4.7	5.1	5.1	5.0
Bahrain	0	0	0	0	160	0.0	0.0	0.0	0.0	0.3
Qatar	333	618	677	587	477	1.0	1.6	1.6	1.4	1.0
Kuwait	1186	1231	1651	1430	2050	3.6	3.2	3.8	3.5	4.5
Saudi Arabia	6291	6253	7209	6644	7372	19.0	16.1	16.8	16.1	16.1
Total	10,515	10,821	12,489	11,514	13,161	31.8	27.9	29.1	27.9	28.7

Data source OPEC Annual Statistical Bulletin 2019 (https://asb.opec.org/)

In recent years, due to the rapid growth of proven oil reserves, crude oil production and crude oil exports in North America, South America, and West Africa, the share of crude oil exports of the GCC countries in the global crude oil export market has declined for a time. In order to maintain its market share, the GCC countries are dedicated to export crude oil vigorously. Recently, the GCC's crude oil market share has rebounded. Since crude oil dominated their main source of economic income, it is extremely important for the GCC countries to maintain and enhance their market share in the crude oil consumption countries. As the world's second largest crude oil consumer, China's market is an important selection for the GCC countries' crude oil export.

3.3.2.3   Essential Factor: Strategic Shift of the GCC Countries Crude Oil Export to the East

In the past, the focus of crude oil export by the GCC countries was in the Western industrial countries or regions represented by the United States of America and the European Union (EU). However, this situation is changed due to the change of the international oil supply and demand pattern. On the one hand, the crude oil demands for the typical industrial countries and regions such as the United States of America and EU have decreased since they have gradually entered the post-industrial era, meanwhile, some newly emerged crude oil exporters have flocked into the international crude oil market weakening the competitiveness of the GCC countries' crude oil exports. On the other hand, the demands for crude oil imports in some emerging economies such as China and India continue to increase attributed to their rapid development of economics and increased consumption of crude oil. Given to this international situation, the crude oil exporters in the GCC countries believe that countries in East Asia are important targets for their crude oil exports [12].

Table 3.8 lists the amount of oil exported by the GCC countries to some countries or regions and the proportion of these amounts to the total oil imports from the world for each region [13]. In 1995, the amount of petroleum exported by the GCC to USA was 9.3 billion US dollars, accounting for 20.5% of the total US petroleum imports. After 1995, the petroleum exported to USA by the GCC continues to increase. In 2010, the petroleum export amount by the GCC to USA reached a peak of 31.9 billion US dollars, however, the share of this amount to the total petroleum imports of USA from the world decreased to 12.0%. In 2018, the petroleum import from the GCC for USA was 28.0 billion US dollars, accounting for 17.2% of its total petroleum imports. In recent years, the United States has gradually reduced its dependence on imported oil from Middle East for the reason of: ①the Trump administration's "energy dominance" policy to rebrand efforts to exploit domestic oil production [14]; ②more choices for oil import due to some newly emerged oil exporter. Similarly, the petroleum import from the GCC by the EU has slightly changed. In 1995, the expenditure of petroleum imports from the GCC by the EU was 9.9 billion US dollars, while in 2005, this value increased to 26.1 billion US dollars. In 2010, the expenditure of petroleum imports from the GCC by the EU dropped to 22.5 billion

Table 3.8 The amount of the GCC's petroleum exports to the main countries or region

Region	Petroleum[a] export amount/billion US dollars					The ratio of petroleum imports from the GCC to its total petroleum imports from the world/%				
	1995	2000	2005	2010	2018	1995	2000	2005	2010	2018
India	2.9	3.9	0.2	31.2	37.7	88.4	53.5	7.6	41.7	35.3
Japan	23.8	34.3	70.2	81.1	76.5	80.4	76.9	88.0	76.7	94.9
Korean	7.7	17.6	36.0	50.4	54.7	71.3	69.6	84.5	73.4	68.1
USA	9.3	13.2	29.2	31.9	28.0	20.5	14.7	15.3	12.0	17.2
EU(28)	9.9	12.1	26.1	22.5	41.0	14.2	10.2	10.5	6.4	12.7
China	0.6	7.0	17.9	41.4	41.1	27.5	46.8	37.5	30.6	16.3

Data source UNCTADSTAT database, https://unctadstat.unctad.org/EN/
Note [a]Petroleum refers to petroleum, petroleum products and related materials

US dollars. In 2018, the expenditure of import from the GCC increased again to 41.0 billion US dollars. Meanwhile, the ratio of petroleum imports from the GCC to EU's total petroleum import from the world decreased from 14.2% in 1995 to 6.4% in 2010, and back to 12.7% in 2018. It can be seen that these developed countries represented by the United States have gradually reduced the market share of oil from the GCC, which has forced the "oil-dependent economy" countries to switch to other oil consumption markets.

The data in Table 3.8 confirmed that "Eastward" is the main change for the GCC countries' petroleum export. In Asia countries like India, Japan, Korean, and China, the cost of petroleum exports from the GCC to these countries keep sustained growth due to their large demand of petroleum imports. India's petroleum imports from the GCC increased from 2.9 billion US dollars in 1995 to 37.7 billion US dollars in 2018, accounting 35.3% of India's total petroleum imports in 2018. Japan imported 80.4% of petroleum from the GCC in 1995, while this ration further increased to 94.9% of Japan's total petroleum import in 2018. Similarly, Korean imported 52.2% of petroleum from the GCC in 1995, while this ratio reached the peak of 71.3% of Korean's total petroleum import in 1995 and slightly deceased to 68.1% in 2018. The expenditure of petroleum imports from the GCC for China increased sharply from 0.6 billion US dollars in 1995 to 41.1 billion US dollars in 2018, while the share of this amount to its total petroleum imports decreased from 27.5% to 16.3%. It is worth mentioning that although the expenditure of petroleum exports from the GCC to Asia countries like Japan and Koreas decreased, the physical quantity of petroleum exports to each region was still increased due to the shrinking of international oil prices since 2015.

In general, Asia is an important oil market for global oil export, and also for the GCC countries' oil export. As far as Eastern Asian countries are concerned, the West Asia where the GCC is located is undoubtedly the richest and nearest oil resources. In the future, these countries including China will face more intense competition over oil in the GCC countries.

3.3.3 The Prospects for China's Crude Oil Import from the GCC Countries

Although there are still many uncertainties in China's crude oil import from the GCC, the scale of China's import of crude oil from the GCC will remain or even continue to grow, regardless of the rigid demand of China's economic development or the inevitability of oil exports from the GCC countries.

3.3.3.1 The Demand of Crude Oil Imports for China Will Continue to Grow

China is a country with very limited oil and natural gas, with low per capita crude oil holdings and limited room for improvement in domestic crude oil production. Although the domestic development and utilization of renewable energy has achieved fruitful development, crude oil is still one of the most important available energy, accounting for 18.9% of China's energy consumption structure in 2018 [11]. As a rigid demand, importing is undoubtedly the best choice when domestic production cannot be met.

Since China became a net oil importer in 1993 and a crude oil importer in 1996, its crude oil imports have soared from 22.6 million tons in 1996 to 464.5 million tons in 2018, with the continuous growth of dependence on imported crude oil from 51.8% in 2009 to 71.1% in 2018 (as shown in Fig. 3.3) [10]. It is predicted that China's future economic growth will depend on external oil markets. The oil demand for will reach 11.6 million barrels of oil equivalent (mboe) per day in 2020, 14.0 mboe per day in 2030, and 16.0 mboe per day in 2040, with an average annual growth rate of 1.8% [15]. In 2040, oil will account for 18.1% of China's energy structure [15]. Although this ratio is the same as the current proportion of oil in China's energy consumption structure, the total energy consumption will be increased as well as the declining of domestic crude oil production, which means that a large amount of oil still depends on imports. BP predicts that China's oil import dependency will increase to 76% in

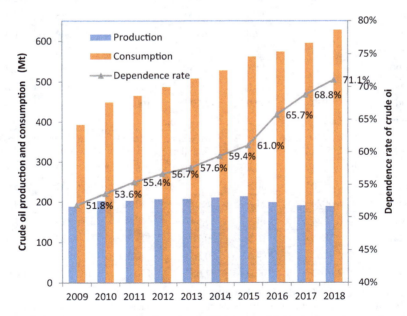

Fig. 3.3 Changes in China's crude oil production, imports and dependence on imported crude oil. *Data source* BP Statistical Review of World Energy 2019

2035, which is higher than the US peak in 2005 [15]. With the increase of crude oil imports, its import risks are increasing. If the source of crude oil imports is relatively single, once the source of import is interrupted, it will easily cause a tight supply situation, which will affect the stable development of the economy and society. For this reason, China has also been working hard to build a safe and reasonable pattern of oil imports.

3.3.3.2 The GCC Countries Still Have the Potential to Improve Oil Exports to China

Table 3.9 summarizes the oil exports of the six GCC countries to major countries and the world in 2018 [13]. Bahrain exported 9037 million U.S. dollars of oil in 2018, of which 16 percent went to Japan, 11.8% to the European Union, less than 5% to major Asian countries and 4.7% to China. Qatar exported 28,143 million U.S. dollars of oil in 2018, of which 30.5% went to Japan, 21.4% to South Korea, 6.5% to the EU(28)

Table 3.9 The GCC countries' oil[a] exports to major countries and the world in 2018

Country/region	Bahrain		Kuwait[b]		Oman	
	Cost/Million U.S. dollars	Share/%	Cost/Million U.S. dollars	Share/%	Cost/Million U.S. dollars	Share/%
China	428	4.7	7408	17.1	18,244	72.5
Japan	1445	16.0	7100	16.4	588	2.3
Korean	250	2.8	12,948	30.0	344	1.4
USA	228	2.5	1907	4.4	300	1.2
EU(28)	1068	11.8	3265	7.6	180	0.7
India	140	1.5	4948	11.5	1822	7.2
World	9037	100.0	43,209	100.0	25,171	100.0
Country/region	Qatar		Saudi Arabia		UAE	
	Cost/Million U.S. dollars	Share/%	Cost/Million U.S. dollars	Share/%	Cost/Million U.S. dollars	Share/%
China	963	3.4	17,305	8.8	4209	4.1
Japan	8570	30.5	32,242	16.3	26,531	25.9
Korean	6024	21.4	25,256	12.8	9926	9.7
USA	524	1.9	23,647	12.0	1370 ara>	1.3
EU(28)	1836	6.5	30,187	15.3	4430	4.3
India	1262	4.5	20,843	10.5	8728	8.5
World	28,143	100.0	197,658	100.0	102,565	100.0

Data source UNCTADSTAT database, https://unctadstat.unctad.org/EN/
Note [a]Oil refers to petroleum, petroleum products and related materials
[b]As the relevant data for Kuwait in 2018 had not been released at the time of drafting, it was replaced by 2017

and 3.4% to China. The UAE exported 102,565 million U.S. dollars of oil in 2018, of which 25.9% went to Japan, 9.7 percent to South Korea, 8.5% to India, 4.3% to the EU(28) and 4.1% to China. Kuwait exported 43,209 million U.S. dollars of oil in 2018, of which 30% went to South Korea, 16.4% to Japan, 4.4% to the United States and 7.6% to the European Union, and 17.1% to China. Oman has a deep oil trade relationship with China. 72.5% of the oil exported in 2018 was exported to China, and the proportion of exports to India was 7.2%. The oil exports from Oman to Japan and South Korea were lower at 3.4% and 2.3%, respectively. Oman exported less oil to the United States and the European Union. In comparison, Saudi Arabia's oil exports in 2018 were 197,658 million U.S. dollars, of which the proportion of exports to Japan, South Korea, India, the United States and the European Union is relatively close, with a percentage of exceeding 10%. The ratio of oil exported to China from Saudi Arabia is 8.8% in 2018. It can be concluded that in addition to Oman, Saudi Arabia, the United Arab Emirates, Kuwait, Qatar and Bahrain all have certain room for improvement in their oil exports to China from the market share.

In summary, from the perspective of resource distribution, export capacity, and trade, the GCC countries are undoubtedly the most ideal source of crude oil imports for China in the future. Since China became a net importer of crude oil in 1996, the GCC countries have become China's main source of crude oil imports, and the importance of the GCC has gradually increased, while the share of oil import from other regions for China have changed significantly. It can be seen that China's crude oil imports are forming a diversified model with "the Middle East as the mainstay, Africa, the former Soviet Union, and South America as the supplement". Although great progress has been made in oil exploration and development in Africa and the Americas in recent years, it has become an important crude oil export region in the world, and its export growth is full of strength. At present, it has become an important source of crude oil imports for China. However, the import transportation distance of oil from these regions is relatively long, and the safety of maritime transportation is easily affected by instability factors. The area where the GCC countries are located not only has sufficient and concentrated oil resources, but also the transportation distance to China is much shorter than that in Africa and the Americas, which can save transportation costs and transportation time. In addition, the official operation of the China-Myanmar crude oil transportation pipeline can more quickly receive and discharge crude oil from the Gulf region. Therefore, the Middle East region represented by the GCC will still be China's most important oil supplier in the foreseeable future.

3.4 Challenges to Energy Cooperation Between China and the GCC

Energy cooperation between China and the GCC is affected by both external factors and the GCC's regional factors and internal factors.

First, energy cooperation between China and the GCC is confined to international situation and regional pattern. The relationship between China and the GCC countries is heavily influenced by the international system and regional pattern and is closely related to the adjustment of China's diplomatic strategies [16]. The cold war pattern during US-Soviet rivalries was a main feature from the 1950s to the 1960s, during which the Gulf pattern was mainly manifested as the contradictions between national revolution and monarchy. Meanwhile, China's Gulf diplomatic policy focused on supporting Gulf's national revolution, hostile to its monarchies. China established diplomatic relations with Iraq and voiced support for Oman's revolutionary organizations in 1958. In the 1970s, Gulf countries achieved independence due to change of US-Soviet rivalries and UK's evacuation from the Gulf region. Plus the intensified Sino-Soviet contradictions and the eased Sino-US relations, China started to develop relations with Gulf monarchies and established diplomatic relations with Kuwait, Iran and Oman successively. In the 1980s, the Soviet Union started Afghanistan War and America responded with "Carter Doctrine". In the meantime, the Iran-Iraq War took place in the Gulf region and six Gulf countries built the GCC for self-protection. Just then China entered the period of reform and opening-up and practiced an independent foreign policy. She upheld a neutral attitude towards the Iran-Iraq War, continued developing the relations with Gulf monarchies and established diplomatic relations with the UAE, Qatar, Bahrain and the Saudi Arabia. In the 1990s, America became the only strongest as a result of dissolution of the Soviet Union and dominated in the Middle East after Gulf War. A triangle relationship among Iraq, Iran and the GCC countries was formed in the Gulf region and the GCC curbed Iraq and Iran under the support of the U.S. At that time, China practiced a "detached" diplomatic strategy for the Gulf situation, improved the relations with the USA and western countries through Gulf War and carried out energy-oriented economic and trade cooperation with the Gulf countries, which indicated the importance of national interest expansion for China's diplomatic relations with the Golf countries. In the first decade of the twenty-first century, anti-terrorism was the US's leading global strategy and consequently the USA was enslaved to Afghanistan War and Iraq War arising from anti-terrorism and declined. The contradictions between the GCC and Iran were intensified by Iraq War, Iran's rise and their safety problems. Confronted with such a complex situation, China practiced "Go-Out" policy and further developed the relationship with the Gulf countries through negotiation with the GCC FTZs and involvement in Iraq's post-war reconstruction and Iran's nuclear negotiation. After the Middle East's change in 2011, the international system changed drastically and the USA initiated "the Asia-Pacific rebalancing" and carried out strategic contraction towards the Middle East. In the Gulf region, the contradictions between the GCC and Iran were sharpened by the "Arab Spring", intensified communal conflicts arising from the U.S.'s evacuation from Iraq, Syria crisis and Iran's nuclear negotiation. After taking power, Chairman Xi Jinping attached greater importance to neighboring diplomacy and advocated the Belt and Road Initiative in order to establish and strengthen partnerships and prosper together with the B&R countries. Since the GCC is in the critical position of B&R, the implementation of the BRI will vitalize the development of China and the GCC.

Then, GCC's internal factors affect safety of energy cooperation between China and the GCC, since the GCC countries are similar in many aspects. For example, economically, the six GCC countries heavily depend on such traditional fossil fuels as petroleum and natural gas. Politically, religion plays an important role in the polity of the six GCC countries. Culturally, they are conservative Musleims, especially Saudi Arabia. Militarily, they rely on developed countries such as the USA for lack of core technology. Therefore, the six GCC countries headed by Saudi Arabia are diplomatically united as one like a clique so as to protect common interests and the GCC has played an important part in internal affairs and foreign affairs over the years. Nevertheless, the GCC countries also conflict with each other due to benefit divergences and different viewpoints. On 5 June, 2017, Bahrain, Saudi Arabia, Egypt, the UAE, Yemen, Libya and Maldives successively declared to break off the relations with Qatar for supporting terrorist activities and destroying regional security in order to protect themselves from being threatened by terrorism and extremism. For this reason, Qatar denied the foregoing evidences groundless. The Ministry of Foreign Affairs of Qatar felt sorry for the "unjust" decision of some Arab states. Qatar has been active in the Gulf affairs in recent years, especially when got involved in a chain of events relating to Muslim Brotherhood and in public voiced support after 2010 till Muslim Brotherhood took power in Egypt. It also has been reported that Qatar has supported the Hamas leadership financially for years with tens of millions of dollars each year and it also kept close contact with Iran, which irritated Saudi Arabia, Egypt and other countries represented by Sunnite [17]. Till now, Qatar has not eased the relationship with Gulf countries. Scholars think that the integrity of the GCC and cooperation between China and the GCC will be challenged if the situation cannot be solved properly.

Furthermore, energy cooperation between China and the GCC is challenged by great powers [18]. Generally speaking, the GCC countries prefer to cooperate with member countries economically, followed by other Arab states as well as the EU countries where the suzerain is located and the USA, the dominant strategic country. Some emerging countries may not be considered as economic partners. However, energy cooperation between China and the GCC will be impeded by western countries and such emerging countries as India to some extent. For example, the EU is the largest trade partner of the GCC and both parties signed the FTA in 2011. The GCC countries have always taken the USA as the "safe box" and have been "deeply stamped with the USA" in military, energy and economy and trade. The USA has exerted influence on OPEC by International Energy Agency and imposed pressure on Saudi Arabia by trade and aid and on OPEC by pricing policy to achieve its aims. In 2004, the USA rejected the GCC's suggestions on the establishment of a bilateral free trade area and persisted in the FTA negotiation with every GCC country, among which Bahrain signed an FTA agreement with the USA. Although the USA has lowered the share of petroleum imported from the GCC countries over the years, it doesn't mean that the USA is willing to witness China's filling in the gaps. Some US scholars even advocate that "China's desire for petroleum is the biggest nightmare of western countries: the combination of 'Islam and Confucianism' [19]. India has a unique link with the Gulf region. Data displays that India has become the largest trade partner of the GCC countries in place of China. The GCC has become the first country of origin of India and the second exported country and India has been the largest food supplier of the GCC. Moreover, Japan and South Korea also keep close contact with the GCC countries. Japan and South Korea, which are energy consumers as important as China, are important trade partners of the Gulf region. For one thing, the Japanese government not only acts in cooperation with main oil & gas countries in the Gulf region and helps them with oil & gas exploration and development so as to control the supply of oil gas. For another, it actively carries out economic and even military cooperation.

In addition, energy cooperation between China and the GCC is also faced with domestic factors, which is mainly reflected in the weak international competitiveness of Chinese petroleum enterprises. Presently, multinational petroleum companies of developed countries engage in oil exploration and development, downstream development and refining and construction of oil storage facilities and sales network; while China falls behind in technology, management and experience due to late "Go Out". Thus, China petroleum companies are still unattractive for the Gulf countries.

References

1. Amadeo, Kimberly. 2019. *Gulf Cooperation Council—GCC Countries.* https://www.thebal ance.com/gulf-cooperation-council-3306357. Accessed 07 Oct 2019.
2. The World Bank data. 2019. *The World Bank.* https://data.worldbank.org/indicator/NY.GDP. MKTP.CD. Accessed 08 Nov 2019.
3. He, Maochun, and Jibing Zhang. 2013. Analysis of the influence of the New Silk Road Economic Belt on National Strategy. *Frontiers* (23): 6–13 (in Chinese).
4. Wu, Sike. 2015. Constructing "One Belt and One Road" to enhancing China and GCC Cooperation. *Arab World Studies* 02: 4–13 ((in Chinese)).
5. International Energy Statistics. 2019. *U.S. Energy Information Administration.* https://www. eia.gov/beta/international/data/browser/. Accessed 25 Nov 2019.
6. World Energy Database. https://www.epschinadata.com/data-resource.html. Accessed 01 July 2019.
7. OPEC. 2019. *OPEC Annual Statistical Bulletin 2019.* Vienna, Austria: Organization of the Petroleum Exporting Countries.
8. World Trade Database. 2020. *EPS China Data.* https://olap.epsnet.com.cn/auth/platform.html? sid=E39413DCC57D2C4A194036EA8BBD7169. Accessed 02 Jan 2020.
9. Cheng, Shujia. 2011. *Evolution of Spatial Pattern of the World's Crude Oil Trade and Strategy to Optimize Spatial Pattern of China's Crude Oil Trade.* Changchun: Northeast Normal University (in Chinese).
10. BP. 2019. *BP Statistical Review of World Energy 2019.* London: BP.
11. NBSC. 2019. *China Statistical Yearbook 2019.* Beijing: China Statistics Press.
12. She, Li. 2012. Analysis of factors and potentials of China's imports of crude oil from the GCC countries. *Forum of World Economics & Politics* 5: 88–98 ((in Chinese)).
13. UNCTADSTAT database. 2019. https://unctadstat.unctad.org. Accessed 31 Dec 2019.
14. DiChristopher, Tom. 2017. *Trump Wants America to be 'Energy Dominant.' Here's What That Means.* Accessed 01 July 2017. https://www.cnbc.com/2017/06/28/trump-america-ene rgy-dominant-policy.html.
15. BP. 2017. *BP Energy Outlook 2017 Edition.* London: BP.

16. Liu, Zhongming. 2016. Historical evolution of the relations between China and the Gulf Region. *Arab World Studies* (02): 17–30+118–119 (in Chinese).
17. *The Solution of Qatar's Diplomatic Crisis Depends on the United States.* 2017–06–17. https://dzb.whb.cn/html/2017-06/17/content_565219.html (in Chinese).
18. Yu, Yong. 2011. The achievements, challenges and prospect of China-GCC trade and economic cooperation. *Arab World Studies* 06: 38–44 ((in Chinese)).
19. Liu, Jiajun, and Chuan Wang. 2013. A study on situation, obstacles and countermeasures of China energy cooperation with Saudi Arabia. *Globalization* 12: 57–66+125 (in Chinese).

Chapter 4
The "Belt and Road" and the Safety of Maritime Energy Transportation Channels

Dehua Wang

Building the transportation system of the Belt and Road is not only the precondition and an important foundation for the implementation of the Belt and Road Initiative and the essential bond and bridge for facilities connectivity, unimpeded trade, and people-to-people bound along the Belt and Road countries, but also the primary strategic task which must be fulfilled [1]. Energy transportation channel is an important link of the transportation system of the Belt and Road, and the safety of energy transportation channel plays an important role in forming the economic spatial pattern and dominating spatial pattern evolution. Whereas petroleum and other energy sources are mainly transported by pipelines and oil tankers throughout the world, this paper, based on the Belt and Road Initiative, will comb construction and operation of worldwide and nationwide main oil and gas pipelines and discuss how to guarantee safety of energy transportation channel in China, especially safety of maritime energy transportation corridor, because sea route has been more important than land route since ancient times. Scholar of Tufts University Phelipe Fernandez-Armesto pointed out that "More goods can be transported by sea routes at less costs" [2]. Scholars also pointed out that "The Maritime Silk Road from Venice to Japan via the Indian Ocean during the Middle Ages and early modern times is of equal importance to the Silk Road across the central Asia" [3].

D. Wang (✉)
Institute of South and Central Asia Studies, Shanghai Municipal Center for International Studies, Shanghai, China
e-mail: dehuawangz@126.com

© Shanghai Jiao Tong University Press 2021
T. Zhang and D. Wang (eds.), *China-Gulf Oil Cooperation Under the Belt and Road Initiative*, https://doi.org/10.1007/978-981-15-9283-6_4

4.1 Construction of Worldwide and Nationwide Oil and Gas Pipelines

Construction and development of oil and gas pipelines can effectively solve the imbalance between production and demand of oil and gas resources. With the increase in the output of unconventional oil and gases such as shale gas, oil sand and offshore oil and gas fields, worldwide oil and gas resources grew steadily in recent years. From the point of regional contribution, the USA intensified the exploration of shale gas, Canada increased the output of oil sand and Russia and the Middle East strived to expand energy export. From the point of oil and gas demand, such emerging economies as China and India accelerated economic growth and increased the energy demand. As a result, the construction of oil and gas pipeline was promoted [4].

4.1.1 Construction of Worldwide Oil and Gas Pipeline

4.1.1.1 Total Distance and Regional Distribution

Data displays that till now total distance of worldwide oil and gas pipelines has reached up to 2,339,200 km, including 562,000 km crude oil pipelines, 351,000 km petroleum product pipelines and 1,425,000 km natural gas pipelines. Natural gas pipelines are the longest, covering 60.9% of the total distance of worldwide oil and gas pipelines; crude oil pipelines and petroleum product pipelines cover 24.0% and 15.0% [5] respectively. According to regional division principle of continental shelf, the earth can be divided into North America, Europe, the Asia-Pacific region, South America, the Middle East, Central Asia and Africa. Based on this, regional distribution of crude oil pipelines, petroleum product pipelines and natural gas pipelines was worked out in 2017 (Table 4.1). As shown in Table 4.1, North America has the longest oil and gas pipelines adding up to 1,052,633 km and covering 42.0% of worldwide oil and gas pipelines, among which length of crude oil pipelines is 185,410 km, that

Table 4.1 Total distance of in-service worldwide oil and gas pipelines

Area	Crude oil pipelines (km)	Petroleum product pipelines (km)	Natural gas pipelines (km)	Total distance (km)
North America	185,409.8	154,785.9	712,437.5	1,052,633
Europe	149,673.8	53,449.2	545,416.3	748,539.3
Asia-Pacific region	61,308.7	32,686.9	187,324.8	281,320.4
South America	38,204.4	21,732.9	74,963.7	134,901
The Middle East, Central Asia and South Africa	97,638.6	31,432.7	159,397.0	288,468.3

Data source Ma and Bai [5]

of petroleum product pipelines is 154,786 km and that of natural gas pipelines is 712,437 km. Three types of pipelines have the world's first total distance. Europe has the second longest oil and gas pipelines adding up to 748,539 km and covering 29.9% of worldwide oil and gas pipelines, including 149,674 km crude oil pipelines, 53,449 km petroleum product pipelines and 545,416 km natural gas pipelines. Oil and gas pipelines of the Middle East, Central Asia and Africa add up to 288,468 km, ranking at the world's third and including 97,638 km crude oil pipelines, 31,433 km petroleum product pipelines and 159,397 km natural gas pipelines. Oil-gas pipelines of the Asia-Pacific region add up to 281,320 km, ranking at the world's fourth and including 61,308 km crude oil pipelines, 32,687 km petroleum product pipelines and 187,325 km natural gas pipelines. South America has the shortest oil and gas pipelines covering 5.4% of worldwide oil and gas pipelines and including 38,204 km crude oil pipelines, 21,733 km petroleum product pipelines and 74,964 km natural gas pipelines.

4.1.1.2 Worldwide Oil and Gas Pipelines Under Construction

As of the end of 2017, the total distance of world's oil and gas pipelines is about 10,800 km, of which 60% are natural gas pipelines, and the total distance of crude oil and petroleum product pipelines only accounts for 40% [5]. This is mainly because natural gas is cleaner than oil, and the price is relatively cheap, and the market demand is increasing. From the perspective of the distribution of pipelines under construction, North America is still the market with the largest demand for oil and gas pipelines, followed by the Asia-Pacific region. It is predicted that the comprehensive growth rate of oil and gas pipelines in North America will be no less than 1.2% in 2017–2022; the growth rate of oil and gas pipelines in the Asia-Pacific region will be no less than 4% [5]. With the rise of shale gas and the increasing demand for natural gas in the world, it is expected that the construction of global natural gas pipelines will be further accelerated in the future. Main world-wide oil and gas pipelines under constructions are as follows:

China-Russia Gas Pipeline It is also called China-Russia eastern gas pipeline, and is the most important gas pipeline project between China and Russia presently. This pipeline is made up of Russian section and Chinese section. The section in Russia is called the Power of Siberia gas pipeline [6]. The section in China is originated from the China-Russian border in Heihe City of Heilongjiang Province and terminates at Shanghai via Heilongjiang, Jilin, Inner Mongolia, Liaoning, Hebei, Tianjin, Shandong, Jiangsu and Shanghai. It was commenced on June 30, 2015 and is predicted to be completed at the end of 2020. With an overall length of 3371 km, it plans to build 3170 km new natural gas pipelines and underground gas storage and utilize 1800 km existing pipelines. With a length of 3000 km, the natural gas transmission system in Russia was commenced on September 1, 2014. The project facilitates the development of Eastern Siberia gas field, extends China's gas supply up to 30 years and realizes an annual transmission capacity of 38 billion m^3 [7]. On December 2,

2019, Power of Siberia was brought into operation and the first-ever pipeline supplies of Russian gas to China were launched [6].

Central Asia-China Gas Pipeline It is the world's largest in-service natural gas pipeline project which is originated from the border between Turkmenistan and Uzbekistan at the right bank of Amu Darya and enters China from Khorgos via the middle of Uzbekistan and south of Kazakhstan. The overall length is about 10,000 km, among which the section in Turkmenistan is about 188 km long, that in Uzbekistan is about 530 km long, that in Kazakhstan is about 1300 km long and that in China is 8000 km long. Sino-Central Asia natural gas pipeline is divided into four sections, among which sections A, B and C have been completed and put into production in 2009, 2010 and 2014 respectively and section D was commenced in September, 2014 and is predicted to be completed at the end of 2020. The annual transmission capacity will reach up to 85 billion m^3 after completion.

TurkStream Pipeline The project is originally built to replace the South Stream pipeline and is aimed at transmitting natural gas from Russkaya compressor station (CS) near Anapa at the north shore of the Black Sea to Turkey. Turkey is one of the largest consumers of Russian gas. At present, Russia supplies gas to Turkey via the Blue Stream and Trans-Balkan gas pipelines. TurkStream is a new export gas pipeline stretching from Russia to Turkey across the Black Sea. The first string of the pipeline is intended for Turkish consumers, while the second string will deliver gas to southern and southeastern Europe. The first and second strings of TurkStream will have the throughput capacity of 15.75 billion cubic meters each. TurkStream's offshore section runs for over 930 km from the Russkaya CS near Anapa across the Black Sea to the Turkish seaboard, with an onshore string for gas transit to be laid up to Turkey's border with neighboring countries. TurkStream pipeline project was commenced on 7 May, 2017 in the Black Sea near the Russian coast and is predicted to be completed and put into operation in late 2019. On 19 November, 2018, construction of the gas pipeline's offshore section was completed [8].

Nord Stream 2 Gas Pipeline Nord Stream 2 is a new export gas pipeline running from Russia to Europe across the Baltic Sea. The entry point of the Nord Stream 2 gas pipeline into the Baltic Sea will be the Ust-Luga area of the Leningrad Region. Then the pipeline will stretch across the Baltic Sea. Its exit point in Germany will be in the Greifswald area close to the exit point of Nord Stream. The route covers over 1200 km. The total capacity of two strings of Nord Stream 2 is 55 billion cubic meters of gas per year. The aggregated design capacity of Nord Stream and Nord Stream 2 is therefore 110 billion cubic meters of gas per year. The promotion of Nord Stream 2 encounters strong disagreements from some new EU members for the reason of unfriendly environment to the Baltic Sea and Geopolitical competition from US and Ukraine. After some unexpected trouble, Nord Stream 2 AG signed the financing agreements for the Nord Stream 2 gas pipeline project with ENGIE, OMV, Royal Dutch Shell, Uniper, and Wintershall in April 2017. These five European energy companies will provide long-term financing for 50% of the total cost of the project. In May 2018, German started construction of the terminal station near Greifswald.

Finland and Sweden have also approved the project. Although Denmark has not yet opened a green light due to environmental issues, it is reported that Nord Stream 2 will be put into operation before late 2019 [9].

Tula Gas Pipeline and Sur de Texas Gas Pipeline The two pipelines operated by TransCanada are both under construction in Mexico [10]. Tula pipeline with a length of 287 km will originate in Tuxpan in the state of Veracruz and extend through the states of Puebla and Hidalgo, supplying natural gas to CFE combined-cycle power generating facilities in each of those jurisdictions as well as to the central and western regions of Mexico. Sur de Texas pipeline will begin offshore in the Gulf of Mexico at the border point near Brownsville, Texas and end in Tuxpan, in the state of Veracruz, connecting with the Tamazunchale and Tula pipelines.

GALSI Gas Pipeline GALSI natural gas pipeline is originated from Algeria and terminates at Italy via Mediterranean. The overall length is about 940 km, including 640 km in Algeria. With an annual transmission capacity of 8 billion m^3 per annum, the project is conducive to safety of Italy's natural gas supply [11]. GALSI pipeline was initially singed between Italy and Algeria on 14 November 2007 and was expected to become operational in 2014. However, this project was laid aide for more than 10 years. In February, 2015, Algeria and Italy reached an agreement in respect of its construction. Nevertheless, not much progress has been made regarding GALSI so far.

India Jagdishpur—Haldia and Bokaro—Dhamra Pipeline This ongoing project with an overall length of 2655 km is conducted by GAIL (India) Limited that is in constant endeavor to expand its pipeline infrastructure across the length and breadth of India. With upcoming of Jagdishpur Haldia and Bokaro Dhamra pipeline project (Pradhanmantri Urja Ganga Pipeline project) GAIL shall cover states of Uttar Pradesh, Bihar, Jharkhand, Odisha and West Bengal. In addition, Vijaipur—Auraiya—Phulpur Pipeline with a length of 670 km and Kochi—Koottanad Bengaluru Mangaluru Pipeline with a length of 879 km are in development by GAIL as well [12].

Turkmenistan-Afghanistan-Pakistan-India (TAPI) Gas Pipeline The TAPI project is a 1814 km gas pipeline which was inaugurated by leaders of four countries in January 2016. It will run from gas fields in Turkmenistan through Afghanistan to Pakistan and India with maximum discharge of 33 billion cubic meters per annum. The project is implemented by the TAPI Limited Company—a group of firms from Afghanistan and Turkmenistan including Afghan Gas Enterprise, Turkmen Gas State Company, and two private companies from Afghanistan, and it will be completed by 2019. Work on the Turkmenistan section is complete while work on the Afghanistan section of the pipeline project started in February, 2018, in Herat—in the west of Afghanistan [13]. It is reported that China is exploring building a spur from Pakistan's territory as an alternative to Beijing's plans to build a fourth China-Turkmenistan pipeline once the multi-country TAPI natural gas pipeline project begins operations [14].

Trans Adriatic Pipeline (TAP) The TAP project was commenced on 17 May, 2016 in Thessalonica after experiencing difficulties [15]. It will start near Kipoi on the border of Turkey and Greece, where it will connect with the Trans Anatolian Pipeline (TANAP). From there, TAP will continue onshore, crossing the entire territory of Northern Greece, its longest stretch, then onwards east to west through Albania to the Adriatic coast. The offshore section of the pipeline will begin near the Albanian city of Fier and it will traverse the Adriatic Sea to tie into Italy's gas transportation network in Southern Italy. TAP will be 878 km in length (Greece 550 km; Albania 215 km; Adriatic Sea 105 km; Italy 8 km). The project is predicted to be able to transmit ShahDeniz natural gas from Azerbaijan to Europe since 2020. At the end of November 2018, the TAP project was 82.4% completed [16].

Keystone XL Pipeline Project The proposed Keystone XL Pipeline operated by TransCanada is a 36-inch-diameter crude oil pipeline with a length of 1906 km, beginning in Hardisty, Alberta, and extending south to Steele City, Nebraska. It is reported that Keystone XL Pipeline will contribute to U.S. energy security, create thousands of jobs and provide a substantial economic benefit to local communities [17]. In January, 2017, president of the US Donald Trump signed an executive order on promoting the construction of Keystone XL pipeline and Dakota pipeline, but he stressed on renegotiating some articles of Keystone XL project. The government of Canada and Alberta attached great importance to the project for popularizing oil sand in the international market and declared that Canada has been well-prepared. Despite of a turnaround, Keystone XL pipeline project is still in development.

4.1.1.3 Ranking of Crude Oil Pipelines

The length of top 10 crude oil pipelines takes up 29.8% of that of worldwide crude oil pipelines, as shown in Table 4.2 [5].

Table 4.2 Ranking of crude oil pipelines of petroleum companies in 2017

Company name	Country	Length (km)	Share (%)
Transneft	Russia	61,000	10.8
Enbridge	Canada	31,245	5.5
PAA	The USA	27,000	4.8
CNPC	China	20,359	3.6
Sunoco	The USA	15,186	2.7
Enterprise	The USA	13,563	2.4
Sinopec Group	China	9561	1.7
ExxonMobil	The USA	7933	1.5
TransCanada	Canada	6321	1.2
Inter Pipeline	Canada	3679	0.5

Ranking first, Transneft is a state-owned transportation enterprise which monopolizes 84% of oil transportation in Russia [18]. Besides, Transneft is also the world's largest petroleum pipeline transportation enterprise. According to statistical data, crude oil pipelines run by Transneft were 61,000 km long in 2017, topping at 10.8% of worldwide crude oil pipelines.

Enbridge has the world's second longest crude oil pipelines and is one of the largest pipeline operating companies in North America. The total distance of oil and gas pipelines owned, held or run by Enbridge is about 103,617 km. Enbridge has 31,245 km crude oil pipelines, covering 5.5% of worldwide crude oil pipelines.

Headquartered in Houston of Texas, PAA has the world's third longest crude oil pipelines and its service covers more than 40 states of the United States and 5 provinces of Canada. It is a petroleum pipeline company integrating oil and gas transportation and sale and covering 4.8% of worldwide crude oil pipelines up to 27,000 km.

China National Petroleum Corporation (CNPC) has the world's fourth longest crude oil pipelines adding up to about 20,359 km and covering 3.6% of worldwide crude oil pipelines.

Founded in 1886 and headquartered in Philadelphia of Pennsylvania, Sunoco has the world's fifth longest crude oil pipelines. It is also the largest oil refinery in the U.S. which mainly engages in exploration and refining of petroleum and natural gas as well as production and sale of petroleum products. Sunoco has 15,186 km crude oil pipelines, covering 2.7% of worldwide crude oil pipelines.

Sinopec Group has 9561 km crude oil pipelines, covering 1.7% of worldwide crude oil pipelines and ranking the world's seventh.

Moreover, Enterprise and ExxonMobil have the world's sixth and eighth longest crude oil pipelines respectively; TransCanada and Inter Pipeline have the world's ninth and tenth longest crude oil pipelines respectively.

4.1.1.4 Ranking of Petroleum Product Pipelines

As shown in Table 4.3, the length of petroleum product pipelines for the top 10 companies exceeds 210,000 km, covering 67.5% of worldwide product oil pipelines [5].

Founded in 1968 and headquartered in Houston, Enterprise has the world's longest petroleum product pipelines and mainly engages in piping and service of liquefied natural gas, onshore natural gas, onshore crude oil and offshore crude oil as well as processing and manufacturing of petroleum and fine chemicals during the intermediate links. Enterprise has 56,228 km petroleum product pipelines, covering 16.0% of worldwide petroleum product pipelines.

Transneft has the world's second longest petroleum product pipelines adding up to 28,817 km and covering 8.2% of worldwide petroleum product pipelines. Phillips 66 has the world's third longest product oil pipelines. Headquartered in Washington, it is a comprehensive transnational energy company which is departmentalized from ConocoPhillips refinery and mainly engages in oil refining, chemicals, gas station, oil

Table 4.3 Ranking of product oil pipelines of petroleum companies in 2017

Company name	Country	Length (km)	Share (%)
Enterprise	The USA	56,228	16.0
Transneft	Russia	28,817	8.2
Phillips 66	The USA	26,357	7.5
Magellan	The USA	22,842	6.2
Kinder Morgan	The USA	21,437	6.1
ONEOK	The USA	20,132	5.9
Sinopec Group	China	18,582	5.7
Buckeye	The USA	15,448	5.3
Colonial	The USA	13,485	5.1
NuStar	The USA	11,073	4.7

and gas pipeline and terminal transportation. Phillips 66 runs 26,357 km petroleum product pipelines, covering 7.5% of worldwide petroleum product pipelines.

Headquartered in Oklahoma, Magellan has the world's fourth longest petroleum product pipelines adding up to 22,842 km and covering 6.2% of worldwide petroleum product pipelines. Located in North America, Kinder Morgan runs 21,437 km petroleum product pipelines, covering 6.1% of worldwide petroleum product pipelines. It is also the largest natural gas pipeline company in North America.

ONEOK has 20,132 km petroleum product pipelines, covering 5.9% of worldwide petroleum product pipelines. Sinopec Group has the world's seventh longest petroleum product pipelines adding up to about 18,582 km and covering 5.7% of worldwide petroleum product pipelines.

Buckeye, Colonial and Nustar have the eighth, the ninth and the tenth longest product oil pipelines respectively. In general, 8 U.S. pipeline companies come out top ten and cover 56.8% of worldwide petroleum product pipelines.

4.1.2 Development of Oil and Gas Pipelines in China

The construction of oil and gas pipelines have developed rapidly in China. Total length of petroleum and gas pipelines was about 8300 km in 1978 and then it increased year by year and reached up to 119,300 km by 2017 with an average annual growth rate of 7.1% [19].

The Chinese pipeline industry has gone through three development stages [20]. The first stage was in the 1970s. Benefiting from the development of Daqing Oilfield, Liaohe Oilfield and Shengli Oilfield, the petroleum pipeline network was formed which covered East China and connected Northeast, North China and East China. The second stage lasted from the 1980s to the 1990s. The western gas line network made a breakthrough from the construction of long-distance oil and gas pipeline and Sichuan-Chongqing gas line network and benefited from the development of western

Table 4.4 Four major oil-gas import channels in China

Channel	Source	Oil channel	Natural gas channel
Northwest	Central Asia	China-Kazakhstan crude oil pipeline	Central Asia-China gas pipeline (sections A/B/C have been put into operation and section D is under construction)
Northeast	Russia	China-Russia crude oil pipeline	China-Russia eastern gas pipeline (under construction)
Southwest	Myanmar	China-Myanmar crude oil pipeline	China-Myanmar natural gas pipeline
Southeast	Middle East/Africa/Latin America/Southeast Asia	Including crude oil import channel and LNG transportation channel via Strait of Malacca and South China Sea	

oilfields such as Sinkiang Oilfield, Tarim Oilfield, Sichuan Oilfield and Changqing Oilfield. In the third stage, pipeline construction of China focuses on imported oil and gas pipeline and natural gas layout with the increase in oil and gas import and the increase of natural gas in the energy structure.

The first pipelines have been severely aged, especially crude oil pipelines, and domestic petroleum and natural gas production cannot satisfy the consumer demand, and so plenty of crude oil and natural gas are imported every year. To ensure safety of energy supply, the Chinese government makes a general layout of energy import channels in the northwest, northeast, southwest and on the sea. Through long-term efforts, land-sea supplementary diversified oil and gas import channels have basically taken shape in China, which effectively lower the risks. Among all these oil and gas import channels, there are three onshore import channels and many offshore channels into southeast coastal harbors [21] (as shown in Table 4.4).

4.1.2.1   Northwest Channel

Northwest channel mainly includes China-Kazakhstan crude oil pipeline and Central Asia-China natural gas pipeline and is used to transport crude oil and natural gas from Central Asia to China. China-Kazakhstan crude oil pipeline is originated from oil fields located in western Kazakhstan to the Dushanzi refinery located in the Sinkiang Province of China. The overall length is 2798 km and the annual design capacity is 20 million tons. Construction of the pipeline was divided into three segments and carried out in two phases. Phase I and Phase II have been put into operation in July, 2006 and July, 2009 respectively [22]. By 11:58 a.m. on March 29, 2018, China-Kazakhstan crude oil pipeline has safely run for 3906 days and transmitted 100 million tons of crude oil to China [23].

According to Sect. 4.1.1, Central Asia-China natural gas pipeline is originated from the border between Turkmenistan and Uzbekistan and enters China from Khorgos of Xinjiang via the middle of Uzbekistan and southern Kazakhstan. It is connected to "West-East Gas Pipeline II". Presently, sections A, B and C of Central Asia-China natural gas pipeline have been completed and put into operation and section D is predicted to be completed in the end of 2020. It's reported that natural gas to be transported by Central Asia-China natural gas pipeline will cover above 40% of imported natural gas [24].

4.1.2.2 Northeast Channel

Northeast channel is mainly used to transport crude oil and natural gas from Russia. China-Russia crude oil pipeline is originated from Skovorodino station of Russian Eastern Siberia—Pacific pipeline and terminates at Daqing via Heilongjiang Province and Inner Mongolia. The annual transport capacity is 15 million tons and the overall length is 999.04 km, including 72 km in Russia and 927.04 km in China. China-Russia crude oil pipeline was put into trial operation on November 1, 2010. On the basic route of China-Russia crude oil pipeline, China-Russia crude oil pipeline II was built with an overall length of 941.8 km from Mohe County of Heilongjiang Province to Yulin County of Daqing City [25]. It was completed on 12 November, 2017 and put into operation on 1 January, 2018. Due to the two crude oil pipelines, the imported oil amount for Russia increases from 15 to 30 million tons per annum.

As shown in Sect. 4.1.1, China-Russia eastern gas pipeline is still under construction. The newly built pipelines in China were approved in phases according to the northern, central and southern sections (Heihe-Changling section, Changling-Yongqing section, Yongqing-Shanghai section). The Heihe-Changling section consist of three branches with a total length of 1067 km, and it is the most difficult project with the highest technical requirements, the most difficult construction and the most difficult construction conditions in the entire China-Russia pipeline project. The construction of this section was started on June 29, 2015 and fully completed on October 16, 2019. The pipeline of Heihe-Changling section was officially put into operation on December 1, 2019. It plans to import 5 billion m^3 of natural gas from Russia in the first year [26]. Heilongjiang, Jilin, Liaoning, Hebei, Tianjin, Beijing and other regions will directly benefit from this section. After the whole project is put into operation, Russia's natural gas resources will be connected with key natural gas markets such as Northeast China, Beijing-Tianjin-Hebei and Yangtze River Delta, and will be interconnected with existing regional gas pipeline networks to provide stable and high quality gas resources to the Northeast, Bohai Rim and Yangtze River Delta regions.

4.1.2.3 Southwest Channel

Southwest channel mainly refers to China-Myanmar oil and gas pipeline project. China-Myanmar crude oil pipeline and China-Myanmar natural gas pipeline were commenced in 2010. The former is originated from Maday Island of Kyaukpyu on the west coast of Myanmar, enters China from Ruili of Yunnan via Rakhine State, Magway, Mandalay regions and Shan State of Myanmar and terminates at Chongqing via Guizhou. The overall length is 2400 km and the designed transmission capacity is 22 million tons per year. On 19 May, 2017, the first batch of crude oil arrived in China through China-Myanmar crude oil pipeline [27]. As of 17 July, 2018, the pipeline had transported more than 10 million tons of crude oil.

China-Myanmar natural gas pipeline mostly overlaps with China-Myanmar crude oil pipeline. They are originated from Kyaukpyu of Myanmar, enter China from Ruili of Yunna and depart from each other in Anshun of Guizhou. Finally China-Myanmar natural gas pipeline extends south and ends at Guangxi. With an overall length of 2500 km and an annual designed transmission capacity of 12 billion m^3, China-Myanmar natural gas pipeline was put into operation in September, 2013.

China-Myanmar oil and gas pipeline project is a leading project of the Belt and Road Initiative in Myanmar, which not only can create considerable economic and social benefits, but also will promote the development of Southwest China. Particularly, China-Myanmar crude oil pipeline transmits oil from the Middle East and Africa to China, which relieves the shortage of petroleum resources of Yunnan, reduces the crude oil transmission distance to Zhanjiang by 1200 km and alleviates overdependence of the oil "lifeline" on the Strait of Malacca [20].

4.1.2.4 Southeast Channel

Southeast channel refers to southwest maritime channel, including crude oil import channel and LNG import channel via the Strait of Malacca and South China Sea. It is the most important channel for energy import of China. According to statistics, China's import volume of crude oil was about 200 million tons before 2011, among which only about 20 million tons was transmitted from Kazakhstan and Russia through pipeline and railway respectively and the rest was shipped through the Strait of Malacca. Thus, China's oil security has been faced with enormous transportation risks. China's import volume of crude oil was about 422.1 million tons in 2017, among which more than 300 million tons was transported by sea [28]. It's visible that safety of crude oil maritime channel is still of great importance for China's energy safety.

4.1.3 Maritime Energy Transportation Channel of China

From the perspective of China's crude oil import pattern, nearly 80% of imported crude oil is transported by sea every year [28]. Presently, there are four major maritime routes in China, west route, south route, east route and north route.

The west route is originated from Shenzhen and Hong Kong in China and arrives in the heart of Europe via the South China Sea and the Strait of Malacca. It is the most complex and the busiest maritime channel in China which connects the Middle East, Africa and Europe and is mainly used to deliver petroleum resources and goods of Central Europe. From the point of petroleum transportation, the west route is divided into Middle East route, African route and Southeast Asian route. The Middle East route starts from the Persian Gulf, enters the Indian Ocean via the Strait of Hormuz and Arabian Sea and arrives in South China Sea via the Strait of Malacca and Chinese Mainland via Taiwan Strait. The Middle East route is mainly used to transport petroleum from the Persian Gulf. The African route has two routes: One starts from North Africa, enters the Indian Ocean from Arabian Sea via the Suez Canal, the Red Sea, Strait of Bab el-Mandeb and Gulf of Aden and arrives in South China Sea via the Strait of Malacca; the other starts from West Africa, enters the Indian Ocean via Cape of Good Hope and arrives in South China Sea via the Strait of Malacca. The African route is mainly used to transmit petroleum from North Africa and West Africa. The Southeast Asian route refers to the route via the Strait of Malacca and Taiwan Strait and to Chinese Mainland. As a matter of fact, the Southeast Asian route is the second half of the Middle East route and the African route.

The south route is the Oceania route from Shenzhen or Hong Kong in China and to Australia and New Zealand via South China Sea, Sunda Strait or Lombok Strait. The south route is mainly used to transport minerals and goods between China and Oceania. The east route, also called the American route, often starts from the areas of Jiangsu and Zhejiang and arrives in North America, Central America and Caribbean Sea via Osumi Kaikyo or Miyako Strait or Bass Strait or Tsugaru Strait. It passes through the disputed areas of East China Sea and is mainly used to transport goods between China and North America, including petroleum resources and mineral resources from South America. The north route starts from coastal harbors of China and arrives in coastal harbors of Russian Far East via Korea and Bering Strait and even Europe via the Arctic Ocean.

As a whole, all these four major routes pass through the world's three largest key channels (the Strait of Hormuz, the Strait of Malacca and the Suez Canal) and are faced with many real, long-term and uncertain risks [29].

4.2 Three Indian Ocean Channels Are Concerned with Energy Transportation Safety of China

As mentioned above, major energy channels of China inevitably relate to the Indian Ocean, especially the Middle East oil channel and two African oil channels. Thus, safety of three Indian Ocean channels is concerned with energy safety of China.

4.2.1 Strategic Position of the Indian Ocean

Along with globalization and regional integration, international strategic channels which connect major economic centers, production bases and consumer bases are regarded as key channels of international passenger and logistics transportation and are highly valued by various countries, because they are transportation corridors and hubs economically and natural moats for attack, bases and shelters for defense and good choices for ambush militarily. The Indian Ocean is one of the most important international strategic channels in the world. Scholars have pointed out that, "Any country that gets hold of the Indian Ocean gets command of Asia.", since the Indian Ocean is the key of 'seven oceans' [30]. Globally, maritime transportation plays a critical role in global trade. Data displays that about 90% of intercontinental trade and 2/3 of oil trade depend on sea transportation [28], indicating the importance of maritime channel in oil trade. Endowed with unique location, the Indian Ocean plays a decisive role in maritime transportation. Besides, 70% of petroleum products are transported along the Indian Ocean from the Middle East in the west to the Pacific in the east [3]. For China, about 90% of crude oil is imported by sea and plenty of transport routes pass the Indian Ocean, indicating the importance of strategic maritime channels in the Indian Ocean for China's energy safety.

4.2.1.1 Geopolitics

From the point of geopolitics, the Indian Ocean is located among Asia, Oceania, Africa and Antarctica and it is vital communication line through Europe, Africa, Asia and Oceania. As the world's third largest ocean, the Indian Ocean covers an area of about 7491.7 km^2 and 21.1% of total ocean area and has an average depth of 3897 m. The Indian Ocean is close to the resourceful South China Sea and is connected to the vast Pacific Ocean via Strait of Malacca in the east; It leans closely against the South Asian Sub-Continent and goes deep into Central Asia, which is "the world's heartland" in the north; It borders on the Persian Gulf and the Middle East and leads to Mediterranean Sea via the Red Sea and the Suez Canal at the northwest corner; And it passes through Gulf of Aden, Arabian Peninsula and the resourceful African Continent and approaches to the Atlantic Ocean at Cape of Good Hope [31]. Besides, the Indian Ocean has three major strategic channels, Strait of Hormuz,

Strait of Mandeb and the Suez Canal. Once a British admiral vividly described: "Among 'five keys of the world' the Indian Ocean have three (the Suez Canal, Strait of Malacca and Cape of Good Hope)." Endowed with unique location, the Indian Ocean becomes one of the world's busiest three strategic transportation channels. Strait of Hormuz on the west of the Indian Ocean and Strait of Malacca are the world's first and second energy channels respectively, for which competition and scramble have been a political focus on the Indian Ocean over the years. Therefore, geopoliticians name it "the last determinant of the world's fate" [31]. According to theories of sea power, "Any country that wants to be a great power must get command of ocean first, especially strategic straits and channels". Once "in command of key navigation channels, straits and maritime channels, they will remain firmly in charge of sources of world wealth and arteries of world economy". Obviously, geopolitic factor arising from strategic channels is the flash point of competition for the Indian Ocean.

4.2.1.2 Geoeconomics

From the point of geoeconomics, the Indian Ocean is rich in resources, and the seabed and surrounding land contain abundant petroleum and natural gas. Petroleum and natural gas of the Indian Ocean are mainly distributed in Arabian Peninsula, Indo-China Peninsula, Indonesia and continental shelves along the coast of Australia. Submarine oil and gas production of the Indian Ocean takes up about 40% of total offshore oil and gas production, among which the Persian Gulf is the world's largest submarine oil producing place known as "the world's petroleum treasury". Saudi Arabia, Kuwait and Iraq along the coast of the Persian Gulf are major oil-gas producers. The Indian Ocean also is an important oil supplier of Europe, the USA, Japan and other developed countries and an intermediate station. The Indian Ocean now has three major petroleum transport routes: The first starts from the Persian Gulf and reaches Western Europe and North America via Cape of Good Hope; The second starts from the Persian Gulf and reaches Japan via Strait of Malacca (or Lombok Strait and Makassar Strait); the last starts from Persian Gulf and reaches Western Europe and North America via the Suez Canal and the Mediterranean Sea. The Indian Ocean also has 1/9 of the world's harbors and 1/5 of cargo throughput. As a whole, the Indian Ocean is an area with the densest maritime channels and its "petroleum transportation channel" and "trade route" is "a strategic lifeline" for China and many other countries. It is by virtue of irreplaceable resources and geostrategic value that the Indian Ocean has become a main battlefield where great powers compete with each other. Any country that attains strategic superiorities of the Indian Ocean can not only protect the lifeline of maritime energy sources and trade routes, but also defeat the rivals and effectively exert influence on the Middle East, South Asia and even Central Asia [32].

4.2.1.3   Geostrategy

From the point of geostrategy, the Indian Ocean becomes the battlefield of great powers by virtue of unique location and abundant petroleum resources. Coveting its benefits, the USA, Russia, UK, France and Japan strengthen the construction of their blue-water navies in the hope of moving about freely and quickly in the Indian Ocean. It's just because of this the Indian Ocean is filled with complicated contradictions and interest disputes and turns turbulent, such as incessant terrorism and antiterrorism, interaction between western civilization and Islamic civilization and fierce competition for oil-gas resources. For example, the United States has maintained a military presence in the Indian Ocean since the 1960s and after that it has strived for a hegemonic position. The Soviet Union also has established military bases in the Indian Ocean since late in the 1960s during the Cold War. As the Soviet Union collapsed, Russia's Indian Ocean policy contracted. However, Russia returned to the Indian Ocean and contended against the U.S.'s dominant strategy after Putin held power in the twentieth century. Considering the importance of the Indian Ocean, Japan also got involved in support of the U.S.'s antiterrorism in order to ensure safety of the maritime transportation "lifeline". India that regards the Indian Ocean as "the ocean of India", accelerated "the control strategy for the Indian Ocean" and strived to strengthen the construction blue-water navies and get command of the Indian Ocean. Despite of different strategies, the USA, Russia, Japan and India all strived to "control the strategic area, get hold of the passages to the Indian Ocean, protect their own channels and attain abundant resources as much as possible" [30].

4.2.2   Great Significance of Three Indian Ocean Channels for China

As a major energy importing country, China is forming a "three-continent one-ocean" energy import pattern (northwest, northeast, southwest and southeast) [14], which relates to China's energy safety. However, the top priority of China's energy safety is how to make major energy channels of the Indian Ocean unimpeded, because it is concerned with sustainable development of China and it is of great practical significance for China to ensure safety of maritime channels of the Indian Ocean.

In the first place, the Indian Ocean is a major transportation channel of energy sources and other resources for China. Among eight major oil-gas producing places three are in the Indian Ocean: the Persian Gulf and its coasts, coasts of Indonesia and northwest continental shelf of Australia [33], among which the Persian Gulf and its coasts are called "star" oil-gas producing places. China imports half of petroleum from the Middle East and Africa along the coast of the Indian Ocean, which demonstrates the importance of energy sources of the Indian Ocean for China. Other than energy sources, the Indian Ocean is also rich in strategic materials such as uranium, gold, diamond, tin, coal, iron ore, tungsten, manganese, copper and zinc, especially precious metals. It has about 85% of Manganese, 60% of Vanadium, 86% of Chrome, 50% of uranium and 25% of ferrum which ranks the world's first [33]. Abundant strategic resources, energy sources and characteristics of transportation channels determine the geo-politic position of the Indian Ocean. It is an importance origin and intermediate station of energy sources and other strategic materials for China.

Then, safety of shipping lanes and arteries of the Indian Ocean relates to China's economic security and social stability. China imports energy sources and other resources mainly through four transportation channels of the Indian Ocean: First, the Middle East channel, which starts from the Persian Gulf and reaches China via Strait of Hormuz, Strait of Malacca and Taiwan Strait; Second, African channel, which starts from North Africa and reaches China via the Mediterranean Sea, Strait of Gibraltar, Cape of Good Hope, Strait of Malacca and Taiwan Strait; Third, Southeast Asia channel, which passes through Strait of Malacca and Taiwan Strait and reaches China; Fourth, the Pacific Ocean channel, which starts from America continent and reaches South China Sea via Panama Canal and Western Pacific. From the perspective of transportation volume [33], about 50% of petroleum is imported from the Middle East channel and 30% is imported from African channel and Southeast Asia channel. In addition, above 40% of global crude oil is transported through Strait of Hormuz and Strait of Malacca. Three channels and corresponding arteries have been long affected by infighting among the USA, Japan, Russia and India for the right of control, and consequently China is deprived of fundamental security assurance. Therefore, vulnerability of Indian Ocean channels becomes a key topic on maritime transportation safety of China.

Third, China's foreign trade highly depends on the Indian Ocean. China has surpassed the US and become the world's largest trading country. As to mode of transportation, about 80% of goods are transported by sea, which makes China an export-oriented economy highly dependent on ocean trade. As to composition of trade partner, most trade partners of China are from Africa, the Middle East and Latin America and their transportation channels must pass through the Indian Ocean. Over 40 countries are located along the coast of the Indian Ocean and can be divided into four parts: South Asia part consists of India, Pakistan, Bangladesh, Maldives and Sri Lanka; Southeast Asia part consists of Indo-China Peninsula, Malay Peninsula and Malay Archipelago; The Middle East part consists of Iran, Saudi Arabia, Kuwait, Iraq, Oman, Bahrain and Yemen; The African part consists of South Africa, Mozambique, Tanzania, Kenya, Sudan, Somalia, Egypt and other African countries. The total volume of bilateral trade between China and these countries obviously increased in recent years. Nevertheless, trade between China and these countries mainly relies on sea transportation and most of them are coastal countries, so maritime channels have a direct effect on commercial intercourse between China and these countries.

Last but not the least, the Indian Ocean is also an important platform by which China practices "Going Out" strategy and builds the status and image of a great power. On the one hand, the Indian Ocean has a huge market. Although the Chinese territory does not border on the Indian Ocean, China has been associated with coastal countries friendly. The Sea Silk Road connected China to India in history and based on this China has kept friendly contact with coastal countries in trade, HR and culture till now. Emerging counties represented by India, South Africa, Indonesia and Saudi Arabia and countries in close contact with China such as Pakistan, Tanzania and Sri Lanka are developable and investible areas and the emphasis of China's "Going Out" strategy, especially the Belt and Road Initiative. On the other hand, abundant maritime resources of the Indian Ocean should be exploited using plenty of advanced technologies. The strong desire of coastal countries to exploit maritime resources is difficult to achieve due to weak strength. With a solid industrial base, China is able to exploit maritime resources of the Indian Ocean and act in economic cooperation with coastal countries, which not only expands national benefits and realizes mutual development and prosperity, but also facilitates to build a "win-win and prosperous" harmonious Indian Ocean and make China a responsible great power [34].

To sum up, the Indian Ocean not only is important channel of traffic, trade and energy channel to South Asia, Middle East, Europe, Africa and Oceania and an important strategic direction and focus of China's maritime security and social stability, but also holds a very important strategic position. Whether petroleum imported from the Middle East or petroleum and mineral resources imported from Africa, Indian Ocean channels are the only way which must be passed. Thus, safety of "energy channel" and "trade route" of the Indian Ocean is closely related to China's economic security and social stability.

4.2.3   Factors Affecting the Safety of China's Indian Ocean Channels

Being eyed by many great powers covetously, the Indian Ocean is confronted with a complicated situation. With different attitudes but the same purpose, countries represented by the USA, Japan and India adopt strategic measures to the Indian Ocean, which certainly will conflict with China's Indian Ocean strategy [35] and consequently will affect safety of its maritime channels. Major influence factors of China's Indian Ocean channels are as follows.

4.2.3.1   The U.S.'s Dominant

As world economy and strategy emphasis transferred from the Euro-Atlantic region to the Asian-Pacific region, the importance and strategic position of the Indian Ocean has increased gradually. Whereas the Indian Ocean has been governed by UK for a long time and the U.S.'s ocean strategy has focused on the Atlantic Ocean and the Pacific Ocean after World War II, the Indian Ocean was "a pool of stagnant water" for the USA over a very long period of time. In the middle of the 1960s, the USA aimed at the Indian Ocean and obtained Diego Garcia for defense through cooperation with UK. The USA took advantage of Diego Garcia to replenish warships and with the development of the Indian Ocean it became an important base for the U.S.'s

Indian Ocean strategy [36]. In the 1970s, oil crisis highlighted the importance of the Indian Ocean for maritime energy channels. Meanwhile, the Soviet Union marched into the Indian Ocean, deployed troops and established strategic cooperation with India, which challenged American interests in the Indian Ocean. For this reason, the USA extensively expanded military base, increased military equipment and strengthened military force centered on Diego Garcia, which symbolized an adjustment of the U.S.'s Indian Ocean strategy. In the end of the 1970s, the Iranian Revolution and the Soviet invasion of Afghanistan threatened safety of maritime energy channels of the USA and other western countries. As a result, the USA no longer rested content with its Indian Ocean strategy but further expanded to coastal areas. After the Cold War, the USA adjusted its Indian Ocean policy by accelerating "forward deployment" and deployed huge blue-water navies in the Indian Ocean, the Red Sea and the Persian Gulf. It also declared that strengthening the military presence in the Indian Ocean was aimed at controlling several important maritime channels such as Strait of Malacca and Strait of Hormuz in war. In the twenty-first century, the USA realized its limited power and turned its military deployment of Indian Ocean policy to cooperation with coastal countries. The USA valued India's strategic position most and actively enhanced US-India strategic cooperation. Besides, it attached importance to the relations among existing military allies and actively promoted the strategic relation with Austria. Presently, the USA has taken an US-Austria-India "triangle" ally into initial shape in the Indian Ocean and vigorously supports allies so as to maintain its strategic interests [37].

The USA transformed its Indian Ocean policy mainly for the following purposes: First, fill in the gap of the Indian Ocean after collapse of the Soviet Union and expand its strategic layout; Second, control maritime channels of the Indian Ocean and cope with the rise of China; Third, take control of petroleum resources of the Indian Ocean, especially the Persian Gulf; Fourth, prevent and strike Islamic military forces and terrorists and deal with non-traditional security threats. The control of the Indian Ocean is conducive to realization of the U.S.'s global strategy. From the angle of antiterrorism, terrorists take the Middle East, East Africa and Southeast Asia as a shelter and the Indian Ocean is a link of them, so in control of the Indian Ocean, the USA can cut off maritime communication channels of terrorist organizations and spread anti-terrorist forces in order to improve antiterrorism efficiency. To contain regional powers, the USA tracks and controls the situation of the resourceful Gulf region and even the Middle East with the aid of the Indian Ocean and coastal countries and can deploy military forces there when necessary. To prevent the rise of great powers, Russia, China and India are identified as latent competitors and in charge of the Indian Ocean's sea supremacy, the USA will hold the deadly weapons against competitors [31]. If the USA is in charge of the Indian Ocean, not only will China's oil delivery channels be controlled, but also an economic blockade will be caused. Being obviously dominant, repellent and interfering, the U.S.'s Indian Ocean policy poses a great challenge to China's interests.

4.2.3.2 Japanese Factors

A security issue of Japan, which is a maritime state, is to expand sea power and maintain safety of strategic maritime channel. The primary cause is identified as severe shortage of energy sources and high dependence on import. According to statistical data, up to 86.3% of crude oil was imported in 2017 in Japan, among which 85.8% was imported from such Middle East countries as Saudi Arabia, the UAE and Kuwait [28]. Since the Indian Ocean is the only transportation channel of crude oil from the Middle East, Japan regards maritime channels via the Indian Ocean and Strait of Malacca as the lifeline. As India, an emerging country, cut a figure in the international arena in recent years, Japan began to value the Indian Ocean and advocated keeping close contact with costal countries. Japanese scholars put forward that, "The Indian Ocean has been called the sea of growth in the last quarter of the twentieth century and had become the sea of growth in the last quarter of the twenty-first century" [38]. Some Japanese scholars also regard the Indian Ocean as an important tie between Japan and African countries. Based on this, Japan is aimed at promoting exchange and cooperation between Japan and other countries such as India centered on the Indian Ocean and collaborating with African countries in maritime economy and maritime military.

Leaders of the Japanese Government voiced concerns about the Indian Ocean more than once. On the one hand, Japan actively developed the relation with India. Japan and India shared the maritime security strategy to maintain safety of maritime energy channels, sought larger regional influence and prevented and contained China's maritime strength. For this purpose, Japan and India reached a series of agreements on maritime security cooperation focused on traditional security and non-traditional security. In terms of non-traditional security, they shared information, protected safety of maritime channels, stroke piracy and maritime terrorism and strengthened maritime environment protection, maritime disaster rescue and maritime communication line protection. In terms of traditional security, they jointly exercised navies and coast guards. On the other hand, Japan made a big fuss about the Indian Ocean in the name of anti-piracy operation. For example, it proposed "Asian Anti-piracy Agreement", passed Anti-piracy Law and dispatched self-defense forces to join Somalia anti-piracy action, etc., took an active part in corresponding international regimes and increased economic aid to Somalia and related areas [39]. Consequently, Japan not only protected safety of Indian Ocean channels, but also expanded its limitary and paramilitary forces and extended its domain in the Indian Ocean [40]. Japanese-India maritime security cooperation cannot be separated from transformation of the United States' Asia-Pacific strategy.

It is worth noting that Japan took actions for the Indian Ocean mainly to "harass" China. In recent years, "the Indo-Pacific strategy", a new concept of geostrategy, was advocated by the United States, Japan and other western countries and was cognized in Japan, of which containing China was an important connotation. Japanese cognition of "Indo-Pacific strategy" featured as follows: First, Japan used "Indo-Pacific strategy" to contain and contend against China. Then, Japanese cognition of "Indo-Pacific strategy" was ocean-oriented and focused on safety of maritime channels of the Indian Ocean and the Pacific Ocean. Third, Japan emphasized on military factors of the Indian Ocean, excluded China from the imagination of regional security cooperation and prevented the rise of Chinese military force in the Indian Ocean. To this end, Japan strengthened its presence in the Indian Ocean through transferring the strategic focus, strengthening southwest defense, intervening with the South China Sea dispute, enhancing Japan-US alliance, promoting Japan-Australia limitary cooperation and developing Japan-India relations and strived to isolate and contain China and its rise, which undoubtedly posed a severe challenge to safety of Chinese Indian Ocean channels.

4.2.3.3 Competitive Factors of India

Among Indian Ocean countries India has the strongest comprehensive national strength. Surrounded by sea on three sides, India has a 7516 km coastline and 1197 islands covering an area of 8249 m^2 and it is adjacent to Bay of Bengal in the east and Arabian Sea in the west. Cape Comorin at the southernmost goes deep into the Indian Ocean for 1600 km. Due to unique geographical features, India highly values and maintains its maritime interests, especially interests in the Indian Ocean. India considers the Indian Ocean as "an inland sea" because of political interest, security interest and economic interest [41]. From the point of political interest, India rises on the bases of the Indian Ocean. Then, India has strived to show its ambition of rise through the pursuit of being a permanent member of the United Nations Security Council, which should be backed by the Indian Ocean countries. Finally, to build a good image, India improves the relations with Islamic states and balances the relationship between Pakistan and the Islamic World. From the point of security interest, India actively copes with traditional security of the Indian Ocean and pays high attention to non-traditional security such as challenges to its energy security and threats from piracy and terrorism. From the point economic interest, India's commercial intercourse is highly dependent on the sea. For all the above reasons, India develops the maritime strategy of "dominating the Indian Ocean and marching the Pacific Ocean eastward".

To dominate the Indian Ocean, India divides it into major waters and minor waters which must be controlled. Major waters include exclusive economic zones and islands such as such as Arabian Sea and Bay of Bengal, main arteries such as Strait of Hormuz, Strait of Malacca, Mandab Strait and Cape of Good Hope and main routes via the Indian Ocean; while minor waters include the Southern Indian Ocean, the Red Sea, South China Sea and the Eastern Pacific Ocean [41]. India stresses on the control over key arteries and attempts to arm itself in the Indian Ocean by "hard power". For example, India adopts "distant-water annihilation" strategy and energetically develops navies so as to maintain an absolute military superiority and cope with threats and conflicts from the Indian Ocean countries. India also stresses on remaining the "frightening" power and "the balance of power" against great powers which covet the Indian Ocean. Meanwhile, it acts in cooperation with extraterritorial powers such as the USA, Japan and Russia and surrounding countries and enhances its dominant status through military exercise. Except for the aforesaid "hard power", India strengthens the relations with Indian Ocean countries using "soft power" such as "Maritime Spice Route" and "Project Mausam" [42].

Exclusiveness is a big characteristic of India's strategic target for the Indian Ocean. In recent years, India regarded China as the main obstacle and rival on the way to dominate South Asia and the Indian Ocean. Especially China has built harbor facilities [42] along the coast of the Indian Ocean in Burma, Bangladesh, Sri Lanka and Pakistan after the proposal of the Belt and Road Initiative, which aroused alertness of India and was interpreted as a challenge to its key benefits and traditional position in the Indian Ocean. It's the reason why India made no response to the Belt and Road Initiative but put up with "maritime route and cultural landscape across the Indian Ocean" [43]. Furthermore, India accelerated its strategic nuclear force by the excuse of "China threat" and "Chinese navy's invasion of the Indian Ocean". In conclusion, India has borne a grudge and taken precautions against China for long and its Indian Ocean strategy and intention will pose a great threat to China's maritime security of the Indian Ocean.

4.2.3.4 Conflicts Among Indian Ocean Countries

Except for India, more than 20 countries such as Pakistan, Bangladesh, Sri Lanka, Maldives, Saudi Arabia, Madagascar, Somalia and Yemen are located along the coast of the Indian Ocean, most of which suffer economic slowdown, overwhelming distractions and internal and external contradictions. Thus, regional conflicts frequently occur among or inside coastal countries, which are key factors for safety of maritime channels. India and Pakistan conflict is the primary regional conflict. For more than half a century, the relationship between India and Pakistan has been sometimes strained or eased. They fought repeatedly in Kashmir and had armed conflicts ceaselessly. Safety of transportation channels of the Indian Ocean was heavily threatened or damaged by a military confrontation or a war between India and Pakistan. Due to a serious imbalance between two countries' military forces, their contradictions and conflicts are difficult to solve in the foreseeable future. The Middle East is another politically turbulent area near the Indian Ocean. Known as "World's Oil Depot", "Ocean of Oil" and "The Heart of Five Oceans and Three Continents", it holds a very important strategic position in politics, economy and military affairs [31]. Under the influence of internal and external factors, various problems are intertwined and hot issues come one after another. Inside the Middle East, Syria crisis, Yemeni Civil War, nuclear issue of Iran and fighting between Saudi Arabia and Iran still remain hard to deal with; Qatar's disconnection crisis and Kurdish region's pursuit for independence are pending issues. Outside the Middle East, the USA and Russia game against each other for the aforesaid issues [44]. Even if "Islamic State" is destroyed in the "state form" and anti-terror campaign makes significant progress, regional and international antiterrorism will become increasingly severe with expansion of terrorist forces.

It's particularly worth mentioning that Saudi Arabia and Iran, which are separated by the Persian Gulf, preside over two disputed Islamic sects and these two oil exporting countries combat again and again for oil dollars. Agents and even both states fought at close quarters in recent years. For example, Saudi Arabia and its allies had a heavy fighting with Houthis, an agent of Iran. Iran's elite Revolutionary Guards and the "opposition faction" backed by Saudi Arabia also bathed in blood for many years in Syria. The GCC countries also have their own problems. When they are grandly armed to exterminate guerrilla forces backed by Iran in Yemen, they have to rely on the USA and other great powers and fail for shortage of ammunitions. What's more, "the GCC" is not a monolithic block, which is proved by Qatar's "disconnection". In this case, a great war among GCC countries headed by Saudi Arabia will cost a lot and seriously disturb petroleum transportation channels, and consequently Strait of Hormuz is apt to be controlled. It's visible that the Middle East still can hardly go through the turbulence due to geographic complexity and severity of problems of coastal countries.

4.2.3.5 Non-traditional Security Factors of the Indian Ocean

Non-traditional security factors refer to a series of negative effects such as maritime terrorism, safety accident, piracy and natural disaster, among which piracy and terrorism are the biggest direct threats to safety of maritime channels of the Indian Ocean. Over the years, piracy incidents took place frequently in the Indian Ocean and Strait of Malacca was a high-prevalence area of piracy and armed attack. Statistical data showed that more than 3700 piracy incidents happened in 21 years from 1984 to 2005 and more than 500 of them happened in Strait of Malacca. After 2005, pirates became increasingly rampant and built a "paradise of terror" in the oceans around Somalia. In 2007, nearly a hundred pirate assaults happened in the Indian Ocean, including 21 in the Strait of Malacca, 31 in Somalia and 42 in Nigeria. During 2012–2015, an average of 163 pirate assaults happened in Southeast Asia every year. Piracy Report in 2016 issued by the International Maritime Bureau Piracy Report Center showed [45] that 191 pirate and armed robberies happened in 2016, which was less than 246 pirate and armed robberies in 2015 and decreased to the lowest level since 1998. The Report also pointed out that kidnapping accidents increased sharply to the highest level in the past decade even if pirating activities decreased to the lowest level for nearly two decades. It's reported that coasts of Somalia in West Africa and East Africa, the Red Sea and Gulf of Aden, coasts of Bay of Bengal, Strait of Malacca and waters in Southeast Asia are called five "waters of terror" and four of them are directly or indirectly related to the Indian Ocean. However, all the five waters of terror are the only way for most Chinese ships. It's just because of this that Chinese ships have been assaulted by pirates and maritime terrorists frequently and suffered heavy property and labor losses.

For example, a Chinese ship was first assaulted by pirates in November, 1998, called "Changsheng" ship event. "Yujia" ship was assaulted by pirates in September, 1999 in northeast of Sri Lanka. "Fuyuan fishing boat No. 226" was hijacked in

Somalia in 2002. A Chinese fishing boat was cannonaded in Sri Lanka on 20 March, 2003, 17 seamen got lost or died, the boat sunk and great losses were caused. A Chinese fishing boat "Tianyu No. 8" was hijacked by Somali pirates along the coast of Kenya on 14 November, 2008 and finally was rescued. A Hong Kong cargo ship "DELIGHT" was hijacked by Somali pirates in Yemen along the coast of the Gulf of Aden on 18 November, 2008. A Chinese cargo ship "COSCO ASIA" was assaulted by lawbreakers in the Suez Canal on 31 August, 2013. A Chinese fishing boat "Lu Rong Yuan No. 917" was hijacked by unknown armed pirates in Ghana on 28 January 2015. Various terrorist attacks that threaten Chinese ships and safety of maritime channels happened in the Indian Ocean every year. In order to protect lives and properties of ships and seamen across the Indian Ocean, Chinese navies escorted Gulf of Aden and Somalia waters these years. The convoy fleet of Chinese navy successfully rescued a foreign cargo ship hijacked by pirates in the Gulf of Aden on 9 April, 2017. China's involvement in fighting piracies and terrorist acts in the Indian Ocean is a boon for maintain safety of maritime channels and peace and stability of the world. The Indian Ocean is also threatened by natural disasters such as earthquake, tsunami and typhoon, which brings potential risks to passing ships.

4.3   Countermeasures for Safety of Chinese Maritime Energy Channels Under the BRI

The Indian Ocean is just covered by the BRI. Considering status quo, challenges and influence factors of Chinese maritime energy channels, it's necessary to discuss how to strengthen and consolidate the relations between China and Indian Ocean countries from the perspective of the BRI so as to protect safety of Chinese maritime energy channels and create a safe external environment for economic development. In view of this, the following countermeasures are proposed to protect safety of Chinese maritime energy channels under the BRI, building an Indian Ocean Rim community, revitalizing three major economic corridors using land and sea transportation and opening up harbors in western China.

4.3.1   Construction of Rim Indian Ocean Community and Safety of Chinese Maritime Channels

As stated above, safety of Indian Ocean channels is closely related to China and has a direct bearing on safety of Chinese trade routes, energy channels and strategic channels. However, safety of Chinese Indian Ocean channels is threatened and challenged in many aspects. From a global view, safety of Indian Ocean channels is of great importance for both China and developed countries such as Japan, the USA and Russia. For this purpose, China should together with countries concerned accelerate the construction of an Indian Ocean Rim community, maintain safety of Indian Ocean channels and build a harmonious Indian Ocean. Concrete measures are as follows:

First, establish a brand new outlook of maritime security based on the BRI

Since new China was founded 70 years ago, China has established the maritime security outlook with Chinese characteristics under the leadership of several generations of the Communist Party of China (CPC) heads. Reviewing the development history of Chinese maritime security outlook, Chinese maritime security strategy has changed from "zero-sum confrontation" to "win-win cooperation" [46]. China had been confronted with complicated internalities and externalities and hostile maritime environment since the founding of new China until the beginning of the 1970s, the first generation CPC heads led by Mao Zedong put forward strategic thoughts of "inshore defense", anti-maritime hegemony and promotion of coast defense based on economic construction, which laid a foundation for maritime security outlook with Chinese characteristics. As UNCLOS (United Nations Convention on the Law of the Sea) came into effect in the 1980s, the fighting for sea power became increasingly sophisticated and took on new features and the second generation CPC heads led by Deng Xiaoping put up with "inshore defense" for coast defense, "highly capable" "useful" naval construction and "seeking mutual development while shelving then sovereignty" for resolution of sea disputes, which took maritime security outlook with Chinese characteristics into initial shape. In the 1990s, confronted with complex and volatile international environment and maritime security situation, the third generation CPC heads led by Jiang Zemin broke limitations of traditional security outlook, recognizes maritime security from a strategic perspective, established a security outlook with maritime economy as the core and proposed to construct the cooperative safety pattern and combine comprehensive means and various measures, which symbolized the formation of maritime security outlook with Chinese characteristics. As the fighting for sea power became increasingly tense and traditional and non-traditional safety threats were intertwined in the twenty-first century, the fourth generation CPC heads led by Hu Jintao came up with the strategic thought of "harmonious ocean", the new coast defense concept of "protection and expansion of maritime interests" and "offshore defense" and the naval construction theory of "powerful people's navy at a national level adapting to the historical mission of armies in the new century and new stage", which elevated the maritime security outlook with Chinese characteristics to a new high [46]. Since 2012, General Secretary Xi Jinping, based on summarizing the thoughts of the previous CPC heads and according to China's current situation and development prospect, has proposed strategic thoughts of "building a maritime power", building a strong sea power, jointly building the 21st Century Maritime Silk Road, building a harmonious ocean and giving play to the role of oceans in cross-strait relations successively, which gives a new meaning to maritime security outlook with Chinese characteristics.

A generally accepted and instructive security outlook has not been formed for the Indian Ocean due to unique location and complicated landform. Chairman Xi Jinping mentioned in the opening ceremony of China-ASEAN (Association of Southeast Asian Nations) Free Trade Area Forum in 2012, "China is always a staunch force for regional and world peace and stability. We firmly defend national sovereignty, security and territorial integrity and devote to peaceful resolution of disputes with neighboring countries about territories, territorial waters and maritime rights and interests through friendly negotiation. We never strive for and seek hegemony. We develop our own through safeguarding world peace and safeguard work peace through self-development, at which China's path of peaceful development is targeted" [47]. The concept[1] that "common, comprehensive, cooperative and sustainable safety" proposed by Chairman Xi Jinping is an effective way to solve matters concerning the Indian Ocean. The new security outlook emphasizes on eliminating scruples among the states based on "mutual trust, mutual benefit, equality and cooperation" and "pursuing common safety through mutual beneficial cooperation".

Safety of Indian Ocean channels should be maintained under the guidance of the security outlook proposed by General Secretary Xi Jinping so as to create an environment for peaceful construction and development. In recent years, with the implementation of the Belt and Road Initiative and the enhancement of Chinese comprehensive maritime strength, some western powers began to fear China and attempted to aim at China deliberately. Some western and Indian media even criticized the submarine base in the South China Sea and hyped "String of Pearls Strategy" of "China's March to the Indian Ocean". Facing such a severe situation, we proposed to construct "a harmonious Indian Ocean" under the guidance of the security outlook and further put forward that promoting the construction of "a harmonious South China Sea" was the best plan to build "an ocean of peace, friendship and cooperation". "A harmonious Indian Ocean" should be built combined with the Belt and Road Initiative, because "win-win cooperation" and "harmony and inclusiveness" are the core idea and guiding principle of the Belt and Road Initiative. Meanwhile, we need to weaken the awareness of "strategy", underline the idea of "win-win cooperation" and "common prosperity" and establish the maritime security outlook of "concordance between land and sea".

Second, strengthen mutual trust with India and promote mutual development
China actively strengthens cooperation with Indian Ocean Countries. Chairman Xi Jinping expresses the determination to kindly treat and keep company with neighboring countries and persist in the policy of creating an amicable, secure and prosperous neighborhood, uphold the neighboring diplomatic concept of amity, sincerity, mutual benefit and inclusiveness and continuously deepen mutual beneficial cooperation with neighboring countries. China hopes to live in harmony with Indian Ocean countries for win-win cooperation.

In the matter of Indian Ocean, China and India are both strategic co-owners and strategic competitors. From the point of strategic interest appeal, China is aimed at protecting safety of energy channels, strengthening economic and trade cooperation with the Indian Ocean countries and realizing regional economic cooperation of the Indian Ocean; while India is aimed at seeking control power and leadership of the Indian Ocean, obtaining economic benefits from lateral extension and "Look/Act East

Policy" and coping with challenges from the rise of China. Different strategic interest appeals to the Indian Ocean between China and India result in strategic competition and contending and even conflict. India considers China's frequent presence in its "backyard" as a huge threat. Both states also compete and conflict with each other in the matter of South Asia, especially the relation with Pakistan. Despite of conflicts and divergences on the aforesaid matters, they share common interests in Indian Ocean strategy. As the USA concentrates more on the Indian Ocean, China and India hope to maintain its stability. Then, Indian "Look/Act East Policy" coincides with Chinese "westward" the BRI and both states may act in cooperation for mutual interests. Last, China and India reach an agreement on non-traditional security and yearn for a safe Indian Ocean.

Along with strategic expansion, China and India should strive to seek mutual interests and ways of cooperation so as to prevent and control of conflicts. In recent years, India felt agonized and conflicted over China. It acted in economic cooperation but remained strategically passive. One reason was that India took China as a rival. It hoped to weaken the control of great powers such as the USA "at the expense of China" but not to "help" China to expand its influence on the Indian Ocean. In view of this, China should reduce and avoid competition and conflict with India in the following aspects [48]. First, China should continue expressing the idea of "a harmonious Indian Ocean" and "standing for peace". China has always persisted in independent and unaligned foreign policy, "always persisted firmly in the path of peaceful development" and always persisted in the policy of creating an amicable, secure and prosperous neighborhood, which was proved by the development history. China will intend to neither dominate the Indian Ocean nor pursue own interests and development at the expense of other states' interests. Second, China should set up an example for living together in amity and cooperation with coastal countries and seek a vaster space for bilateral cooperation so as to build a wider cooperation platform, reduce strategic distrust and expand Sino-India cooperation. Third, China should seek opportunities for Sino-India cooperation and jointly build BRI especially the 21st Century Maritime Silk Road as the tie of common interests between China and India, since both states have common interest appeals to the Maritime Silk Road. Both states should politically trust each other, culturally integrate and communicate with each other and realize greater mutual benefits and win-win outcomes based on cultural recognition.

Third, develop good neighborly and friendly relations with Indian Ocean countries

Besides India, China still needs to maintain the relations with other Indian Ocean countries. In South Asia, she needs to keep friendly relations and cooperation with Pakistan, Bangladesh, Maldives and Sri Lanka. China and South Asian countries not only enjoy geographical proximity and cultural affinity, but also help each other in defense work and act in close cooperation. Geographically, South Asia extends in all directions and directs the progress of the BRI. The BRI now takes on a solid basis for cooperation, highly consistent cooperation needs, a "complex and broad" cooperation architecture and diversified forms of cooperation and will guide, demonstrate, support, promote and popularize the implementation of BRI [49]. First, we should persist in quality, efficient, sound and ordered fundamental principle and ensure smooth implementation of some flagship projects in South Asia. Then, we should concern about trends of states concerned, act in close cooperation with them and handle interest relationships properly. Finally, we should strengthen public diplomacy of think tank, academic circle and media and build a good public opinion atmosphere. Furthermore, China should pay close attention to the Indian Ocean countries in Southeast Asia, Middle East and Africa and remain on friendly and cooperative relations with coastal countries so as to maintain safety of Indian Ocean channels and build a "harmonious Indian Ocean".

To strengthen friendly and cooperative relations with coastal countries, China should promote multilateral cooperation on safety of Indian Ocean channels. Due to various limitations, the Indian Ocean lacks an effective and binding multilateral cooperation mechanism. Generally geopolitical balance and complexity of the Indian Ocean is based on various geographical characteristics and cultural characteristics and covers such multilateral cooperation mechanisms such as ASEAN, the South Asian Association for Regional Cooperation (SAARC), the Southern African Development Community (SADC), the GCC, Indian Ocean Commission, African Union, the Asia-Pacific Economic Cooperation (APEC) and the ASEAN Regional Forum [31]. The Coastal countries and extraterritorial great powers are intertwined with these organizations and dominate regional development. Therefore, we can promote multilateral cooperation on safety of Indian Ocean channels as follows: First, strengthen negotiation and dialogue with coastal countries, develop and improve rules and procedures for maintenance of maritime security; then, strengthen strategic cooperation with countries which Indian Ocean channels must pass and establish the cooperation (cooperation on maritime affairs at different levels) framework for protection of maritime channels; last, under UN's guidance for safety control of maritime channels, act in cooperation and strive to build a multilateral cooperation framework.

Fourth, handle the relations with extraterritorial great powers properly
To maintain safety of Indian Ocean channels, China also needs to handle the relations with extraterritorial great powers properly, especially the relation with the United States. With sustainable development of the Asia-Pacific strategy, the Indian Ocean has attracted great attention of the USA. It actively cozies up to India to contain China while accelerating expansion of Asia-Pacific strategy and maintaining its superiorities in the Indian Ocean [29]. In her illusion to this, China should deal with the relations with extraterritorial great powers such as the USA mainly through negotiation and cooperation, energetically developing the relations and enhancing long-term and stable relationship and cooperation on political mutual trust, economic cooperation and cultural integration with coastal countries.

To improve Sino-US relations, we should further promote the development of a new type of major-power relationship. In December, 2012, Xi Jinping, General Secretary of the Central Committee of CPC, stressed while meeting with Jimmy Carter, a former President of the United States, "Under the new situation, China and the USA should be fearless of hardship, have the courage to bring forth new ideas, strive to build mutually respectful and beneficial partnership and create a new pattern of relationship between China and the USA". In May, 2013, Chairman Xi Jinping met with Obama, the former President of the United States, in Mar-a-Lago of Florida, defining the developing direction of Sino-US relations during the new era. In November, 2013, President Trump paid a visit to China, during which Chairman Xi Jinping expressed "a better future" of Sino-US relations. The development concept of Sino-US relations initiated by Chairman Xi Jinping orients the policy to the USA and defines the aim of Sino-US relations as win-win cooperation. It also can be completely used as a guideline for the Indian Ocean cooperation. In other words, it can be used to neutralize Sino-US opposition and solve the conflicts on the Indian Ocean through international cooperation.

China and the United States should cooperate on regional issues such as matters concerning the Indian Ocean and global issues based on strategic mutual trust so as to achieve win-win development. Both states have cooperated on regional security mechanisms based on strategic mutual trust and achieved demonstrable results. For example, China got involved in nuclear issue of Iran as a member of the negotiation mechanism consisting of six countries and came up with constructive proposals for US-Iraq agreement. As to regional hot spots, Afghanistan became a "new highlight" of Sino-US cooperation. As to the South China Sea dispute, China and the USA also strive to agree on maintaining safety of the South China Sea and protecting safety of South China Sea channels. As to global issues such as energy source and climate change, both states are seeking ways of cooperation. Thus, both states can seek an appropriate entry point and ways of cooperation to safeguard peace and stability of the Indian Ocean and realize win-win cooperation with Indian Ocean countries.

Fifth, strengthen naval construction of China and protect safety of Indian Ocean channels

For the need of changing times and protecting national interests, China came up with that naval construction was the focus of maritime construction in "the 18th National Congress of CPC". She also proposed in the report of "the 19th National Congress of CPC" to "persist in building a strong army with Chinese characteristics", including a strong navy. The maritime security outlook of Chairman Xi Jinping also embodies the idea of building "a strong arm" and "the Chinese dream" based on the "naval dream", which attaches importance to protection of Chinese maritime interests. As Chinese interest expands to the Indian Ocean, a strong navy is needed to protect safety of China's Indian Ocean channels and maintain its interests.

First, China builds up blue-water navies not for seeking hegemony. In history, the diplomatic activity that the imperialists conducted foreign affairs and popularized their colonial invasion by force was called gunboat policy. Gunboat policy focused on colonialism and aimed to contend for colonies the last century, but now it focuses on hegemonism. To maintain its domination, the USA sets up military bases all around the world. It must be noted that China has no condition, potential and occasion to maintain safety of maritime channels by military means; while military measures are often adopted just in case, since necessary military force is the bottom line of safety. Moreover, both international cooperation and military deterrence cannot be separated from a strong navy. China gets involved in the Indian Ocean with the aim of carrying out economic activities and maintaining regional stability and safeguarding critical interests of all parties with military aid.

Then, it's a practical need for acquiring sea supremacy and maintaining peace of Indian Ocean channels to set up blue-water navy. Threat from other countries, piracy and terrorist attack bring challenges to Indian Ocean channels of China. Additionally, many marine outfalls are narrow and easy to be intercepted and blocked, if without enough maritime military force China will be seriously impacted when conflicts occur. Once an Indian military source said, "If conflicts occur between China and India in the northern land of India, India will take actions against Indian Ocean channels of China so as to make up its onshore weaknesses", which indicates that Indian Ocean channels of China are vulnerable to be controlled. Therefore, China must set up blue-water navy in order to fight against piracies and terrorist attacks, protect safety of Indian Ocean channels and resist invasion of other powers.

Finally, there is a need for maintaining and expanding national interests and acting as a great power to build up blue-water navy. With the enhancement of comprehensive strength, China has changed the role in the international arena and is undertaking more and more responsibilities. Blue-water navy can not only protect safety of Indian Ocean channels of China and other countries through striking piracies and dealing with maritime crises, but also offer humanitarian aid and cope with maritime natural disasters such as tsunami so as to build the image of a responsible great power. For instance, Chinese navy rescued a hijacked foreign cargo ship in Somalia in 2017 and saved a Vietnamese fisherman who was suddenly seriously ill in January, 2018 in Xisha sea area. Obviously, Chinese navy is able to protect safety of maritime channels and take on an internationally responsible role.

4.3.2 Revitalize Three Economic Corridors by Land and Sea Transportation: Open Up Marine Outfalls in Western China

As mentioned above, maritime channel related the Indian Ocean has dominated the cargo freight for China. As the way of maritime transportation is not only high cost and long time, but also high uncertainty risk, more reasonable transportation mode is needed not only for China, but also for the countries along the B&R routes. One effective way to solve this problem is to revitalize three economic corridors, open up marine outfalls in Western China, and combine land and sea transportation. In other word, it is an irresistible trend for China to seek marine outfalls of the Indian Ocean. Three economic corridors including China-Pakistan Economic Corridor (CPEC), Bangladesh-China-India-Myanmar Economic Corridor (BCIM-EC) and Himalaya Rim Economic Corridor are the focus to open up marine outfalls in Western China and a highlight of "the Belt and Road Initiative", among which China-Pakistan Economic

Corridor and Bangladesh-China-India-Myanmar Economic Corridor are top choices among six economic corridors along the B&R routes.

4.3.2.1 China-Pakistan Economic Corridor

The China-Pakistan Economic Corridor was first proposed by Pervez Musharraf, the former President of Pakistan. When Premier Zhu Rongji visited Pakistan in 2001, Pervez Musharraf expressed the wish to help China build Gwadar Port for the purpose of boosting Pakistan's economy and opening up a cargo and energy corridor for China. When Pervez Musharraf visited China in 2005, he came up with the construction for "national trade and energy corridor" in the hope of building Pakistan a trade and transportation corridor between China and the Middle East, Africa, Central Asia and other energy producing countries and transporting petroleum and other energy sources from Gwadar Port to Sinkiang of China by land. However, both plans remained undone for a variety of reasons. The concept of China-Pakistan Economic Corridor was formally put forward until Premier Li Keqiang visited Pakistan in May, 2013. When Chairman Xi Jinping proposed "the Belt and Road Initiative" in the end of 2013, China-Pakistan Economic Corridor became the top choice and was considered as an important supplement to the Belt and Road Initiative and its strategic importance was further elevated. On 20 April, 2015, the construction of CPEC project was officially stared. A network of trade, industry, energy and traffic [50], which starts from Kashi of Xinjiang in the north and reaches Gwadar Port of Pakistan in the south and connects China, Central Asia and South Asia, and whose overall length is 3000 km, will be formed by 2030 when China-Pakistan Economic Corridor is completed. The construction of China-Pakistan Economic Corridor is not only conducive to interests of China and Pakistan but also of great significance for the development of regional and even global economy.

Till now, key projects of China-Pakistan Economic Corridor have made great progress. From the angle of policy, China and Pakistan drew up Long-term Plan for China-Pakistan Economic Corridor (2017–2030), which offers macro guidance to stable development of CPEC. From the view of energy, several collaborative projects are actively carried out (shown in Table 4.5) [51]. For instance, 2×660 Mega-watts (MW) coal-fired power plants at port Qasim and Sahiwal 2×660 MW coal-fired power plant have been put into operation, one of the power generator unit at Hub coal-fired power plant has been successfully connected to the grid, Karot and Sukki Kinari hydropower station are under construction, nearly 1000 MW solar power and 300 MW wind farm are commercially operated. Besides, several energy projects are under construction or in the early stages of preparation.

From the angle of transportation infrastructure, connectivity is in full wing between China and Pakistan and inside Pakistan. Karakoram Highway (KKH) Phase II (Thakot to Havelian Section), the first key highway project of China-Pakistan Economic Corridor, was commenced in September, 2016 and will be completed by March 2020. Karachi-Peshawar motorway (Multan-Sukkur Section), the largest road infrastructure project of China-Pakistan Economic Corridor, was commenced in

Table 4.5 Major energy projects along the China-Pakistan economic corridor

No.	Project name	Install capacity (MW)	Estimated cost (billion US$)	Status (commercially operated date)
CPEC-energy priority projects—Coal-fired power related				
1	Sahiwal coal-fired power plant	2 × 660	1.6	Commercially operated (May, 2017)
2	Qasim coal-fired power plant	2 × 660	1.9123	Commercially operated (June 8, 2017 for phase I; April 25, 2018 for phase II)
3	CPHGC coal-fired power plant at Hub, Balochistan	2 × 660	1.912	Commercially operated (February, 2019 for phase I; August, 2019 for phase II)
4	Engro Thar Block II coal-fired power plant	2 × 330	0.9954	Under construction (June, 2019)
	TEL Thar mine mouth lignite fired power plant at Thar Block II	1 × 330	0.4977	
	ThalNova Thar coal power plant	1 × 330	0.4977	
	Surface mine in block II of Thar Coal field, 3.8 million tons/year	–	1.47	Under construction (December, 2018)
5	Imported coal based power project at Gwadar	300	Yet to be determined	Approved for construction
6	SSRL Thar coal block-I 6.8 mtpa and SEC Mine Mouth power plant	2 × 660	1.912 + 1.3	Under construction (2019 for mine production; 2018/2019 for plant COD)
7	Thar Mine Mouth Oracle Power Plant and surface mine	1320	Yet to be determined	In consideration
CPEC-energy priority projects—Hydropower				

(continued)

Table 4.5 (continued)

No.	Project name	Install capacity (MW)	Estimated cost (billion US$)	Status (commercially operated date)
1	Karot hydropower station	720	1.698	Under construction (December, 2021)
2	Sukki Kinari hydropower station	870	1.707	Under construction (December, 2022)
CPEC-energy priority projects—Solar power				
1	Quaid-e-Azam solar park (Bahawalpur)	300	1.302	Commercially operated (June 16, 2017)
		600		
		100		
CPEC-energy priority projects—Wind farm				
1	Hydro China Dawood wind farm	50	0.11265	Commercially operated (April 5, 2017)
2	UEP wind farm	100	0.25	Commercially operated (June 16, 2017)
3	Sachal wind farm	50	0.134	Commercially operated (April 11, 2017)
4	Three Gorges Second Wind Power Project	50	0.15	Commercially operated (June 30, 2018)
	Three Gorges Third Wind Power Project	50		Commercially operated (July 9, 2018)
CPEC-energy priority projects—Transmission line projects				
1	Matiari to Lahore ± 660 kV HVDC Transmission Line Project	/	1.658	Under construction (March, 2021)
	Matiari (Port Qasim)—Faisalabad Transmission Line Project	/	1.5	Under construction (2018/2019)
CPEC-energy actively promoted projects				
1	Kohala Hydel Project, AJK	1100	2.364	Preliminary preparations (2025)

(continued)

Table 4.5 (continued)

No.	Project name	Install capacity (MW)	Estimated cost (billion US$)	Status (commercially operated date)
2	Rahimyar khan imported fuel Power Plant	1320	1.6	LOI by GoP issued
3	Cacho Wind Power Project	50	–	LOI stage
4	Western Energy (Pvt.) Ltd. Wind Power Project	50	–	LOI stage
CPEC-potential energy projects				
1	Phandar Hydropower Station	80	–	Under review of experts from both sides
2	Gilgit KIU Hydropower	100	–	Under review of experts from both sides

August, 2016 and will be completed in August 2019. Lahore Orange Line project, a rail traffic project of Pakistan, is a demonstration project of China-Pakistan Economic Corridor and the first trains were delivered to Lahore on October 9, 2017. Orange line project is currently in trial operation and will be put into use soon. Both states also signed an agreement in respect of rehabilitation and up-gradation of Karachi-Lahore Peshawar (ML-1) railway track including a newly built Havelian Dry port. At present, the preliminary design of this project was completed in May 2017 and it will be put in to commercial operation in 2022 [52].

Gwader Project is another important and comprehensive project of CPEC. It consists of several projects including construction of Breakwaters, dredging of berthing and channels, Pak China Friendship hospital, Gwadar Smart port city master plan, Gwadar livelihood project, etc. Among them, Gwadar East-Bay expressway is under construction and will be finished by October, 2020. New Gwadar international airport project is at its early stage and will be commenced in 1st quarter of 2019. In addition, China and Pakistan established an expert group in charge of in-depth cooperative research on 9 CPEC Special Economic Zones (SEZs), such as China Special Economic Dhabaji, Rashakai Economic Zone, Bostan Industrial Zone and so on. Moreover, both states enlarged cultural and educational exchanges and obtained popular support. China offered staff training to Pakistan and dispatched Red Cross to Gwadar Port. China-Pakistan Government Primary School Faqeer Colony funded by China Foundation for Peace and Development has been put into operation and the meteorological station contributed by Karamay Municipal Government has been put into use.

China-Pakistan Economic Corridor became a demonstration project of the Belt and Road Initiative in the past four years. Heads of two states have conversations

.frequently about maintaining and strengthening bilateral relations and laying a solid foundation for China-Pakistan Economic Corridor. Since proposed China-Pakistan Economic Corridor has become a flagship project and sample project of BRI and was highly valued by heads of both states. When meeting with President of Pakistan on February 20, 2014, Chairman Xi Jinping put forward the construction of BRI and a Sino-Pakistan community. Premier of the State Council Li Keqiang mentioned when meeting Premier of Pakistan Nawaz Sharif that China-Pakistan Economic Corridor was a flagship project for China to establish and strengthen partnerships with neighboring countries. When Chairman Xi Jinping visited Pakistan in April, 2015, both states formed '1 + 4' cooperation model centered on China-Pakistan Economic Corridor and focused on Gwadar Port, energy and traffic infrastructure and industry cooperation, which brought about a new situation for the construction of China-Pakistan Economic Corridor. Chairman Xi Jinping and President of Pakistan exchanged congratulatory messages on the 65th anniversary of diplomatic relations on 21 May, 2016. Xi Jinping said, "China takes Pakistan as an important BRI partner and the construction of CPEC will lay a solid foundation for Sino-Pakistan community". China hoped to make common efforts with Pakistan for a better bilateral relationship. The accordance between "the Belt and Road Initiative" and "Pakistan 2025 Vision" accelerates the construction of China-Pakistan Economic Corridor.

Despite of remarkable achievements, China-Pakistan Economic Corridor is also faced with risks [53]. First, Pakistan is trapped in political instability and different political parties have different opinions about the construction of CPEC. Next, Pakistan, as an underdeveloped country, focuses on service industry and its weak industrial strength and poor investment environment put off the construction of China-Pakistan Economic Corridor. Third, Pakistan faces many uncertain safety problems, especially Balochistan where Gwadar Port is located. Baluch and other insurgents rise in revolt in Balochistan which comprises various nationalities. Sinkiang also has hidden dangers as "Three Evils" are ready to make trouble. Last, extraterritorial great powers represented by the USA, India and Iran may interfere with the construction of CPEC.

China-Pakistan Economic Corridor cannot be built overnight or by either side but through concerted efforts to cope with the risks. First of all, we should recognize safety problems and domestic situation of Pakistan correctly, rationally and profoundly and based on this conduct systematic field research to obtain accurate and reliable information. Considering various nationalities of Pakistan and its intimacy with China, any adverse events may be maliciously hyped by western media. Second, we should connect with think tank, media and political parties of Pakistan. We need to keep on good terms with them without interference in internal affairs and with their aid build up a positive image. Third, we should help Pakistan with infrastructure construction so as to gain popular support and lay a solid foundation for the construction of China-Pakistan Economic Corridor. Fourth, we should together with Pakistan protect us from being disturbed by voices of extraterritorial great powers. Thermal power project and hydropower project among many energy projects of China-Pakistan Economic Corridor have been often criticized by western media for environmental damage. In this case, China should strengthen environmental cooperation with Pakistan so as to rectify the name of overseas energy projects. Finally, both states should continue enlarging cultural and educational exchanges [54]. Above all, preventing CPEC project from becoming an empty shell is the key for both China and Pakistan.

4.3.2.2 Bangladesh-China-India-Myanmar Economic Corridor (BCIM-EC)

When visiting India in May, 2013, Premier of the State Council Li Keqiang proposed to build Bangladesh-China-India-Myanmar Economic Corridor, India, Bangladesh and Myanmar made an active response. Bangladesh-China-India-Myanmar Economic Corridor was formerly named "China-India-Myanmar-Bangladesh Economic Cooperation Forum" initiated by Chinese and Indian scholars. The first meeting of BCIM-EC work group was held in December, 2013 in Kunming of Yunnan, in which minutes and research program were signed and the cooperation mechanism was formally established. The second meeting of BCIM-EC was held in December, 2014 in Cox's Bazaar of Bangladesh, in which prospect, priority and development direction were discussed. The 12th BCIM Cooperation Forum was held in February, 2015 in Rangoon of Myanmar, in which a joint statement was made on further promoting Bangladesh-China-India-Myanmar cooperation in resource development, trade and transportation facilitation and tourism cooperation. China introduced Vision and Action to Promote the Construction of Silk Road Economic Belt and 21st Century Maritime Silk Road in March, 2015, including BCIM-EC in six economic corridors. The 3rd meeting of BCIM-EC work group was held on 27 April, 2017 in India. The research report which was prepared by four countries and described the construction of BCIM-EC in detail was discussed, four countries agreed to arrange for negotiation after completion of the report and planned to call the 4th meeting in the first half of 2018.

Geographically, BCIM-EC covers Bangladesh, Southwest China, Northeast India and Myanmar and exerts profound effect on connectivity, economic and trade cooperation and regional development of four countries. First, the construction of the BCIM-EC is conducive to improvement of regional development environment and enhancement of economic strength. Then, the economic corridor will elevate the connectivity level of these areas and even wider areas after completion. Third, promoting the construction of the BCIM-EC facilitates joint development of four countries. Fourth, successful implementation of the BCIM-EC can enhance political mutual trust, narrow the wealth gap and help to create a stable and harmonious borderland [55]. Construction basis for BCIM-EC has been constantly deepened and construction conditions became increasingly mature in recent years. For one thing, the cooperative mechanism has been improved and the "Bangladesh-China-India-Myanmar Economic Cooperation Forum" changed from an academic exchange platform into a regional cooperation platform. Besides, large exchange activities such as China-South Asia Expo accelerated the construction of the economic corridor.

For another, the scope of economic and trade cooperation continuously extended, the connectivity level continually improved and exchange visits became intensified, which widened scope and form of multilateral cooperation and fostered mutual trust.

Bangladesh-China-India-Myanmar Economic Corridor has made great progress recently. With regard to connectivity, the economic corridor is aimed at promoting connectivity of highway, railway, waterway, air transport and pipeline transport. But now there is no high-level land channel and four countries mainly conduct bilateral cooperation. With regard to air transport, China has been connected with three other countries, but it's still hard to keep trade contacts among four countries due to high cost of air transport. Highway transport and waterway transport are still interrupted by external factors. Railway transport also has not been placed on the agenda due to dissenting voices of Myanmar and India. With regard to pipeline transport, China-Myanmar oil and gas pipeline has been put into production and it is a pilot project of Bangladesh-China-India-Myanmar Economic Corridor under the Belt and Road Initiative. Four countries also have strengthened cultural, educational and technical exchanges to gain popular support. For instance, an automobile race which had been planned for 6 years was held in 2013. Chinese Foreign Ministry sponsored "Friendly Exchange and Investigation Activity for Bangladesh-China-India-Myanmar Young Diplomatists" in 2014, which boosted a common understanding among them. "Bangladesh-China-India-Myanmar Health and Disease Control Cooperation Forum" was held twice in Yunnan of China during 2015–2016 and a communication platform was built for health and disease control [56]. Besides, many cross-regional forums on agriculture, animal husbandry and economy have been held, which strengthened exchange and interaction and set the stage for the construction of BCIM-EC. With regard to economic and trade cooperation, bilateral trade was driven by BRI to grow steadily, the same was true of energy cooperation. Economic and trade cooperation parks have been initiated one after another, among which Myanmar Kyaukpyu industrial park and deep-water port project were the most representative. What is stated above symbolizes the maturity of the BCIM-EC and the economic corridor is expected to be the second largest demonstration project of the BRI.

Bangladesh-China-India-Myanmar Economic Corridor makes slower progress than China-Pakistan Economic Corridor, since Pakistan is the only partner for the latter; while the former relates to India, Bangladesh and Myanmar. So BCIM-EC faces severer challenges and difficulties in the area of overland and sea-transport connectivity, trade barriers, and security issues [57]. First is a low degree of political mutual trust between four countries, especially China and India. India has been envious of and kept a distance away from the BRI and has regarded China as a major competitor; while China has been open-minded to promote joint development. When meeting with Premier of India Narenda Modi in July, 2014, Chairman Xi Jinping extended an olive branch and put forward "promoting the construction of BCIM-EC and ushering in regional economic integration"; while India made a pessimistic response. Even though India made a response, it was still about the proposal. Second, a low connectivity level among four countries and backward land transport obstruct economic and trade development. Third, an internal impetus is needed for the construction of the BCIM-EC and economic and trade cooperation is confined to trade friction and barrier. Fourth is strategic interference from extraterritorial great powers such as the USA, Japan and Russia [11]. What's more, the BCIM-EC is also disturbed by religion, terrorism and other non-traditional safety factors.

For this purpose, we should develop corresponding policies in order to ensure smooth implementation of the BCIM-EC. First, we should strengthen policy communication and enhance political mutual trust on the basis of common interests. What's most important is to correctly recognize conflicts and contradictions with India, locate common interests, strengthen policy communication and understanding, build a consensus and uniformize strategic objectives. Then, we should facilitate trade and investment of the BCIM-EC, enhance regional cooperation and build a feasible multilateral cooperation mechanism [58]. We can refer to "N-X" mechanism of ASEAN economic cooperation, practice "4-X" mechanism and give play to the leading effect of top-level design. Third, we should establish and strengthen partnerships among four countries, accelerate the construction of the cross-border highways, ports and railways, raise air service ability and create sea-land-air flagship project and demonstration project. Fourth, we should enlarge the cooperation scope and degree of cultural and educational exchanges, build an interactive platform for education, deepen non-governmental exchanges and improve popular feelings through cultural exchange. Fourth, we should continue exploring the cooperative potential of four countries, elevate the level of economic and trade cooperation and maximize mutual benefits and win-win outcomes. Fifth, four countries should cope with threats from extraterritorial great powers and regional threats through establishing and improving security cooperation mechanisms using cooperative organizations and platforms and strengthening information sharing and joint exercise.

4.3.2.3   Himalaya Rim Economic Corridor (HREC)

It is known that China proposed to construct six economic corridors linking China-Mongolia-Russia, China-Central and Western Asia, China-Indo-China Peninsula, China-Pakistan and Bangladesh-China-India-Myanmar as well as the New Eurasian Land Bridge to promote Asia-Europe connectivity. As mentioned above, CPEC and BCIM-EC are the two main corridors for improving the safety of the Indian Ocean for both China and the countries along the routes. To maximize benefits and safety, it is necessary to promote the construction of the third route—Himalaya Rim Economic Corridor—towards the India Ocean in the long run.

Scholars have pointed out that, in a narrow sense, Himalaya the Rim economic cooperation refers to developing frontier trade, international tourism, characteristic agriculture and animal husbandry and cultural industries with Bangladesh, Nepal, India and Bhutan rooted in Zhangmu, Jilong and Pulan in southwest Tibet and centered on Lhasa and Shigatse. In a broad sense, it refers to extending from Himalaya economic area to Bangladesh-China-India-Myanmar-centered South Asia and Southeast Asia. It can be seen that the HREC is a big channel to South Asia and an extension of the BCIM-EC. It can not only promote the development of Tibet and other western areas and pioneer inland opening of the B&R, but also promote the development of the B&R countries such as Bangladesh, Nepal, India, Bhutan and Myanmar and connect South Asia, Southeast Asia and East Asia so as to promote joint development. Thus, with the sluggish recovery of global economy facilitating the development of the Himalaya Rim Economic Corridor is a growing trend of regional integration and complies with people's needs and benefits.

The Himalaya Rim Economic Corridor is not so mature as CPEC and BCIM-EC and a consensus remains to be reached mainly because a wide coverage and underdevelopment of related countries, as well as such fundamental issues as low economic aggregate, poor infrastructure, weak industry basis, policy diversification, irrational tax system and natural environmental factors. Western countries' potential intervention with related countries also competes against the development of China. So we should give consideration to internal and external challenges and adopt corresponding countermeasures after identifying these basic contradictions.

The most important thing to solve this problem is to root out strategic doubts of related countries and relieve or eliminate their doubts about strategic intent for the construction of the HREC. For example, India proposed Monsoon Project, Spice Road and Cotton Coad and was suspicious of "Corridor Construction" and "the Belt and Road Initiative" proposed by China. Indian Express reported on 9 May 2017 that India has difficulty in giving a deep consideration. That is, the BRI will greatly elevate the influence of China on commerce, economy, politics and security of India's neighboring countries and consequently regional advantages of New Delhi will be marginalized. The BRI is more than land "road" and maritime silk "road" which connects Eurasia to the Indian Ocean and the Pacific Ocean, it relates to China's output of capital, labor, technology, industrial standard, business regulation, RMB internationalization, port, industrial park, special economic zone and military installations, which poses a great threat to New Delhi. In fact, India's involvement in Asian Infrastructure Investment Bank (AIIB) signifies its partial involvement in the BRI. Nevertheless, some neighboring countries can't stand the sight of China's involvement in the construction of large channels and suspect that China takes this opportunity to expand its power, intentionally politicize economic issues and even militarize some maritime projects and ports. On this occasion, China should positively publicize the true meaning of BRI and weaken its strategic significance just as what is repeatedly initiated by state leaders. We can also launch a few feasible projects or plans in the HREC according to regional characteristics so as to improve the radiating capacity of the HREC. For example, according to regional advantages and features of neighboring countries and through reference to the development pattern of the BCIM-EC, we can launch China-Nepal-India cooperation corridor first in Tibet, attract domestic and foreign investments and increase openness of neighboring countries so as to vitalize border areas and enrich the people. Once demonstration projects succeed, we can head south and open up the channel to South Asia.

Finally, three economic corridors will combine sea and land transportation, get China out of high dependence on the Indian Ocean and spread the risk of Chinese energy channels.

Note

1. The 4th summit of Conference on Interaction and Confidence-Building Measures in Asia was held on May 21, 2015 in Shanghai. Chairman Xi Jinping took the chair and addressed a keynote titled *Actively Establishing a Security Outlook of Asia and Creating a New Security Cooperation Situation*, which was interpreted by exports as: "According to what CPC described about inheritance and innovation of diplomatic strategy in the 18th National Congress and other heads' foreign activities, the new session CPC heads advocate 'a new security outlook'. That is, respect civilization and systems of various countries, seek mutual development and build a harmonious world and surroundings. From Russia, Africa, ASEAN and Central Asia to Europe and four Latin American countries, foreign activities and simple and unadorned speeches made by Chairman Xi Jinping tried to convey new thought and new pattern of China's diplomatic strategy transformation. New thought means to focus on "win-win cooperation" while dealing with international relations and pursue gambling and cooperative "equal relations" while dealing with the relations with great powers such as America so as to national core benefits and good external relations and build strong safety barriers. New pattern means to chiefly strengthen Sino-Russian strategic cooperative partnership, establish 'a new type of major-power relationship with America without confrontation and conflict and with mutual respect and win-win cooperation', maintain a stable and progressive relationship with EU and build a 'intimate, honest, reciprocal and tolerant community' with other countries and neighboring countries." Reported by foreign media: "New Security Outlook" of Xi Jinping deserved a great power, China Daily, May 30, 2014.

References

1. Dong, Suocheng, Hao Cheng, Peng Guo, Fujia Li, Yu. Li, Zehong Li, and Xiaoxiao Zhang. 2016. Transportation industry patterns and strategy of the Belt and Road. *Bulletin of Chinese Academy of Sciences* 31 (06): 663–670 (in Chinese).
2. Fernández-Armesto, Felipe. 2007. *Pathfinders: A global history of exploration.* New York: W. W. Norton & Company.
3. Kaplan, Robert D. 2013. *Monsoon: The Indian Ocean and the future of American power.* Trans. Zhaoli Wu and Yue Mao. Beijing: Social Sciences Academic Press (China).
4. Yan, Lin, Yunfeng Zhao, Peng Sun, Mingshun Liu, and Qi. Wang. 2017. The distribution status and development trend of global oil & gas pipelines. *Oil & Gas Storage and Transportation* 36 (05): 481–486 (in Chinese).
5. Ma, Gang, and Rui Bai. 2018. Global oil and gas pipeline distribution and development prospect. *Welded Pipe and Tube* 41 (03): 6–11 (in Chinese).
6. Gazprom. Power of Siberia. https://www.gazprom.com/projects/power-of-siberia/. Accessed 04 Jan 2020.

7. CNPC. 2015. China-Russian eastern natural gas pipeline starts in China. https://news.cnpc.com.cn/system/2015/06/30/001548371.shtml. Accessed 30 June 2015 (in Chinese).
8. Gazprom. TurkStream. https://www.gazprom.com/projects/turk-stream/. Accessed 04 Jan 2019.
9. Gazprom. Nord Stream 2. https://www.gazprom.com/projects/nord-stream2/. Accessed 04 Jan 2019.
10. TransCanada. Operations Maps. https://www.transcanada.com/en/operations/maps/. Accessed 08 Jan 2019.
11. Zhu, Quezhi, Chao Wu, Qiuyang Li, Xueqin Zhang, Libo Zeng, and Shanbo Gao. 2017. Current situations and future development of oil and gas pipelines in the world. *Oil & Gas Storage and Transportation* 36 (04): 375–380 (in Chinese).
12. Limited, GAIL (India). 2019. Natural gas. https://gailonline.com/BV-NarutalGas.html. Accessed 08 Jan 2019.
13. Mohammadi, Zarmina. 2018. Thousands of security forces deployed to ensure TAPI safety. https://www.tolonews.com/business/thousands-security-forces-deployed-ensure-tapi-safety. Accessed 14 Mar 2018.
14. DAWN. 2018. Beijing interested in joining Tapi pipeline project. https://www.dawn.com/news/1425900/beijing-interested-in-joining-tapi-pipeline-project. Accessed 09 Aug 2018.
15. TAP-AG. Trans Adriatic Pipeline route. https://www.tap-ag.com/the-pipeline/route-map. Accessed 08 Jan 2019.
16. TAP-AG. Project progress. https://www.tap-ag.com/pipeline-construction/project-progress. Accessed 08 Jan 2019.
17. TransCanada. Keystone XL pipeline. https://www.transcanada.com/en/operations/oil-and-liquids/keystone-xl/#collapse_id_b48416fe-20e2-443d-9c65-5222a872e93e. Accessed 07 Jan 2019.
18. Transneft. Company introduction. https://en.transneft.ru/about/. Accessed 08 Jan 2019.
19. NBSC. 2018. *China statistical yearbook 2018*. Beijing: China Statistics Press.
20. Wang, Hongju, Quezhi Zhu, and Yanping Zhang. 2015. Overview of oil and gas pipelines in the world. *Oil & Gas Storage and Transportation* 34 (01): 15–18 (in Chinese).
21. Gao, Shixian, Yuezhong Zhu, et al. 2016. *To deepen international energy cooperation via the Belt and Road Initiative*. Beijing: China Economic Publishing House.
22. Kazakhstan-China crude oil pipeline. https://www.hydrocarbons-technology.com/projects/kazakhstan-china-crude-oil-pipeline/. Accessed 09 Jan 2019.
23. CNR. 2017. The Kazakhstan-China crude oil pipeline has accumulated 100 million tons of oil and officially entered the "100 million tons era". https://china.cnr.cn/gdgg/20170329/t20170329_523682920.shtml. Accessed 29 Mar 2017 (in Chinese).
24. CNPC. The cumulative gas transport amount of Central Asia-China natural gas pipeline has exceeded 100 billion cubic meters. https://news.cnpc.com.cn/system/2014/11/18/001516264.shtml. Accessed 09 Jan 2019 (in Chinese).
25. Chinanews. 2016. The second line of China-Russia crude oil pipeline was put into operation at the end of 2017, with an annual output of 15 million tons. https://www.chinanews.com/cj/2016/12-20/8099398.shtml. Accessed 20 Dec 2016 (in Chinese).
26. The northern section of the Sino-Russian East natural gas pipeline will be put into use on December 1, 2019. 2019. https://www.yidaiyilu.gov.cn/xwzx/gnxw/106425.htm. Accessed 16 Oct 2019.
27. Xinhuanet. 2017. China-Myanmar crude oil pipeline put into operation. https://www.xinhuanet.com//english/2017-04/11/c_136199129.htm. Accessed 11 Apr 2017.
28. BP. 2018. *BP statistical review of world energy 2018*. London: BP.
29. Liang, Dongxing, and Shiping Chen. 2017. The impact of US Asia-Pacific strategy on the competitive situation of the Indian Ocean. *Theory Monthly* 12: 177–183 (in Chinese).
30. Cottrell, Alvin J., and R.M. Burrel. 1972. *The Indian Ocean: Its political, economic, and military importance*. Shanghai: Shanghai People's Publishing House.
31. Wang, Lirong. 2009. The Indian Ocean and the Chinese strategy for maritime security. *South Asian Studies* 03: 46–54 (in Chinese).

32. Wang, Dehua. 2015. Analysis on "One Belt and One Road" and the IOR community building—Study on construction of the China—IOR energy supply chain. *Indian Ocean Economic and Political Review* 04: 74–91 (in Chinese).
33. Zhu, Cuiping. 2012. China's India Ocean strategy: Motivation, strategy, and response. *South Asian Studies* 03: 1–14 (in Chinese).
34. Zhao, Xiyuan. 2014. *The research of China's Indian Ocean maritime security strategy.* Qingdao: Ocean University of China (in Chinese).
35. Xu, Ke. 2011. The threat of maritime piracy in the Indian Ocean and China's Indian Ocean strategy. *South Asian Studies* 01: 2–14 (in Chinese).
36. Sun, Xianpu. 2013. U.S. Indian Ocean strategy. *Pacific Journal*, no. 06: 28–38 (in Chinese).
37. Wang, Xiaowen. 2014. American Indian Ocean strategy and American hegemony in the 21st Century. *Forum of World Economics & Politics*, no. 04: 20–32 (in Chinese).
38. Zhu, Xiaoqi. 2015. Maritime strategy studies in Japan: Core issues and research trends. *Journal of International Studies*, no. 06: 85–98+156 (in Chinese).
39. Jiang, Xudong. 2017. On Japan's participation in anti-piracy action off the coast of Somalia—Motivation, path and Impact. *Journal of International Relations*, no. 02: 85–98+156 (in Chinese).
40. Li, Xiushi. 2014. An analysis of Japan's strategic expansion in the Pacific and Indian Oceans: From "anti-piracy" to "defending" the maritime channels about the two oceans. *International Review*, no. 02: 121–134 (in Chinese).
41. Shi, Hongyuan. 2013. India's dream of marine power. *International Studies* 03: 104–119 (in Chinese).
42. Tao, Liang. 2015. "Project Mausam", India's Maritime strategy and the "21st Century Maritime Silk Road". *South Asian Studies*, no. 03: 95–110+157–158 (in Chinese).
43. Yang, Siling. 2015. On how India views Sino-Indian relations under the "One Belt One Road" Initiative. *Frontiers* 09: 37–50 (in Chinese).
44. Zhu, Yue. 2018. 2017: Another year of Middle East turmoil. *Contemporary World* 01: 62–64 (in Chinese).
45. China Ocean News. 2017. Global report on piracy in 2016: The kidnapping of seafarers is the highest in a decade. 17 Jan 2017 (in Chinese).
46. Liu, Yonglu, and Lvshan Xu. 2011. From "zero-sum confrontation" to "win-win cooperation": Historical evolution of marine safety concept with Chinese characteristics. *Military Historical Research* 04: 125–132 (in Chinese).
47. Xi, Jinping. 2012. China never strive for and seek hegemony but safeguards peaceful development. https://www.china.com.cn/international/txt/2012-09/21/content_26591813.htm. Accessed 21 Sept 2012.
48. Zhu, Cuiping. 2014. China-India engagement in the Indian Ocean: Mutual needs and potential conflict. *South Asian Studies Quarterly*, no. 04: 8–15+14 (in Chinese).
49. Du, Youkang. 2017. International cooperation: The "Belt and Road" Initiative and South Asia. *Frontiers* 08: 59–69 (in Chinese).
50. Liu, Zongyi. 2016. Construction of the China-Pakistan Economic Corridor: Progress and challenges. *International Studies*, no. 03: 122–136+138 (in Chinese).
51. CPEC-Energy Priority Projects. https://cpec.gov.pk/energy. Accessed 23 Jan 2019.
52. CPEC Infrastructure Projects. https://www.cpec.gov.pk/infrastructure. Accessed 25 Jan 2019.
53. Yao, Yun. 2015. China-Pakistan Economic Corridor: A risk analysis. *South Asian Studies*, no. 02: 35–45+155 (in Chinese).
54. Li, Xiguang, and Lizhou Sun. 2015. The strategic value and security situation of the China-Pakistan Economic Corridor. *Frontiers* 12: 32–50 (in Chinese).
55. Chen, Lijun. 2015. BCIM economic corridor and the construction of "One Belt, One Road". *Southeast Asia & South Asian Studies*, no. 04: 54–62+109 (in Chinese).
56. Liu, Zhen, Yingtian Liu, Binxiu Cheng, and Fengwei Zeng. 2017. The Belt and Road Initiative and the construction of Bangladesh-China-India-Myanmar Economic Corridor. *Journal of Boundary and Ocean Studies* 2 (06): 49–61 (in Chinese).

57. Deepak, B.R. 2018. Bangladesh, China, India, Myanmar Economic Corridor (BCIM-EC): Security dilemma rider to regional economic integration. In *China's global rebalancing and the New Silk Road*, ed. B.R. Deepak, 51–68. Singapore: Springer.
58. Li, Yanfang. 2016. An analysis of the strategic significance and feasibility of promoting trade and investment in BCIM Economic Corridor. *Pacific Journal* 24 (05): 61–70 (in Chinese).

Chapter 5
Development Status of Oil Stockpiling of Major Developed Countries and China

Tingting Zhang

Since ancient times, energy has been essential for production and life of human and played a critical role in the development of national economy. Accounting for 1/3 of energy sources, petroleum will be a major energy source in the foreseeable future. The energy safety of China is challenged by energy supply, energy transportation, energy distribution and use and environmental protection. Domestically, main challenges are as follows: First, energy sources such as petroleum and natural gas highly depend on foreign trade. Then, energy production and consumption are imbalanced. Third, extensive energy utilization pattern exerts pressure on the ecological environment. Internationally, our energy safety is challenged by externalities. On one side, China imports petroleum mainly from turbulent areas such as the Middle East and North Africa, where different political forces engage in an intense game. On the other side, China transports petroleum mainly through Indian Ocean channels, which increases the risk for energy transportation. To protect energy safety, we should take precautions while keeping good partnership with oil producing countries and ensuring safety of energy channels. Thus, having a certain amount of oil reserves is an important way to protect energy safety and economic development. Presently, China has built and had a certain amount of oil reserves and is able to cope with the risk of oil supply failure to some extent; while the oil reserve system remains to be improved compared with developed countries. In view of this, this Chapter emphatically introduces developed countries' experience in oil reserve and summarizes the development history and main problems of Chinese oil reserve.

T. Zhang (✉)
International Energy Research Center, Shanghai Jiao Tong University, Shanghai, China
e-mail: zhangtingting@sjtu.edu.cn

© Shanghai Jiao Tong University Press 2021
T. Zhang and D. Wang (eds.), *China-Gulf Oil Cooperation Under the Belt and Road Initiative*, https://doi.org/10.1007/978-981-15-9283-6_5

5.1 Overview of Oil Reserve

Oil reserve means that countries, the society and enterprises reserve a certain amount of oil as planned so as to ensure sustainability and safety of oil supply, maintain normal operation of national economy and satisfy the need for national defense.

5.1.1 Traceability of Oil Reserve

The Oil reserve was originated from before World War II (WWII) and France came with up oil reserve first. To satisfy the need for fuels for military use, the French Government requested domestic the oil operators to reserve a certain amount of oil. On 10 January 1925, France passed a law of "National Liquid Fuel Agency" on control of oil reserve. As the situation changes, French oil reserve was aimed at no longer meeting military need but avoiding the impact of energy shortage on domestic economy. UK also reserved oil during WWII with the aim of satisfying the need for war. Egypt resumed the jurisdiction over the Suez Canal on 19 September 1956. In the meantime, an oil pipeline was ruined by Syria and consequently oil price soared, which was a heavy blow to UK, France and other European countries. After that, oil companies in some European countries attached importance to oil reserve so as to avoid the impact of oil supply failure on national economy.

The Fourth Middle East War broke out in October 1973, during which the USA support for Israel infuriated Arab countries. Oil exporting countries stroke Israel and countries in support of Israel with an oil embargo and raised the oil price substantially. The oil crisis caused an economic recession to western countries. According to statistics, economic growth rate of the USA decreased by 4.7% and GDP of Europe declined by 2.5%. As a result, the international oil market was out of order and oil consuming countries realized their weakness in oil supply. Specific to the oil embargo, the OECD established the IEA in 1974 against oil crisis. As stipulated by the IEA, member countries must have an emergency capacity of oil reserve equal to an import volume of 60 days.

The Iranian Revolution took place in the 1980s. From the end of 1978 to the beginning of March, 1979, the Pahlavi Dynasty was overturned. As a result, Iranian oil export paused for 60 days and the international oil market suffered a panic purchase for oil shortage. Iraqi air force bombed Iran and the Iran-Iraq War on 20 September 1980, and consequently oil supply fell short of demand in the international oil market due to oil supply failure. Meanwhile, the OPEC was broken and most member countries raised oil price in line with market conditions; while Saudi Arabia stood for increasing production and forcing prices down. However, the OPEC failed to turn the scale and the supply-demand balance of the international crude oil market was broken again. The second oil crisis triggered and aggravated the work economic crisis and further highlighted the weakness of western oil-oriented economies. Hence, the

IEA requested member countries to raise the emergency capacity of oil reserve equal to an import volume of 90 days.

IEA's oil reserve system gradually improved and the reserve scale of member countries further enlarged hereafter. As stipulated by the IEA, the member countries should reserve a certain amount of oil from the angle of national defense and economic security, according to national conditions, systems and financial conditions and through combining government leadership with private participation, and they should offer mutual support when necessary. Since the IEA established oil reserve system, member countries have employed their oil reserves in different ways in face of oil supply risk. For example, the U.S. Government sold 33 million barrels of crude oil during the Gulf War in 1991. The emergency oil reserve enables member countries to effectively weaken the deterrent force of oil producing countries, reduce or inhibit human factors of oil shortage. Facing an oil crisis, they can drawndown oil reserve to the market to stabilize oil price, maximize the impact of oil supply, relieve the market pressure and ensure economic and political stability. We can see that the IEA's emergency oil reserve system has become the most important and the most effective weapon for energy conservation, economic development and social stability of western countries.

5.1.2 Classification of Oil Reserve

The oil reserve can be classified according to different standards. According to ownership, the oil reserve can be classified into the Strategic Petroleum Reserve (SPR) and the Commercial Oil Reserve (COR) (as shown in Table 5.1).

The SPR refers to petroleum reserved by a country to cope with emergencies such as oil supply disruption. Owned by government, it is also called governmental reserve or national petroleum reserve. As defined by IEA, the SPR refers to "the total inventory of crude oil and main oil products owned by governments, non-government institutions and petroleum enterprises of member countries, including the stocks in pipelines and transfer stations (excluding 10% of unusable oil)" [1]. Obviously, the SPR includes governmental reserve and enterprise reserve and it is essentially a resource which is controlled by the government and embodies the will of a state. Therefore, the SPR can be neither abused nor used for commercial purposes, it must be used under emergencies such as oil shortage, deadly natural disasters or war. As

Table 5.1 Comparison between SPR and COR

Item	SPR	COR
Subject	Government	Enterprise
Financing	Government-dominated	Enterprise+ government
Management method	Government-regulated	Enterprise-dominated
Category	Crude oil and main varieties	Crude oil and main varieties

to management, the SPR undergoes government-oriented centralized management and overall arrangement and only government is entitled to determine scale, layout, structure, transaction time, quantity and capital of the SPR. As to capital, the SPR is often subsidized by government. As to function, the SPR can resist risk, protect safety, balance supply with demand and retrain oil price in case of oil shortage and other emergencies. It is also a strong deterrent to stability of international oil price and policy regulation of petroleum exporting countries.

The COR, also called non-governmental oil reserve or enterprise oil reserve, refers to the minimum inventory of oil retained by petroleum production and circulation enterprises according to legal provisions so as to undertake social responsibilities. The COR is aimed at stabilizing oil price fluctuation and protecting national energy security. As to composition, COR mainly includes unusable oil reserve and usable oil reserve. The former refers to crude oil and product oil necessary for normal operation of petroleum production and circulation enterprises and the latter refers to the COR subtracting by unusable oil reserve. Confined to cost and income, usable oil reserve has a smaller size than unusable oil reserve. As to function, unusable oil reserve is an important guarantee for normal social and economic order and usable oil reserve is essential for enterprises to enhance operation safety and economic effectiveness. Usable oil reserve can partly resist oil shortage or oil prices surge; while usable oil reserve has absorptive capability in case of oil surplus or oil prices drop and can ensure operation safety of enterprises. As to management, the COR is usually free from government interference and its quantity, scale, operation, warehouse equipment and routine management are determined by production and operation activities. As to fund raising, cost of the COR is mostly borne by enterprises with the compulsory obligation to reserve a certain amount of oil. Generally, governmental subsidies will be offered to enterprises to cover the cost of the COR [2].

5.2 Oil Stockpiling System of Major Countries

Considering the contributions of oil stockpiling to national energy security, economic development and social stability, governments represented by western developed countries make much account of oil reserve and have their own oil stockpiling systems. There are three typical oil stockpiling systems at present: national stockpiling, agency stockpiling, and private sector stockpiling (as shown in Fig. 5.1). National stockpiling system is a system whereby government taxes are used, directly by government or through stockpiling organizations, to operate and maintain stockpiling bases and stockpiled oil,such as U.S. oil stockpiling system, New Zealand oil stockpiling system and Czech oil stockpiling system. Agency stockpiling system is a system in which a public stockpiling agency established by law implements stockpiling, such as oil stockpiling system in Germany, Hungary, Belgium, Estonia, Ireland, and Slovak Republic. Agencies' roles and legal positions differ from country to country depending on the market structure and government. Private sector stockpiling system is a system applying to private companies which are required by law

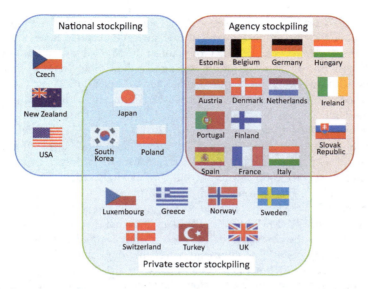

Fig. 5.1 Current stockholding systems of IEA member countries [3]. *Data source* IEA. 2014. Energy Supply Security: Emergency Response of IEA Countries 2014. Paris, France: International Energy Agency

to stockpile a specified amount of oil using their own facilities and at their expense. Stockpiling systems in UK, Sweden, Switzerland, Greece, Luxembourg, Norway and Turkey are typical private sector stockpiling system. The oil stockpiling systems in some countries are usually a combination of different stockpiling systems. For example, the oil stockpiling systems in Japan, South Korea, and Poland are a combination of national stockpiling and private sector stockpiling, while the oil stockpiling systems in Austria, Denmark, Netherlands, Portugal, Finland, Spain, France, and Italy are a combination of Agency stockpiling and private sector stockpiling. The pattern and scale of the oil stockpiling in different countries are mainly related to government system, oil dependence and marketization degree of energy in each country.

5.2.1 U.S. Petroleum Stockpiling System

As the world's largest petroleum consuming country and the world's largest petroleum importing country, the U.S. Government has regarded the establishment of emergency stockpiles of crude oil and petroleum products as an important measure to protect energy safety in the event of a commercial supply disruption. The emergency stockpiles of the United States are managed by the Department of Energy (DOE)'s Office of Petroleum Reserves (OPR). The OPR manages four kinds of stockpiles: the Strategic Petroleum Reserve, the Northeast Home Heating Oil Reserve (NEHHOR), the Northeast Gasoline Supply Reserve, and the Naval Petroleum and oil Shale Reserves. The SPR is the most important stockpile in the United States.

Early in WWII, the U.S. intended to establish the SPR and it put it into practice till the first oil crisis. The cutoff of oil flowing into the United States from the Arab members of OPEC, in response to the U.S.'s aid to Israel during the Yom Kippur War, sent economic shockwaves throughout the Nation. In the aftermath of the oil crises, the United States established the SPR. In 1975, the United States Congress passed *Energy Policy and Conservation Act (EPCA)*. The legislation declared it to be the U.S. policy to establish a reserve of up to one billion barrels of petroleum with an initial size target of 500 million barrels (MMbbl). On July 21, 1997, the first oil—approximately 412,000 barrels of Saudi Arabian light crude—was delivered to the SPR [4]. Fill of the Nation's emergency oil reserve had begun. Presently, the U.S. has about 713.5 MMbbl of crude oil design storage capacity with a crude oil inventory level of 635 MMbbl as of February 28, 2020 [5]. At the current level, U.S. SPR, holding the equivalent of 168 days of import protection (based on 2017 net petroleum imports of 3768 thousand barrels per day) and 1195 days of import protection (based on 2019 net petroleum imports of 531 thousand barrels per day) [5], is the largest government-owned stockpile of emergency crude oil in the world.

According to pattern and composition, the U.S. petroleum stockpiling is government-bearing type and includes governmental SPR and COR. According to category, it includes crude oil, petroleum products such as diesel and gasoline, and heavy oil, among which crude oil accounts for the largest proportion. According to form, the federally-owned SPR are stored mainly in huge underground salt caverns along the coastline of the Gulf of Mexico, while the petroleum products stocks are mainly stored in aboveground oil tanks in the Northeast region of the country. The asset of U.S SPR comprise four underground storage sites located along the Gulf Coast in Texas and Louisiana including the Bryan Mound and Big Hill sites in Texas and the West Hackberry and Bayou Choctaw sites in Louisiana [6]. The SPR's crude oil inventory is stored in 62 underground caverns spread across these sites. The sites vary in size and design drawdown rate, as illustrated in Fig. 5.2.

5.2.1.1   Operation and Management of U.S. Oil Reserve

After many years of development, the United States has established a management system for energy crisis coping mechanism which is dominated by the Federal Government and with which state governments act in close cooperation, of which energy crisis emergency mechanism is the main part and the SPR is the core. The organization of the U.S. SPR is illustrated in Fig. 5.2. As a part of DOE's Office of Fossil Energy, the organization of OPR includes a Program Office located at DOE headquarters in Washington, D.C., a Project Management Office (PMO) located in New Orleans, and four field storage sites. The OPR operates under the direction and leadership of the Deputy Assistant Secretary for Petroleum Reserves. As for management, the Program Office has responsibility for program management of the SPR and NEHHOR. In this capacity, the office has executive oversight of all aspects

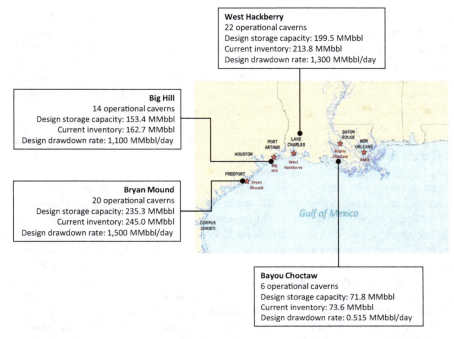

West Hackberry
22 operational caverns
Design storage capacity: 199.5 MMbbl
Current inventory: 213.8 MMbbl
Design drawdown rate: 1,300 MMbbl/day

Big Hill
14 operational caverns
Design storage capacity: 153.4 MMbbl
Current inventory: 162.7 MMbbl
Design drawdown rate: 1,100 MMbbl/day

Bryan Mound
20 operational caverns
Design storage capacity: 235.3 MMbbl
Current inventory: 245.0 MMbbl
Design drawdown rate: 1,500 MMbbl/day

Bayou Choctaw
6 operational caverns
Design storage capacity: 71.8 MMbbl
Current inventory: 73.6 MMbbl
Design drawdown rate: 0.515 MMbbl/day

Fig. 5.2 Locations of SPR storage sites in the United States [4, 6]. *Data source* DOE, Long-term Strategic Review of the U.S. Strategic Petroleum Reserve (Report of Congress). Washington, D.C.: United States Department of Energy; Strategic Petroleum Reserve, https://www.energy.gov/fe/ser vices/petroleum-reserves/strategic-petroleum-reserve

of the program, including major engineering projects; oil distribution planning and analysis; environmental, safety, security, and occupational health issues; the drawdown and operations of the SPR and NEHHOR; strategic planning, policy analysis and engages with domestic and international stakeholders, etc. The PMO is mainly responsible for operating and managing the SPR's filed activities. As for operation, marketization mechanism is established and oil company and base management company are selected by public bidding. Oil company is responsible for procurement and launch and base management company is responsible for daily operation, management and safety protection of the base.

In the aspect of legislation, the U.S. has established a comprehensive legal energy emergency system. As stipulated by *Energy Policy and Conservation Act* enacted in 1975, Federal Energy Administration was equipped with Petroleum Reserve Office which took charge of SPR base construction, procurement, drawdown and equipment maintenance and enabled launch of petroleum reserves under emergencies as directed by the President. The Department of Energy Organization Act enacted in 1977 assembled several energy agencies including Federal Energy Administration into Department of Energy and put Petroleum Reserve Office under centralized management of DOE [7]. The EPCA specified the SPR-related authorities of the Secretary of Energy (as originally enacted, the Administrator of the Federal Energy Administration), including the details of initial oil acquisition and storage, and certain characteristics and requirements of the SPR. Subsequent to the enactment of the EPCA in 1975, the law has been amended several times to address SPR-related issues. For example, the United States Congress amended EPCA in 1990, relaxing the requirements on the SPR by the excuse that "the strategic importance of SPR for national economy security declines" [6]. Except for EPCA, other laws and regulations, such as *Energy Policy Act (2005), Bipartisan Budget Act (2015), Fixing the U.S.'s Surface Transportation Act (2015)* have been issued to assist the development of the U.S.'s SPR. So far the U.S. has formed an energy emergency legal system centered on EPCA and assisted by other laws and regulations.

In the aspect of operation, the U.S. petroleum reserve system undergoes strict planning and management and its operation mechanism can be generalized as government-owned, government-dominated and marketized. Section 165 of the EPCA requires the Secretary of Federal Energy Administration (renamed Department of Energy) to report annually to the President and the Congress on the activities of SPR utilization, including budget enforcement, construction and maintenance of facilities, management of reserve inventory, legislation and policy adjustment. In case of petroleum supply interruptions and other emergencies, the President is entitled by the EPCA to carry out the plan for SPR drawdown. A full or limited drawdown must be authorized by the President through a Presidential Finding. The Secretary also has the authority to release the SPR petroleum products for the purpose of conducting test sales and exchanges. Should the President order an emergency sale of SPR oil, the DOE can conduct a competitive sale, select offers, award contracts, and be prepared to begin deliveries of oil into the marketplace within 13 days. Therefore, aside from coping with domestic petroleum supply disruptions, the other core mission of the U.S. SPR is to carry out the U.S. obligations under the International Energy Program, the 1974 treaty that established the IEA [6].

In the aspect of constitution system, the U.S. petroleum Reserve system can be divided into governmental SPR and COR. The U.S. Government offers financial support to SPR and saddles with heavy financial burden due to huge investment and high operating cost of SPR. To ease the burden, the United States began to commercialize oil reserve in 1995 through renting reserve facilities from enterprises for cost reduction and offering storage services to foreign users for income increase. Governmental SPR is independent from enterprise oil reserve in operation. The COR is free from government interference and is commercialized according to operational characteristics. Presently, the governmental SPR accounts for 1/3 of total reserve and the COR accounts for 2/3 in the U.S. petroleum reserve system.

5.2.1.2   Procurement and Release of SPR

The EPCA directs the Secretary of Energy to develop procedures to acquire petroleum to fill the authorized petroleum reserve capacity. The SPR and the COR are purchased in different ways. To lower the purchase cost, The SPR is purchased by public bidding.

The OPR discloses purchase plan and tender time to the public and qualified oil companies participate in the bidding. The bid winner will sell oil at market price, the Ministry of Finance will charge the purchase cost to the account of oil reserve funds and oil will be used to replenish oil reserve. 40% of oil is purchased from oil companies with long-term contractual relationship and other is purchased by invitation to bid in the market. Enterprise oil reserve is nothing more than a market behavior and its quantity and the time to market are determined by market supply and demand and strength of enterprise.

According to the EPCA, the President of the United States has the right to order a full or limited drawdown from the SPR, while the Secretary has the authority to release the SPR petroleum products for the purpose of conducting test sales and exchanges. Release of the U.S. SPR mainly includes full drawdown, limited drawdown, test drawdown and sale or exchange, and exchange [6]. Full drawdown—Only the President can make the decision on full drawdown of the SPR. According to amendment of the EPCA, an authority of full drawdown can be issued only in the case of "severe energy supply interruption". So-called "severe energy supply interruption" refers to a national energy supply shortage which the President determines (a) is, or is likely to be, of significant scope and duration, and of an emergency nature; (b) may cause major adverse impact on national safety or the national economy; (c) results, is likely to result, from (i) an interruption in the supply of imported petroleum products, (ii) an interruption in the supply of domestic petroleum products, or (iii) sabotage or an act of God [6]. ② Limited drawdown—Only the President can make the decision on limited drawdown of SPR. The President can make a decision on limited drawdown of the SPR, if the President finds that (i) A circumstance, other than those described for a full drawdown exists that constitutes, or is likely to become, a domestic or international energy supply shortage of significant scope or duration, (ii) Action taken would assist directly and significantly in preventing or reducing the adverse impact of such a shortage; and (iii) The Secretary of Defense has found that action taken will not impair national security. ③ Test drawdown and sale or exchange—The Secretary of DOE has the right to conduct a test drawdown and sale or exchange of SPR. Test drawdown and sale is aimed at preventing failure arising from emergency release and checking whether storage facilities and systems and selling processes run normally. Such a test drawdown and sale may not exceed 5 million barrels of petroleum products and the petroleum products can be sold to the market or enterprises as a loan or swap. ④ Exchange—As another form of the U.S. SPR, temporary exchange happens between COR and SPR and it is aimed at solving quality issues of oil or the delivery problem of oil supply enterprises in the short run.

Since the establishment of the SPR, the U.S. has released crude oil from the SPR repeatedly at different levels (as shown in Table 5.2) [8]. The release activity is grouped into four category types: emergency drawdowns, test sales, exchange agreements, and non-emergency sales. The United States has participated with other IEA members to release strategic petroleum stocks as part of an IEA collective action under the IEP on three occasions. The first, in 1991, with the commencement of Operation Desert Storm, resulted in a release of 17.3 MMbbl of oil from the SPR. The second release came after Hurricane Katrina, in 2005, and resulted in a release

Table 5.2 The historical release activity of crude oil from the SPR in the United States

Date	Release volume/MMbbl	Purpose
Emergency drawdowns		
January, 1991	17.300	Desert Storm: supply oil for U.S. army during Persian Gulf War
September, 2005	11.000	Hurricane Katrina: President George W. Bush issued a Finding and authorized the sale of 30 MMbbl as part of an IEA collective action
June, 2011	30.640	IEA coordinated release: President Barack Obama issued a Finding and directed DOE to offer crude oil to offset Libya's production curtailment as part of an IEA collective action
Test sales		
November, 1985	0.967	After extending the EPCA in June 1985, Congress authorized DOE to conduct test sales for up to 5 MMbbl to involve the private sector in the competitive sales process for the first time
September, 1990	3.900	Desert Shield: President George H. W. Bush ordered a 5 MMbbl test sale to "demonstrate the readiness of the [Reserve] system under real life conditions." Only 3.9 MMbbl were sold
March, 2014	5.000	The secretary authorized a test sale to evaluate the ability of SPR drawdown and distribution mechanisms
Exchanges agreements		
May, 1996	12.800	ARCO Pipe Line company singed an emergency crude oil lease exchange agreement with DOE due to the pipeline blockage and returned the oil with an equivalent grade within six mounts
September, 1999	11.000	DOE exchanged 11 MMbbl of Maya crude for 8.5 MMbbl of other higher value of crude oil to improve the SPR's oil quality and operational efficiency
June, 2000	1.000	DOE exchanged 0.5 MMbbl each with CITGO and Conoco refiners in the event of Calcasieu ship channel closure

(continued)

Table 5.2 (continued)

Date	Release volume/MMbbl	Purpose
September, 2000	2.840	DOE exchanged crude oil to pay for the first year of tank-storage and stocks for establishing NEHHOR
October, 2000	30.000	DOE exchanged with oil companies to concern over low distillate levels in the Northeast
October, 2002	0.980	DOE exchanged with Shell Pipeline Company to secure Capline storage tanks in advance of Hurricane Lili
September, 2004	5.400	DOE exchanged sweet crude with 5 companies due to disruptions in the Gulf of Mexico caused by Hurricane Ivan
September, 2005	9.800	DOE approved 6 requests for emergency loans of crude oil to address oil supply shortages caused by oil production and distribution facilities being shut ahead of Hurricane Katrina's landfall
January, 2006	0.767	DOE exchanged sour crude with Total Petrochemicals USA due to closure of the Sabine Neches ship channel to deep-draft vessels after a barge accident in the channel
June, 2006	0.750	DOE exchanged sour crude with ConocoPhillips and Citgo due to Calcasieu ship channel closure
September, 2008	5.389	Following Hurricanes Gustav and Ike, DOE loaned nearly 5.4 MMbbl to Marathon, Placid, ConocoPhillips, Citgo, and Alon USA after their supplies had been cut off due to shutdown of the petroleum industry in the Gulf region. The companies repaid the loans with a premium of 93.35 Mbbl
September, 2012	1.000	Marathon Petroleum Company had an exchange contract to request an emergency loan due to the Hurricane Isaac
September, 2017	5.200	DOE conducted crude exchange with Gulf Coast refineries due to Hurricane Harvey.

(continued)

Table 5.2 (continued)

Date	Release volume/MMbbl	Purpose
Non-emergency sales		
January, 1996	5.100	After becoming geologically unstable, DOE decided to decommission the Weeks Island SPR site and offset the decommissioning costs by selling oil
April, 1996	12.800	Reducing the federal budget deficit
October, 1996	10.200	Reducing the federal budget deficit
January, 2017–April, 2017	6.280	Raise funds for SPR modernization program
May and June, 2017	9.890	Mandated sale under section 5010 of the twenty-first Century Cures Act
May, 2018	5.000	Mandated sale under section 5010 of the twenty-first Century Cures Act
April and May, 2018	4.740	Raise funds for SPR modernization

of 11 MMbbl of SPR oil. The third, a release of 30.6 MMbbl, occurred in June 2011, in response to oil supply disruptions driven by hostilities in Libya [6]. The SPR has also conducted Test Sales to ensure the readiness of the Reserve and its personnel to carry out a Presidentially-ordered drawdown [8]. This has occurred three times since the establishment of the SPR. The first test sale of approximately 1 MMbbl of oil occurred in 1985. The second sale of 3.9 MMbbl of oil occurred between Iraq's invasion of Kuwait in August 1990 and the beginning of Operation Desert Storm in January 1991. The third test sale of 5 MMbbl of oil, the statutory maximum under the EPCA, took place in May 2014 [6]. U.S. crude oil from the SPR can also be released under exchange arrangements with private companies. In an exchange, an entity borrows SPR crude oil for a short time period due to exigent circumstances and later replaces it in full along with a premium of an additional quantity of oil. About 13 times of the SPR drawdown have been made through exchange agreements [8] (see Table 5.2). The purpose of most exchange agreements between the DOE and the companies are averting a temporary shutdown of the refineries due to occasional accidents, such as severe weather events, pipeline blockages, ship channel closures, during the creation of the NEHHOR, and so on. Besides, the SPR oil has also been sold to meet the SPR-specific and general government fiscal purposes.

5.2.2 Japanese Petroleum Stockpiling System

Japan was the world's second largest oil consuming country and oil importing country in earlier times. Due to adjustment to Japanese energy structure in recent years, Japan became the world's fourth largest oil consuming country and oil importing country following the USA, China and India in 2017 [9]. It is reported that 99.68% of crude oil, 97.56% of natural gas, 99.35% of coal, 100% of Copper and 100% of Zinc are imported for Japan in 2018 [10]. Specific to poor oil resource endowment and extremely high foreign-trade dependence, Japan established huge oil reserves after two energy crises so as to ensure oil supply safety. According to statistical data of international petroleum institutions, Japan is able to survive by existing oil reserves if oil import channels were blocked.

5.2.2.1   History of Japanese Petroleum Stockpiling

Japanese petroleum stockpiling has gone through five stages: the preparatory phase (from the 1950s to the beginning of the 1970s), the initial stage (from the beginning of the 1970s to the end of the 1970s), the expansion stage (from the end of the 1970s to the end of the 1980s), the consolidation stage (from the beginning of the 1990s to the end of the 1990s) and the improvement stage (since the end of the twentieth century).

Japanese energy supply structure was dominated by coal in the 1950s and oil imported was restricted by using exchange quota system. With the involvement in the General Agreement on Tariffs and Trade (GATT) in 1955, Japan opened the energy market under the pressure from public opinion and the oil import volume began to increase. Oil has become the main force of Japanese energy supply structure since the 1960s and up to the first oil crisis Japan has formed oil-oriented energy supply system, among which oil took up above 75%.

As international oil prices soared and the oil crisis broke out in the beginning of the 1970s, Japan deeply realized the importance of enhancing oil reserve. The Ministry of International Trade and Industry (MITI) requested private enterprises to reserve oil equal to an import volume of 60 days prior to 1974 in 1971 and raised it to IEA's standard equal to an import volume of 90 days in 1974. The *Oil Stockpiling Act* enacted in December, 1975 symbolized the legalization of Japanese petroleum reserve.

As the second oil crisis broke out in the end of 1978, Japanese oil reserve entered the expansion stage. Plus extremely high foreign-oil dependence, Japan realized that an oil reserve equal to an import volume of 90 days dissatisfied the domestic safety need. Hence, Japan began to further enlarge the scale of oil reserve. Whereas oil reserves equal to an import volume of 90 days were borne by private enterprises, Japan decided to establish national petroleum stockpiling to relieve their pressure to further enlarge petroleum stockpiling. National petroleum stockpiling was run by new oil companies through renting offshore tankers and idle oil tanks from private enterprises for temporary storage and constructing permanent oil reserve bases. During that period of time, Japan established oil reserves equal to an import volume of 50 days.

Japan took the oil reserve pattern combining government-controlled petroleum stockpiling and non-governmental petroleum stockpiling into initial shape in the 1990s, including 30 billion liters of national petroleum reserve, non-governmental petroleum reserve equal to an import volume of 90 days and non-governmental liquid petroleum (LP) gas reserve equal to an import volume of 50 days, which played an important role in coping with the Gulf War. Japan continuously solidified and improved petroleum stockpiling at that time and increased petroleum stockpiling to 50 billion liters at the end of the 1990s.

Japan has further adjusted and optimized the petroleum stockpiling pattern according to the OPEC's and IEA's international situation since the twenty-first century, during which oil supply was strained due to artificial or natural disasters such as "911", the Iraq War, Hurricane Katrina and Libya Crisis. Japan, as a member country of the IEA, discharged the duties and proved the emergency capacity of petroleum reserve with an active response to IEA's contingency plan through petroleum reserve adjustment.

Up to now, Japan has established a fairly complete stockpiling system including petroleum stockpiling and LP gas stockpiling (as shown in Fig. 5.3). The stockpiling of petroleum in Japan is performed in three programs including national petroleum stockpiling, private-sector petroleum stockpiling, stockpiles held jointly with oil-producing nations. The three programs have a combined stockpile of approximately 75.08 million kiloliters (KL) (46.83 million KL for national stockpiling and 28.25 million KL for private stockpiling) of petroleum (equivalent to approximately 210 days of domestic consumption, as of the end of March 2018) [10]. As of the end of March 2018, the strategic government reserves consist of 131 days' worth of crude

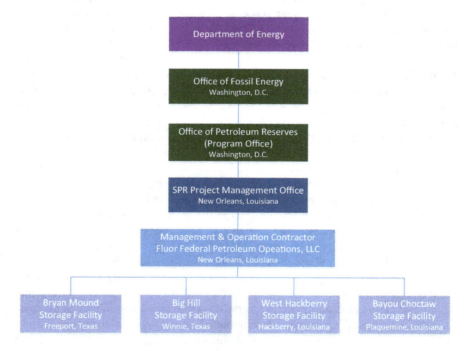

Fig. 5.3 The SPR organization of the United States

Table 5.3 National petroleum stockpiling base in Japan

No.	Petroleum stockpiling site	Technique types	Stockpiling capacity[a] (ten thousand KL)
1	Tomakomai-Tobu	On-round tank	640
2	Mutsu-Ogawara	On-round tank	570
3	Akita	In-ground tank	450
4	Kuji	Underground rock cavern tank	175
5	Fukui	On-round tank	340
6	Kikuma	Underground rock cavern tank	150
7	Shirashima	Floating tank	560
8	Kamigotou	Floating tank	440
9	Kushikino	Underground rock cavern tank	500
10	Shibushi	On-round tank	175

Note [a]refers to the data as the end of March 2014

oil and petroleum products stored in 10 national petroleum stockpiling bases [11] (shown in Table 5.3) and in the tanks leased from the private sectors. Meanwhile, private-sector reserves comprise 79 days' worth of crude oil and petroleum products in their tanks. In addition, there are stockpiles of 5 days' worth of crude oil held jointly in collaboration with oil-producing nations (the United Arab Emirates and Kingdom of Saudi Arabia) [10].

5.2.2.2 Organization and Operations of Japanese Petroleum Stockpiling

Japanese petroleum stockpiling management mode has undergone a series of adjustments. Japanese petroleum stockpiling adopted "direct national management" before 2004, under which Agency for National Resources and Energy (ANRE) of MITI—Japan National Oil Corporation (JNOC)—national petroleum stockpiling companies (or private-sector petroleum stockpiling)—stockpiling base four-level management system was adopted. The ANRE of MITI was the main-body of decision-making which formulated objectives and policies of petroleum stockpiling, determined its storage and utilization, approved its construction cost and budget, coordinated the relations between departments and supervised the implementation. The JNOC was the management main body which developed the plan for construction and operation of national petroleum stockpiling, supervised operation of petroleum stockpiling base, collected and supervised non-governmental stockpiling, managed national petroleum stockpiling corporation and offered financial aid to it. The National petroleum stockpiling companies was the executive body which organized construction and equipment commissioning for petroleum stockpiling, stored and released oil and drew up annual financial plan for governmental stockpiling. Stockpiling base was responsible for storage and release of petroleum reserve, including maintenance of base facilities and operation safety of stockpiling base, etc.

Japanese petroleum stockpiling adopted "direct national management" mode during that period of time. As to management hierarchy, the hierarchical management mode was adopted. As to nature of operating body, ANRE of MITI was a government agency attached to Japanese Central Government, the JNOC is a state-owned oil company which exercised the rights on behalf of the government, national petroleum stockpiling companies were founded with a 70% capital investment by the JNOC to build and operate stockpiling bases and the know-how of the private sector was used by the JNOC to run national petroleum stockpiling safely and efficiently [11]. As to property ownership of petroleum stockpiling, the JNOC owned the national stockpiling petroleum and lands for national stockpiling base and national petroleum stockpiling companies owned relevant base facilities lands. It can be seen that Japanese petroleum stockpiling adopted "direct national management" mode before 2004 whether in management hierarchy or operational body or ownership of base and its properties.

Nevertheless, the foregoing "direct national management" mode has a series of disadvantages due to the complexity and specialty of petroleum stockpiling system. First, government intervention with petroleum stockpiling operation system lowers the management efficiency and affects the decision-making ability of the JNOC. Then, it's hard to control reserve cost since the JNOC is a state-owned and administrative organization and consequently heavy losses will be caused. Third, the JNOC's poor performance aroused strong dissatisfaction in Japan. Finally, the Japanese Cabinet restructured concerning national stockpiling through the Plan for Reorganization and Rationalization of Special Public Corporations enacted in December, 2001. The original objective of national stockpiling, which was "to maintain stockpiled petroleum safely and efficiently, and to release them safely and promptly in emergencies, in order to stabilize Japanese oil supplies", remains unchanged and continues to be carried out.

In 2004, the Japan Oil, Gas and Metals National Corporation (JOGMEC) was founded with the objective that it would take over the operations of the JNOC and perform integrated management operations for national stockpiling, which indicating that Japanese oil reserve management system turned into "principal-agent" system. The other roles of the JOGMEC is to support private stockpiling and cooperate with international community on oil stockpiling and strength collaboration with other international oil stockpiling organizations. "Principal-agent" system consisted of ANRE of Ministry of Economy, Trade and Industry (METI), the JOGMEC and operation service companies, among which ANRE of METI was the decision layer, the JOGMEC was the management layer and operation service companies was the executive layer. As to operation mode, ANRE of METI was mainly responsible for formulating petroleum stockpiling policies and the JOGMEC which signed national stockpiling management consignment contract and facility management consignment contract with government and was authorized by the METI, was responsible for management of petroleum stockpiling and subject to government supervision. Operation service companies were responsible for management and operation of government crude oil and facilities upon the authorization of JOGMEC by signing base operation consignment contract. As to nature of operational body, the predecessor of ANRE of METI, ANRE of MITI, was also a government agency. JOGMEC was no longer subordinate to the government but was an independent administrative institution with the right of self-decision. Operation service companies was not long attached to JOGMEC but was an independent operation service company sponsored by private capital. Compared with "direct national management" mode, "principal-agent" system had obvious advantages of government-enterprise separation, responsibility division, unified supervision and marketization so as to reduce the cost and improve the efficiency of petroleum stockpiling [12].

In order to build a response system that enables a prompt and smooth release of stockpiled oil in times of emergency, since the founding of the former JNOC, the JOGMEC have been conducting emergency release exercises by mooring tankers at a National Petroleum Stockpiling Base and performing loading and unloading of oil, in conditions comparable with potential emergency scenarios [11]. The Minister of METI has been authorized to drawdown the Japanese petroleum stockpiles. In the event that is a shortage or could be a shortage in the supply of oil in Japan, the demand suppression is the priority choice, followed by the drawdown of private sector petroleum stockpiling through reducing the target petroleum reserve and national petroleum stockpiling. During the 1991 Gulf War, about 15.7 MMbbl of petroleum products were drawdown by Japanese government in response to IEA's Co-ordinated Emergency Response Measures. In 2005, in order to alleviate the tight supply situation in the international market caused by Hurricane Katrina, Japan has voluntarily released a total of 7.3 MMbbl of private sector petroleum reserves.

5.2.2.3 Japanese Petroleum Stockpiling Features "Third-Party Reserving"

Japan creates the "third stockpiling reserving" mode which means that oil is reserved by Japan and oil producing nations. To be specific, the Japanese Government provides capital and venue and rents oil tanks to state-owned oil companies of oil producing countries for intermediate reserve of crude oil exported to East Asia. In turn, oil producing countries need to keep half of oil tanks and Japan has the preferential right to purchase and receive oil supply in the event of a supply crisis. The "third stockpiling system" was first presented by Japanese Prime Minister Shinzo Abe when visiting Saudi Arabia in April, 2007 and ANRE of METI reached a consensus on "jointly holding" with the supreme oil council of Saudi Arabia in June, 2010. Saudi Aramco began to store crude oil in Okinawa petroleum stockpiling base after February, 2011 and sold oil to China and Korea, etc. The new *Strategic Energy Plan* issued by Japan officially defined "third stockpiling system" in April, 2014, which was functionally equal to "quasi-national petroleum stockpiling". Up to now, Japan has signed two "third stockpiling system" contracts with Saudi Arabia and UAE with a total reserve capacity of about 126 million barrels.

Japan puts forward the "third stockpiling system" mainly for the following reasons: First, international oil prices soared in the beginning of the twenty-first century; Second, rapid growth of emerging economies intensified the competition of energy sources; Third, some oil exporting countries upheld resource nationalism and intended to contain oil importing countries from exploration and exploitation. To avoid the aforesaid adverse effects, Japan must find a new way to guarantee stability and safety of domestic oil supply and it selected Saudi Arabia and UAE since more than 50% of oil is imported from the Gulf countries. Experience shows that petroleum stockpiling jointly with oil producing countries not only facilitates oil trade of oil producing countries and enhances the partnership, but also endows the oil stockpiling country with the preferential right in case of a crisis and effectively evades and weakens the threat from traditional and non-traditional risks of energy safety.

5.2.3   German Oil Reserve System

Germany is one of net oil importers around the world. In 2017, its crude oil production and petroleum products demand were 43,170 barrels/day and 2,504 million barrels/day respectively, with a foreign-trade dependence up to 98% [13]. Crude oil is imported into Germany via four transnational crude oil pipelines as well as the ports of Wilhelmshaven, Brunsbüttel, Hamburg and Rostock. To protect safety of domestic energy supply, the German Government began to adjust energy strategy and policy after the first oil crisis, among which an important step was to establish and improve petroleum stockpiling and emergency mechanism.

5.2.3.1   History of German Oil Reserve

The Federal Republic of Germany has made legal provision for a strategic oil reserve since the 1960s due to the high degree of dependency on mineral oil imports. In 1966, German formally introduced compulsory oil reserve system. With the 1970s oil crisis, this strategic reserve took on greater importance and has since been expanded several times. In 1974, Germany enacted energy safety law and first established a national petroleum reserve base of 4 million tons using underground Etzel salt caverns near Wilhelmshaven in North German Plain. As requested by European Community in 1975, West Germany raised the compulsory oil reserve of oil refineries and oil importers and extended it to small-sized oil importers, which was opposed by all manufacturers and failed to increase the scale of German oil reserve. In 1975, the precautionary obligation was set at 90 days for the primary product groups in order to meet commitments made to IEA.

The *Petroleum Stockholding Act (PSA)* enacted by the German Government in 1978 laid a foundation for modern German oil reserve and stipulated that Germany shall establish the Petroleum Stockpiling Association (Erdölbevorratungsverband, EBV), which was an oil reserve organization subordinate to the federation and needs to reserve oil equal to 65 days' product oil consumption. It also affiliated all oil refineries and importers to EBV and requested them to reserve oil equal to 25 days' import volume or processing volume while discharging the obligation of oil reserve. *The Regulation on Oil Reserve of Power Plant* enacted in 1981 requested fuel oil power plants to reserve oil for 30 days' power generation. In 1987, the Petroleum Regulation was amended to increase the EBV stock requirement from 65 to 80 days and reduce manufacturers' compulsory stocks from 25 to 15 days. In practice, this resulted in an increase in total inventories, as inventories of manufacturers did not decrease to the same extent [14].

Since October 1990, the oil stockpiling law was also applied in the new federal states. After expiry of a transitional period of eighteen months, the obligation to provide stock has been fully met in eastern Germany since April 1992. In 1998, a new version of the PSA came into force, which increased the stockpiling obligation of the EBV from 80 to 90 days and at the same time abolished the compulsory stocking of the manufacturers. This change has improved the quality of national stockpiling, as EBV stocks are always fully available to the members of the EBV (and ultimately to the consumer). At the same time, this change brought with it a bit of administrative simplification by eliminating reporting obligations. In 2012, the PSA was heavily amended, clarifying the subject responsible for oil reserve, further strengthening government-regulated oil reserve, elevating the marketization degree of oil reserve and improving cooperativity with EU and IEA. By then, Germany has formed an economical and efficient oil reserve and emergency mechanism specifically for internal centralized management and external collaboration.

5.2.3.2 Capacity of German Oil Reserve

The oil reserves in Germany can be held as crude oil or as products, namely gasoline, diesel, heating oil, and aviation fuel. At least one-third of the stockholding has to be in products. As of March 31, 2018, the oil reserve in Germany was reported to be 22.74 million tons of crude oil equivalent, including 13.77 million tons of crude oil and 11.50 million tons of petroleum product [15]. A significant portion of national oil reserves in Germany are held by the EBV.

Based on the principle of regional balance and economic security, German oil reserve is mainly distributed in east, north, northwest, southwest and south (shown in Table 5.4) [14]. The crude oil is mainly stored in salt caverns in Northern Germany which are logistically connected to refineries and product oil is mainly stored in surface oil tanks. 90% of oil reserves are owned by the EBV and up to 10% of the reserves are met by the association with quantities paid by the oil companies earmarked (contracts for delegation volumes). Germany has reached an agreement on oil reserve with other European countries such as Belgium, France, Italy and

Table 5.4 The distribution of oil reserve in Germany

Region	Location
East	Mecklenburg-Vorpommern, Brandenburg, Berlin, Saxony-Anhalt, Thuringia and Saxony
North	Schleswig-Holstein, Hamburg, Bremen and Lower Saxony
Northwest	North Rhine-Westphalia and parts of Hesse
Southwest	Baden-Württemberg, Saarland, Rhine Land-Pfalz and parts of Hesse
South	Bavaria

Luxembourg. That is, the EBV can rent oil storage facilities from these countries in case of an emergency.

5.2.3.3 Operation and Management System for German Oil Reserve

For more than five decades, the German oil reserve system was becoming mature, sound and rigorous and was functioning flexibly with a clear division of power and responsibility.

From the point of composition, the German oil reserve system can be divided into governmental strategic reserve system and non-governmental reserve system. As to management and operation, the German oil reserve system takes the PSA as the core principle, the EBV as the responsible subject and the Federal Ministry for Economic and Energy as the supervising subject. Founded in 1978 under the PSA in Hamburg, the EBV is a public corporation comprised of general meeting, the Advisory Board and Management Board. Members of general meeting are members of the EBV. All companies that produce relevant products domestically or that import such products into Germany with a production or import volume of above 25 ton are compulsory members of the EBV. General meeting shall be called yearly with the aim of drawing up and revising regulations, determining appointment and dismissal of directors by votes and auditing annual report. The Advisory Board consists of at least nine individuals and includes between one and at most three representatives from the Federal Ministry of Economic Affairs and Energy, one representative each from the Federal Ministry of Finance, and the German Bundesrat, as well as six representatives from the petroleum industry. The representatives from the petroleum industry are elected by the Members' Assembly for terms of three years. A deputy is elected or appointed for each member of the Advisory Board. The Advisory Board is mainly responsible for supervising behavior of management and auditing annual business plan. The EBV's two-person Management Board is appointed by Advisory Board and are mainly responsible for operation of the EBV.

The EBV Management Board and Advisory Board are advised by an Economic Committee and a Stockholding Committee. The committees are composed of representatives of the EBV member businesses. The Economic Committee reviews the draft business plan and the amount of membership fees upon which it is based as well as the annual reports. In addition, the Economic Committee advises regarding special circumstances which are related to financing the EBV. The Stockholding Committee advises the EBV Management Board and Advisory Board with respect to questions of overall stockholding and its cost effectiveness, quantity planning and stockholding, increases and decreases [16].

From the point of fund raising, the German oil reserve is mainly supported by bank loan and membership fee instead of governmental subsidy. The former is mainly used for purchase of crude oil and product oil and construction of storage facilities and the latter is mainly used for interest payment of bank loan and current expenses of the EBV. Membership fee is mainly paid by the EBV members. According to legal provisions, the EBV members must report category and quantity of imported or produced oil before the end of every month and pay membership fee before the end of next month. *Petroleum Stockholding Act* also stipulated that the EBV needs not to repay bank loans but cover the interest. The government shall assume the debts of the EBV in case the EBV were dissolved due to law revision.

From the point of utilization, the German oil reserve must be released according to the *Petroleum Stockholding Act*. The EBV signs contracts on spaces for purchase, rent and storage of oil and reserves oil according to consumption structure, consumer distribution, storage space, category and quantity. At any time, the EBV must ensure oil reserve can be utilized and cannot be utilized without permission. The *Petroleum Stockholding Act* also requested to keep oil transportation channels clear and ensure continuous supply of crude oil within 150 days and product oil within 90 days. As stipulated by the *Petroleum Stockholding Act*, oil reserve should be utilized under any of the following situations: First, oil is an acute shortage of; second, energy supply suffers an immediate threat; third, oil supply of EU or IEA remains to be balanced. In this case, the Federal Ministry of Economy and Labor can order to release oil reserve. In case actual oil reserve is more than 5% higher than compulsory oil reserve, the excess part can be transferred at market price. In case actual oil reserve is no more than 5% higher than compulsory oil reserve, the excess part can be transferred with the permission of the Federal Ministry for Economic and Energy. The oil reserve should be supplied to members in the proportion of payments made to the EBV and at market price instead of competitive price. Economy and Export Administration can order the EBV to supply oil to specific organizations so as to ensure the supply of life necessities and services necessary for common people and public facilities. The EBV has not right to utilize oil reserve more than half a year but an approval must be obtained from Bundesrat. Evidently, SPR is strictly controlled by the German Government and it is utilized specifically for military purposes or a shortage of 90 days stipulated by IEA.

5.2.4   French Oil Reserve System

France is a net oil importer as well. With a foreign-trade dependence up to 99%, its crude oil production and demand were 15,167 barrels/day and 1707 thousand barrels/day respectively in 2017 [13]. In parallel with the diversification of supplies, strategic stocks are an essential instrument to ensure the security of France's supplies of petroleum products in the event of a crisis. These strategic stocks consist of storing a quantity of various petroleum products to overcome a temporary break in supply. They can be used at the initiative of the International Energy Agency after agreement of all the member nations of the agency or at the instigation of the only French public authorities, in case of exceptional dysfunction of the circuits of supply that may lead to a shortage or a risk of shortage of petroleum products.

5.2.4.1   History of French Petroleum Stockpiling

France got involved in World War I (WWI) in 1914 and cost plenty of national power and financial resources. Since then, the French Government has attached importance to petroleum, which is a strategic material, and planned to build up petroleum stockpiling. The French Government enacted a government decree in 1923, requesting domestic oil and oil product operators to reserve oil at least for normal operation, which indicated the establishment of legal petroleum stockpiling. In January, 1925, the Parliament passed an act and put forward the establishment of "National Liquid Fuel Agency" for management of petroleum stockpiling. During the war French petroleum stockpiling was aimed at satisfying the need for military fuels and after that most countries were busy with economic resurgence. As the effect of oil was further highlighted, France changed the aim of petroleum stockpiling from satisfying the military need to preventing energy supply shortage from impacting national economic development, which attracted the attention of other developed countries and was imitated by Europe and even other countries.

In 1968, France commenced a stockpiling program at Manosque north of Marseille. Here, 34 solution-mined cavities in salt are used for crude oil and middle distillate stocks. This storage is principally but not wholly operational, with stocks being periodically drawn down and later replenished. This site is believed to have in excess of 14 million m^3 of storage capacity making it one of the largest facilities of its kind. In addition to the Manosque project, an iron mine near Caen has been converted to use for storage of up to five million m^3 diesel fuel [17]. During the first oil crisis, the French Government stipulated a petroleum stockpiling equal to 90 days' domestic petroleum consumption and requested overseas departments to reserve oil equal to 73 days' consumption. The IEA began to popularize petroleum stockpiling policy among member countries in 1974, which gradually improved the development of petroleum stockpiling in France. In 1988, a security stocks agency, Société anonyme de gestion des stocks de sécurité (SAGESS), was created to take control over one-half of France's petroleum stockpiling obligation.

Since then, the French oil reserve system has been basically complete. The purpose of its oil reserve system is to enable France to meet its commitments to the European Union (EU) and the IEA in the area of energy security. According to the IEA, France held on average an inventory volume equivalent to 114 days of net imports in crude oil equivalent in 2015, while according to EU accounting rules, France had on average

97 days of net imports (EPB). The 17-day differential with the IEA stocks represents commercial stocks of oil operators [18]. By 6 December 2016, the total amount of France's oil stockpiling was about 18.76 Mt of crude oil equivalent (shown in Fig. 5.4), of which 75% of the oil was stockpiled by SAGESS [19]. From the oil distribution of SAGESS stocks, about 38.1% of the oil is stored in the port, 41.4% of the oil reserves are stored in the caves, and 17.2% of the oil is stored in petroleum refineries across France [19] (Fig. 5.5).

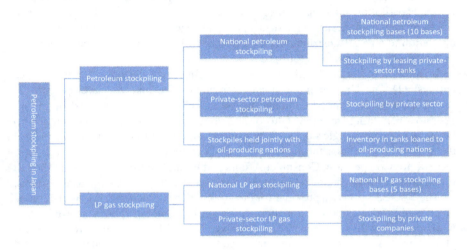

Fig. 5.4 The stockpiling of petroleum system in Japan

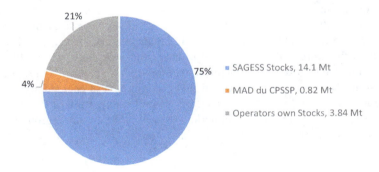

Fig. 5.5 The strategic inventory structure in France by 2016

5.2.4.2   The Organization and Management of French Petroleum Stockpiling

French regulations make the obligation to build and maintain strategic oil stocks based on operators carrying out operations for home use. Among them, distributors with the status of authorized warehouse keepers must delegate the management of part of these stocks to the Professional Committee for Strategic Oil Stocks (CPSSP), which mainly uses the services of the Société anonyme de gestion des stocks de sécurité for the constitution and conservation of these stocks; they manage the remainder of stocks by their own means. Other distributors delegate the entire management of their obligation to CPSSP. Distributors pay to the CPSSP a remuneration corresponding to the services they perform for their benefit.

In addition to the oil distributors, who are obliged, the system is based on three entities: (1) The CPSSP, professional committee of economic development. (2) SAGESS, a public limited company whose shareholding is constituted by the oil operators benefiting from the status of authorized warehouse keeper and subject to the obligation of strategic stocks. (3) The public authorities that supervise and control the system, in particular through the Energy Directorate (DE) and the Directorate-General for Competition, Consumer Affairs and Fraud Control (DGCCRF). The DE is responsible for the organization of the system and authorizes the release of stocks.

The SAGESS acts as a provider for the CPSSP and, as such, carries out purchases or sales of products and ensures their storage through storage contracts established with operators with storage capacity. The inventories to be serviced represent 29.5% of the volumes of finished products released for consumption in a calendar year and consist of finished products, crude oil or intermediate refined products.

The effectiveness of strategic stocks is intimately linked to the quality of the storage or transport infrastructure that allows them to be stored and circulated, whether to put them in place, to maintain their quality, or to use them. Currently, inventories are distributed in refineries, import depots and mesh deposits. Their distribution therefore makes it possible to have stocks as close as possible to the consumption zones. SAGESS is therefore required to have at least 10 days of gasoline consumption and 15 days of diesel fuel consumption in each zone of defense and security. Despite this distribution effort, a significant portion of these stocks is nevertheless concentrated in the refineries, as well as in the underground storage facilities of the company GEOSEL near Manosque.

5.2.5   United Kingdom's Oil Reserve System

Oil has been one of the dominant—although declining—energy sources in the United Kingdom [20], accounting for 40.0% of the country's total primary energy supply in 2018 [21]. The United Kingdom has significant levels of domestic crude oil production before the year 1999 peaking at 2.9 million barrels per day. Since then, the proved oil reserves and daily production have gradually declined, as well as the total oil demand. During the decade of 2006–2016, the UK's proved oil reserves, oil production and oil demand all maintained negative growth, with growth rates of −4.3%, −4.8% and −1.3%, respectively. In 2005, UK became a net importer of oil. In 2018, the oil production and consumption of the UK was 50.8 Mt and 74.2 Mt [21], respectively, and the net import dependency was 36.0% [22]. Compared to other IEA countries such as Germany and Japanese, the oil dependency on imported oil of the UK is not high. Besides, the self-sufficiency score of crude oil for the UK was reported to be 0.92 and was above the OECD (Organization for Economic Co-operation and Development) average of 0.41 [23]. These data mark the difference of oil reserve system between the UK and other countries mentioned above.

There are no public stocks and the country does not have a public stockholding agency in the UK. The UK's strategic oil reserves are owned, established and maintained by oil companies. The British government does not directly own the strategic oil reserve, but the government has clearly stated that all large-scale petroleum product producers and retailers have the responsibility to establish and maintain a certain amount of strategic oil stockpiling. The structure of the UK's petroleum stocks is in three ways: by the company itself in the UK, by third parties, on behalf of the company within the UK, or by the company, by an affiliate or by third parties in another EU member state, provided that the affected stocks are held under a bilateral agreement between the United Kingdom and the relevant member state [20].

Figure 5.6 shows the stocks structure trends of the UK including stocks held abroad for use under approved bilateral agreements and the equivalent stocks held

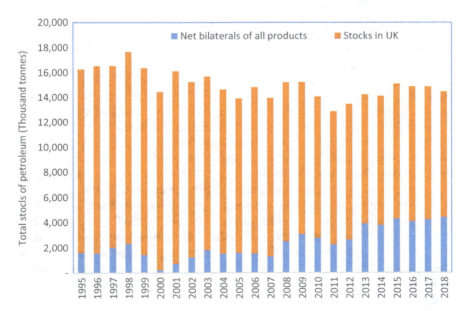

Fig. 5.6 The petroleum stocks of the UK. *Data source* BEIS, Energy trends: September 2019. London: Department for Busiiness, Energy & Industrial Strategy

Table 5.5 The primary oil storage sites of the United Kingdom [20]

Region	Location
North	Sullom Voe, Flotta, Nigg
Middle	Glasgow, Grangemouth, Tyne, Workington, North Tees, Lindsey, Bootle, Eastham, Stanlow, Warrington, Wisbech
South	Milford Haven, Barry, Avonmouth, Shell Haven, Isle of Grain, Harwich

Data source IEA, Energy Supply Security: Emergency Response of IEA Countries 2014

in the UK for foreign use [22]. From 2013 onwards, the EU Directive 2009/119/EC came into effect and this has lead to changes in how the UK companies manage their stock-holding. The increase in crude stocks held abroad was at the expense of a decrease in product stocks held under similar agreements. At the end of Q2 2019 total stocks for all oil were up 0.2% (0.3 million tonnes) compared to the same point in 2018, of which about 51% of stocks was product stocks. Stocks of primary oils were down 9.2%, primarily because of a decrease in stocks held at terminals. In contrast, product stocks were up 11% with an increase in volumes held under bilateral agreements offsetting a fall in physical stocks of motor gasoline and kerosene. At the end of the Q2 2019 the UK held stocks broadly equivalent to two months of demand, or 180 days of net imports [22].

The main storage facilities for crude and oil products of the UK are located at refineries. A number of major product distribution terminals also serve as self-contained, separate storage and distribution facilities. Altogether, the refinery and stand-alone terminals comprise a total of 59 primary distribution terminals, some of which are listed in Table 5.5 [20]. They are collectively supplied by pipeline (51% by volume), rail (15%), and sea (34%) from the UK refineries and—in some cases—from overseas [20].

The Department for Business, Energy & Industrial Strategy (BEIS) replaced the Department of Energy and Climate Change (DECC) in July 2016 and is now responsible for coordinating the country's response to oil supply emergencies. Within the BEIS, there is a team which serves as the national emergency strategy organization (NESO). The role of this team is responsible for maintaining and implementing emergency response measures in an oil supply disruption [20]. To function as the NESO, the legal basis for the BEIS during an oil supply disruption is the *Energy Act 1976*. The Act provides powers, subject to an order in council, for the Secretary of the BEIS to regulate or prohibit the production, supply, acquisition or use of fuel in a domestic oil supply emergency, or in order to enable the United Kingdom to meet its international obligations in the event of an IEA collective action through a compulsory stockholding obligation (CSO) on oil companies [20]. The Act also required refining companies to hold stocks equivalent to 67.5 days of their supplies during the previous four quarters, while importing companies must hold stocks equivalent to 58 days [20].

The oil companies and importers are required to submit monthly oil returns to the DECC. The costs of compulsory oil stocks are financed by the companies operating in the market, and thus implicitly passed on to consumers through market prices. Once the NESO has been activated in the event of an emergency, drawing down oil stocks by lowering the CSO on industry and instigating demand restraint measures are the two primary emergency response policy options for the UK government. The government's preferred option for responding to an emergency is to draw down oil stocks—and there is a six-stage process in place to activate this option. During the implementation stage of a stockdraw, companies are obliged to develop an implementation plan and notify the BEIS. Stocks would be expected to be drawn down within an agreed timeframe—usually one month. The BEIS's preference is for implementation plans to be made on a voluntary basis, but in the event that acceptable company-specific implementation plans cannot be agreed on, the BEIS would use its legal authority to direct companies to release stock. During the IEA collective action in 2005 following Hurricane Katrina and again in 2011 during the Libyan crisis, the United Kingdom met its IEA obligations by reducing the CSO on industry and drawing down oil stocks [20].

5.3 Development Status of Chinese Oil Reserve

The energy consumption is an impetus for national economic growth. Chinese energy demand has grown rapidly since the reform and opening-up in 1978. Especially after the accession to the World Trade Organization (WTO) in the beginning of the twenty-first century, Chinese energy demand further grew and China became increasingly dependent on the international energy market especially the oil market. Oil dependence broke through 60% in 2015 and further increased to 65.4% in 2016 and further up to 69.8% in 2018 [24]. Thus, China pays high attention to energy supply safety.

5.3.1 Development History of Chinese Oil Reserve

Chinese oil reserve has a late start when measured against developed countries. Since China became a net oil importer in 1993, the construction of the SPR has been discussed on reducing the effect of oil supply failure disruption on domestic consumption. *Ninth Five-Year Plan for National Economy and Social Development of PRC and Outline of Long-range Objective by 2010* approved in the 4th session of the 8th National People's Congress on 17 March 1996 put forward "constructing the SPR and maintaining national energy safety". In November, 2000, General Secretary Jiang Zemin explicitly requested in the Central Economic Working Conference to accelerate demonstration and implementation of projects relating to the construction of the SPR. In 2001, Premier Zhu Rongji came up with "accelerating the establishment of reserve systems for oil and other strategic resources" from the perspective of resource strategy in the government work report of the 4th Session of the 9th National People's Congress. In the meantime, the State Development Planning Commission organized related departments and experts to thoroughly study feasibility, management system, fund guarantee and layout of oil reserve and make suggestions to the State Council, which were approved at the end of 2002. The State Economic and Trade Commission introduced the *"Tenth Five-year Plan" for Petroleum Industry* in 2003 on gradually establishing and improving the development route of strategic reserve system. The National Development and Reform Commission Petroleum Reserve Office was put into operation in May, 2003, which officially launched SPR of China.

5.3.1.1 SPR in China

China began to construct the first SPR in 2004. On account of a vast territory and differences in economic development level and petrochemical productivity, China first made experiments of oil reserve and then popularized it. According to the requirements for "establishing national petroleum reserve base in the light of integrated planning, rational distribution, standard management and gradual progress and making the most of existing facilities", oil reserve base phase I was constructed in eastern coastal China mainly because of a large oil demand, a variety of refinery plants and convenient sea transportation. Phases II and III were constructed in western China.

Table 5.6 shows distribution and scale of the Chinese SPR [25]. The oil reserve base phase I was commenced in March, 2004 in eastern coastal China and consisted of four bases: the Zhenhai National Petroleum Reserve base with a capacity of 5.2 million m^3 was completed in August, 2006; the Zhoushan National Petroleum Reserve base with a capacity of 5 million m^3 was completed in December, 2008; the Huangdao National Petroleum Reserve base with a capacity of 3.2 million m^3 was completed in November, 2008; the Dalian National Petroleum Reserve base with a capacity of 3 million m^3 was completed in December, 2008. With a total capacity of 16.40 million m^3, four bases were comprised of 100,000 m^3 large steel tanks and can store 12.43 million tons of crude oil. They were completed and put into operation during the end of 2007 to the beginning of 2008. The *Medium-term and Long-term Planning for National Petroleum Reserve* passed by the State Council in 2008 proposed to construct a petroleum reserve base by three stages by 2020, of which phase I, phase II and phase III have a capacity of 12 million tons, 28 million tons and 28 million tons respectively. The oil reserve will be equal to a net import volume of 100 days and the total investment is predicted to exceed 100 billion Yuan.

According to phase II national petroleum reserve planning, oil reserve site gradually turns from coastal areas to inland areas. Table 5.6 shows the basic information of phase II national petroleum reserve base. In addition to the petroleum reserve extension project in Zhoushan and the underground storage cavern project in Huangdao, phase II national petroleum reserve base spreads over Dushanzi of Sinkiang, Zhanjiang and Huizhou of Guangdong, Lanzhou of Gansu, Jintan of Jiangsu, Jinzhou

Table 5.6 Overview of national petroleum reserve base in China

Planning period	Base name	Detail	Completion time	Undertaker
Phase I	Zhenhai National Petroleum Reserve Base	52 100,000 m^3 oil storage tanks with a capacity of 5.2 million m^3 and 3.78 million tons of crude oil	August, 2006	Sinopec
	Zhoushan National Petroleum Reserve Base	50 100,000 m^3 oil storage tanks with a capacity of 5 million m^3 and 3.98 million tons of crude oil	December, 2008	SINOCHEM
	Huangdao National Petroleum Reserve Base	32 100,000 m^3 double-disc floating-roof oil tanks and auxiliary projects with a capacity of 3.2 million m^3 and 2.5 million tons of crude oil	November, 2008	Sinopec
	Dalian National Petroleum Reserve Base	30 100,000 m^3 oil storage tanks with a capacity of 3 million m^3 and 2.17 million tons of crude oil	December, 2008	CNPC
Phase II	Dushanzi National Petroleum Reserve Base	The planning capacity is 5.4 million m^3, 30 100,000 m^3 oil storage tanks with a total capacity of about 2.2 million tons are built in the first period	November, 2011	CNPC
	Lanzhou National Petroleum Reserve Base	30 100,000 m^3 oil storage tanks with a capacity of 3 million m^3	2011	CNPC
	Tianjin National Petroleum Reserve Base	The capacity is 5 million m^3 and 3.2 million m^3 is built in the first period	End of 2013	Sinopec
	Underground storage cavern project in Huangdao National Petroleum Reserve Base	Underground oil storage with a capacity of 3.0 million m^3	2015	Sinopec

(continued)

Table 5.6 (continued)

Planning period	Base name	Detail	Completion time	Undertaker
	Petroleum storage extension project in Zhoushan National Petroleum Reserve Base	The capacity is about 3.0 million m³	May, 2016	SINOCHEM
	Jinzhou National Petroleum Reserve Base	The first large underground oil storage in China with a design capacity is 5 million m³ and consisting of 8 caverns. 2.6 million tons of crude oil will be storaged	August, 2018	CNPC
	Underground water storage cavern project in Zhanjiang Petroleum Reserve Base	90–20 m deep underground oil storage with a capacity of 7 million m³ and 5 million m³ is planned to be built in the first period	–	Sinopec
	Huizhou National Petroleum Reserve Base	Underground oil storage with a planning capacity of 5 million m³	–	CNOOC
	Jintan National Petroleum Reserve Base[a]	Underground salt cavern with a planning capacity of 3.0 million m³	–	CNPC
	Shanshan National Petroleum Reserve Base[a]	10 100,000 m³ external floating-roof oil tanks and auxiliary facilities with a total capacity is 8 million m³ and the capacity of Phase I is 1 million m³	Phase I was completed in the end of 2008	CNPC
Phase III	Phase IIInational petroleum reserve base is in construction			

Note All the information is collected from internet; [a]indicates it has not been officially confirmed of Liaoning and Tianjin. Sinkiang Dushanzi Petroleum Reserve Base initiated in 2009 officially launched phase II national petroleum reserve base. Till now, some of these bases have already been put into operation while some of these are still under construction.

The phase III national petroleum reserve base has been into preparation and construction since the phase II national petroleum reserve bases were still in construction. In 2014, *Strategic Action Plan for Energy Development (2014–2020)* introduced by the State Council pointed out "the construction of the phase II national petroleum reserve base and the initiation of the phase III". The detailed sites for petroleum reserve are not officially announced. However, it is reported that the possible sites for the phase III national petroleum reserve base were located in Daqing of Heilongjiang province and Rizhao of Shandong province. These two bases were undertaken by CNPC in 2012. Another project for the phase III national petroleum reserve was reported to be an extension project in the Huizhou National Petroleum Reserve Base. As of 5 March, 2019, the project publicized the candidate for the successful bidding in the geological survey of the scientific research stage.

After more than ten years of hard work, the China's SPR has achieved certain achievements. The data of National Energy Administration shows that 9 national petroleum reserve bases including Zhoushan, Zhoushan extension, Zhenhai, Dalian, Huangdao, Dushanzi, Lanzhou, Tianjin and Huangdao had been completed by May, 2017 [26].

5.3.1.2 COR in China

The COR, also called non-governmental oil reserve, is an important part of Chinese oil reserve system and is high valued by the Chinese Government. According to the *"Tenth Five-year Plan" for Energy Development*, we must "encourage enterprises to enlarge oil reserve" for "certain SPR capacity", "accelerate the construction of governmental oil reserve, construct compulsory COR timely and encourage the development of COR" and "study the construction of compulsory COR". The *"Twelfth Five-Year Plan for Energy Development"* states that it is necessary to "research and establish a corporate obligation reserve." The *Guiding Opinions of the National Development and Reform Commission about Strengthening Operation and Management of the COR* issued by the National Development and Reform Commission in January, 2015 requested that "all crude oil processors which produce oil products using crude oil must reserve crude oil of no less than 15 days' processing volume. When international oil price exceeds USD 130/barrel, they can lower the inventory to no less than 10 days' processing volume." The significance of the COR was further highlighted: guaranteeing national energy safety and stable operation of the oil market. The *"Thirteen Five-year" Plan for Energy Development* issued by the National Development and Reform Commission and the National Energy Administration in December, 2016 came up with "accelerating the construction of oil reserve system and constructing phase II national petroleum reserve base", encouraging the development of the COR and scaling up the COR reasonably. Meanwhile, the

Energy Production and Consumption Revolution Strategy (2016–2030) issued by the National Development and Reform Commission and the National Energy Administration pointed out "establishing an energy reserve mechanism laying equal stress on governmental reserve and commercial reserve, separating central reserve and local reserve, combining resource reserve and technical reserve, giving consideration to strategic reserve and emergency response and integrating domestic reserve and international reserve" and "accelerating the construction of petroleum reserve base and scientifically determine the reserve scale". The aforesaid policies indicated that the Chinese Government attached increasing importance to the development of the COR.

State-owned petroleum enterprises such as CNPC, Sinopec, Sinochem and CNOOC are main forces of COR (as shown in Table 5.7). In June 2008, Sinopec's first commercial reserve oil company, Sinopec Group Petroleum Commercial Reserve Co., Ltd. was incorporated; in July of the same year, CNPC Commercial Reserve Oil Branch was incorporated. The establishment of the two petrochemical companies marks the official start-up operation of the commercial oil reserve projects. CNPC Tieling Commercial Crude Reserve Base with a capacity of 1.16 million m^3, the first COR project in China, was commenced in June, 2007. Afterwards, PetroChina, Sinopec and other major oil companies established COR depots successively and Chinese COR boomed. So far, the COR depots of major oil companies spread over Guangzhou, Tianjin, Hebei, Jiangsu, Liaoning, Gansu, Yunnan and Hainan.

Not only the state-owned oil companies but also the private enterprises make contributions to the construction of COR. Despite of high enthusiasm, only a few private enterprises engage in COR due to small size and capital shortage. For example, the National Petroleum Reserve Center called for bids of national oil reserve qualification in May, 2010 and three private enterprises won the bid with an oil reserve of 1.5 million tons, which indicated the involvement of private enterprises in the construction of national COR system [27]. In January, 2013, Zhejiang TYLOO Energy Co., Ltd. and Zhoushan Zhongji Chemical Engineering Co., Ltd. were qualified for storage of crude oil reserve [1], which indicated that private enterprises stepped into oil storage and laid the root for private enterprises to expand oil import. According to the public information from the Ministry of Commerce of the People's Republic of China, more than 10 private companies have obtained crude oil storage qualifications as of October 2019, such as Longkou Jinggang Oil Storage and Transportation Co., Ltd., Ningxia Lingwu Pagoda Dagu Storage and Transportation Co., Ltd., Wanxiang Petroleum Storage and Transportation (Zhoushan) Co., Ltd., Hainan Huaxin Petroleum Base Co., Ltd., and so on.

It is observed that the Chinese oil reserve system focuses on the SPR and is assisted by the COR. Controlled by the central government, the SPR mainly functions on preventing oil supply failure, drastic oil price fluctuation and oil supply disruption arising from natural disasters and emergencies and ensuring stable domestic oil supply. The COR means that enterprises based on normal operation assume the obligation of oil reserve according to legal provisions. The COR functions on maintaining stability of the oil market and stabilizing its fluctuation. The statistical data shows that 37.73 million tons of crude oil has been reserved using 9 national oil reserve bases and non-governmental oil reserve depots by the middle of 2017 [26].

Table 5.7 Overview of major COR depots in China

Company name	Oil depot name	Description	Construction period
Sinopec	Lanshan Commercial Crude Reserve Base (Zhejiang province)	38 100,000 m³ crude oil storage tanks with a total capacity of 3.8 million m³	Completed and put into operation in November, 2008
	Baishawan Commercial Crude Reserve Base (Zhejiang province)	The capacity of phase one is 950,000 m³ including 4 150,000 m³, 3,100,000 m³ and 1 50,000 m³ crude oil storage tanks, while phase two is planned to newly built a capacity of 450,000 m³ including 1 150,000 m³ and 3 100,000 m³ crude oil storage tanks	Phase one was completed and put into operation in 2009, and phase two is under construction
	Rizhao Commercial Crude Reserve Base (Shandong province)	28 100,000 m³ floating roof tanks for crude oil reserve	Commenced in June, 2010 and put into operation in June, 2012
	Tianjin Commercial Crude Reserve Base	32 100,000 m³ floating roof tanks for crude oil reserve	Commenced in June, 2011 and put into operation in September, 2013
	Tianjin Dagang Commercial Crude Reserve Base	13 100,000 m³ floating roof tanks with a total capacity of 1.3 million m³	Commenced in March, 2013 and put into operation in 2015
	Tianjin Shihua Commercial Crude Reserve Base	Total capacity is 1.2 million m³	Commenced in July, 2012 and put into operation in September, 2017
	Dongjiakou Commercial Crude Reserve Base (Shandong province)	16 100,000 m³ external floating roof tanks with a total capacity of 1.6 million m³	Commenced in 2016 and completed on April 23, 2019
	Caofeidian Commercial Crude Reserve Base (Hebei province)	32 100,000 m³ large floating roof tanks with a total capacity of 3.2 million m³	Commenced in May, 2010 and put into operation in the end of 2012
	Hainan Commercial Crude Reserve Base (Hainan province)	25 100,000 m³ and 1 50,000 m³ single-disc floating roof tanks with a total capacity of 2.55 million m³	Commenced in January, 2013 and put into operation in November, 2014

(continued)

Table 5.7 (continued)

Company name	Oil depot name	Description	Construction period
	Cezi Island Commercial Crude Reserve Base (Zhejiang province)	13 100,000 m^3 and 1 50,000 m^3 oil storage tanks with a total capacity of 1.35 million m^3	Completed in October, 2013
	Lianyungang crude oil COR base (Jiangsu province)	16 single-disc external floating roof tanks with a total capacity of 1.6 million m^3	Commenced in March, 2012
	Maoming Commercial Crude Reserve Base (Guangdong province)	15 125,000 m^3 oil storage tanks with a total capacity of 1.875 million m^3	Commenced in March, 2010 and completed in April, 2011
	Beihai Commercial Crude Reserve Base (Guangxi province)	The total capacity is 3.2 million m^3, among which phase I and phase II is 1.6 million m^3 respectively	Commenced in November, 2010, phase I was completed and put into operation in October, 2011 and phase II was completed and put into operation in November, 2013
CNPC	Tieling Commercial Crude Reserve Base (Liaoning province)	8,100,000 m^3 crude oil storage tanks were newly built and the total crude oil storage capacity was increased to 1.16 million m^3	Commenced in July, 2007 and completed and put into operation in October, 2008
	Shanshan Commercial Crude Reserve Base (Sinkiang province)	The planning capacity is 2 million m^3, among which phase I and phase II is 1 million m^3 respectively	Phase I was put into production in December, 2008 and phase II was commenced in 2009
	Linyuan Commercial Crude Reserve Base (Heilongjiang province)	12 100,000 m^3 double-disc external floating roof tanks with a total capacity of 1.2 million m^3	Commenced in April, 2008 and completed in April, 2010
	Changqing Commercial Crude Reserve Base (Shanxi province)	The design capacity is 1.2 million m^3 including 0.8 million m^3 of the COR storage and 0.4 million m^3 of production and running storage	Commenced in July, 2008 and completed in 2010
	Tianjin Nangang Commercial Crude Reserve Base	10 100,000 m^3 crude oil storage tanks with a total capacity of 1 million m^3	Completed in December, 2010

(continued)

Table 5.7 (continued)

Company name	Oil depot name	Description	Construction period
	Jinzhou Port Commercial Crude Reserve Base (Liaoning province)	6 100,000 m³ oil storage tanks	Commenced in April, 2008 and completed in January, 2010
	Jidong Oilfield Commercial Crude Reserve Base (Hebei province)	The design capacity is 1 million m³ including 10 100,000 m³ crude oil storage tanks	Commenced in January, 2009 and put into operation in June, 2010
	Qinzhou Commercial Crude Reserve Base (Guangxi province)	With a total planning capacity is 20 million m³, the project is constructed by two stages. The capacity for phase I was 10 million m³ of which the first batch consists of 40 oil storage tanks with a total capacity of 4.2 million m³	Commenced in February, 2009 and the first batch of phase I was put into operation in August, 2010
	Lanzhou Commercial Crude Reserve Base (Gansu province)	18 100,000 m³ crude oil storage tanks with a total capacity of 1.8 million m³	Commenced in February, 2009 and completed in November, 2011
	Yunnan Petrochemical Commercial Crude Reserve Base (Yunnan province)	100,000 m³ double-disc external floating roof tanks with a total capacity of 1 million m³	Invited for bid in 2013
CNOOC	Changyao Island Commercial Crude Reserve Base (Fujian province)	The total capacity is 9.8 million m³. The capacity of phase I is 2.2 million m³, including 1 million m³ of aboveground storage tanks and 1.2 million m³ of underground cave depots. The capacity of phase II is 3.0 million m³ of underground cave. The capacity of phase III is 4.6 million m³, including 2.6 million m³ of aboveground storage tanks and 2 million m³ of underground cave depots	Phase I was planned to be constructed during January, 2014 to December, 2016 and put into operation in 2017; phase II was planned to be put into operation in 2020

(continued)

Table 5.7 (continued)

Company name	Oil depot name	Description	Construction period
CEFC China Energy Company Limited (CEFC China)	Hainan Yangpu Commercial Crude Reserve Base	With a total capacity of 2.8 million m³, phase I consists of 24 100,000 m³ oil storage tanks and 8 50,000 m³ product oil tanks	Commenced in October, 2013 and put into production in 2016

Note A large part of the information are referenced from [25], while some of these are updated from internet

5.3.2 The Management of Chinese Oil Reserve

The Chinese oil reserve system consists of the SPR and the COR, while the SPR consists of governmental SPR and non-governmental SPR, as shown in Fig. 5.7. The SPR mainly includes government-dominated petroleum reserve bases and non-governmental SPR includes petroleum and petroleum product producers and distributors, oil refineries and oil importers.

Management of Chinese SPR is becoming mature now. The *"Eleventh Five-year" Plan for Energy Development* pointed out that "China will establish a three-level oil reserve management system through reference to international experience: National Development and Reform Commission Energy Bureau, national oil reserve center and national oil reserve base from top to bottom". The existing Chinese SPR management structure consists of decision layer, management layer and operation layer. The decision layer, which is the top layer under the charge of the National Development and Reform Commission Energy Bureau Oil & Gas Department (national oil reserve office), is mainly responsible for reserve policy and planning. The National oil reserve center, which is the executive layer, is responsible for project implementation, operation and management. The operation layer, which is an authorized state-owned enterprise, is responsible for construction, management and safety of oil reserve bases.

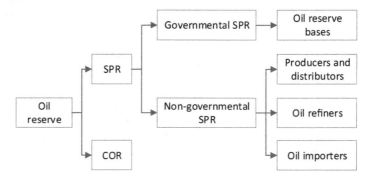

Fig. 5.7 Composition of Chinese oil reserve system

Founded in 2003 and attached to the National Energy Administration, national oil reserve office is the leader of oil reserve system. The National Energy Administration is responsible for drawing up oil reserve policies and objectives, including "drafting, implementation and management of national oil and natural gas reserve plans and policies, monitoring of supply-demand change of domestic and overseas markets, presentation and implementation of national oil and natural gas reserve plans and policies, approval or audit of oil and natural gas storage facilities projects and supervision on commercial oil and natural gas reserve". After National Energy Administration draws up oil reserve policies and objectives, national oil reserve office is responsible for specific work. Founded on 18 December 2007 and incorporated into National Energy Administration in August 2008, national oil reserve center is an executing agency in charge of construction and management of national oil reserve. It exercises the rights of contributor, takes responsibility for construction and management of national oil reserve base, undertakes storage, replacement and utilization of the SPR and monitors supply-demand change of domestic and overseas oil markets. National oil reserve base is the operation layer of oil reserve. According to relevant provisions for construction of national oil reserve base, the national oil reserve office makes investments on behalf of the government. Phase I SPR bases reside in Zhenhai of Zhejiang, Zhoushan of Zhejiang, Dalian of Liaoning and Huangdao of Shandong by virtue of management of local refineries and in consideration of project construction management and operation management. As to fund raising, the SPR project is mainly sponsored by national finance. First, the National Development and Reform Commission releases an investment plan for national oil reserve base construction project and the authorized oil company creates a special account. Then, the oil company establishes and improves financial and accounting systems according to provisions of the Central Government on investment in infrastructure. Last, the oil company appropriates construction funds to the authorized oil reserve base in line with fund using plan and in strict accordance with project progress, fund demand and relevant contracts. National oil reserve base will be run and managed by enterprises after completed and put into operation. As to management rules for relevant expenses, it is referred to the *Interim Procedures for Fiscal and Financial Management of National Oil Reserve introduced by the Ministry of Finance.*

The COR, as an important part of international oil reserve, plays a critical role in elevating the level of domestic oil supply, guaranteeing stable operation of the oil market and protecting safety of national energy supply. The Chinese COR includes commercial reserve subordinate to state-owned oil companies and oil reserve of other small and medium-sized enterprises, among which state-owned oil companies are main forces of the COR and small and medium-sized enterprises are an important supplement. The Chinese COR is under unified management of the National Energy Administration and is run by oil enterprises under two operation modes: one is management mode combining reserve depot with production depot and the other is independent management mode. The PetroChina adopts the former and the Sinopec adopts the latter. Both have their own advantages and disadvantages. For example, management mode combining reserve depot with production depot is highly flexible, by which oil can be renewed and replaced during normal operation. Not only is operating cost of reserve depot substantially lowered, but also responsiveness of reserve depot under emergencies is enhanced. However, it has unclear management interface and is difficult to supervise. On the contrary, independent management mode can overcome the difficulty of supervision, but it makes it hard to renew and replace oil. As to fund raising, commercial reserve of state-owned oil enterprises is fully subsidized by national finance. 30% of purchase fund is subsidized by national finance and operation cost and dissipation fee of reserve library are borne by enterprises. Besides, government pays the rent for oil and storage facilities rented from social organizations.

5.3.3 Main Problems of Chinese Oil Reserve

A certain size of oil reserve can not only maintain safety of national oil supply and intensify governmental regulation on the oil market, but also boot China's speaking right to involve in matters concerning international energy and global energy management. After more than ten years of development, the characteristics of Chinese oil reserve has taken its own shape but also has many problems.

First, the oil reserve guarantee capability is still weak. For more than a decade, China has made great achievements in construction of oil reserve base and crude oil storage. It was just upon completion of phase I oil reserve base that international oil price suffered a setback, during which China purchased plenty of cheap crude oil for the SPR. By the middle of 2017, China has reserved 37.73 million tons of crude oil in 9 national petroleum reserve bases and some commercial oil depots [26]. The data of BP Statistical Review of World Energy 2019 shows that net oil import of China in 2018 was 461.8 million tons which equals to 9.22 million barrels per day [21]. According to IEA's oil reserve standard equal to import volume of 90 days, Chinese oil reserve should reach about 459.156 million tons. But the current oil reserve is just 37.73 million tons equal to 22 days' domestic oil consumption (Crude oil consumption for China in 2018 is about 1.72 million tons per day [21]), and far from the IEA's oil reserve standard. The *Medium-term and Long-term Planning for National Petroleum Reserve* put up with an oil reserve of China equal to 100 days' net oil import and that of the USA, Japan and other developed countries more than 100 days' net oil import. It shows a large room for Chinese oil reserve.

Second, the non-governmental oil reserve remains to be expanded. Chinese oil reserve now focuses on "governmental oil reserve" and non-governmental oil reserve is not brought into fullest play. Relatively speaking, non-government institutions and commercial oil enterprises take a larger part in the oil reserve system of developed countries and regions such as the USA, Japan, Korea and Europe. For example, non-governmental oil reserve of the United States accounts for 2/3 of total oil reserve, while that of Japan accounts for 46.4%. But most oil depots of Chinese private oil enterprises are idle. Chinese private enterprises fall far behind developed countries in involvement in oil reserve. It's worth mentioning that non-governmental oil reserve made modest progress under the support of national policies in recent years. Presently, private enterprises get involved in national oil reserve in two ways: private enterprises construct reserve tanks and rent them for the SPR and a part of the COR or they obtain the qualification for crude oil storage and then import crude oil and store commercial oil. In 2013, private enterprises such as Zhejiang TYLOO Energy Co., Ltd. and Zhoushan Zhongji Chemical Engineering Co., Ltd. obtained the qualification for crude oil storage, indicating that private enterprises' intervention with national oil reserve. There were only 3 private enterprises among 27 enterprises which engaged in crude oil storage by June, 2016. However, the number for private enterprises engaging in crude oil storage was increased to 11 by October 2019. Obviously, scale and involvement of Chinese private enterprises in oil reserve need to be further strengthened.

Third, the oil reserve operation mechanism remains to be improved. Chinese oil reserve has a late start and a short development course, scale as well as conditions, opportunities and procedures for renewal and utilization of oil reserve are unclear, relevant facilities and methods are unsound, and operation mechanism and management method for oil reserve are still under research. As to oil reserve operation mechanism, conditions, opportunities and procedures for storage, renewal and utilization of oil reserve are unclear and relevant facilities and methods are unsound, so we should learn from overseas oil reserve operation experience. For example, the *Energy Policy and Conservation Act* of the United States explicitly stipulates release of oil reserve, presents three SPR utilization modes (comprehensive utilization, restricted utilization and trial sale) and strictly limits different utilization conditions and quantities. As to operation management of oil reserve base, Chinese oil reserve management introduced by the National Development and Reform Commission, Ministry of Finance and relevant authorities still focuses on base construction and management methods stress bidding, management and fund use of oil reserve base projects instead of specifying production management and operation mode of bases, which go against standardized and orderly production and operation of oil reserve bases.

Last but not the least, legal provisions for Chinese oil reserve are decentralized and a special legal system for oil reserve is needed. Overseas oil reserve systems are often established and improved through legislation, such as the *Energy Policy and Conservation Act* of the United States, *Oil Stockpiling Act* of Japan, *Petroleum Stockholding Act* of Germany and *Oil Supply Safety Law* of France. However, China needs to make improvement in this aspect. The *Energy Law (exposure draft)* includes oil reserve, but it has not been formally introduced for more than ten years. The 6th meeting of the Leading Group for Financial and Economic Affairs hosted by General Secretary Xi Jinping in June, 2014 studied our energy security strategy and pointed out accelerating "legislation, amendment and annulment of laws and regulations on energy". This demonstrates that the decision layer has envisaged disadvantages of existing energy system and plan to find a practical way out of the situation. The *Regulations on National Petroleum Reserve (Exposure Draft)* issued by the National Energy Administration in May, 2016 specified utilization, supervision, management and legal liability for governmental reserve, compulsory reserve of enterprise and national oil reserve [28]. At present, this regulation has been submitted to the legislative department of the State Council for legislative review [29]. Even though it has not been formally introduced either, it indicates another step towards legislation of Chinese oil reserve.

In addition, the China's oil emergency management system remains to be improved. The IEA has rich experience in oil emergency management. Since becoming a net oil importer, China has valued the construction of oil emergency system. The oil emergency management system now mainly includes the SPR, establishment of oil reserve organization, formulation of legal regulations and participation in international cooperation. Oil emergency management research and practice fall behind IEA's mature oil emergency management system mainly in formulation of emergency policy and oil reserve, especially the studies of oil emergency activities and correlations [30]. The *Energy Production and Consumption Revolution Strategy (2016–2030)* [31] issued by the National Development and Reform Commission and National Energy Administration in December, 2016 mentioned "improving energy early warning and emergency system", "drawing up contingency plan, improving emergency exercise and scheduling mechanism, enhancing energy emergency response capability and effectively reducing losses arising from energy supply failure." This indicates that the decision layer have been aware of the importance of oil emergency management system and has taken action.

References

1. Announcement No. 3 of 2013 from Ministry of Commerce of the People's Republic of China. 2013. http://www.mofcom.gov.cn/article/b/c/201301/20130108518753.shtml. Accessed 8 Jan 2013.
2. Rui, Zhiduo. 2002. Thoughts on China's reserve management and operation system. *International Petroleum Economics* (08): 40–44 + 64. (in Chinese).
3. IEA. 2007. *Oil Supply Security: Emergency Response of IEA Countries 2007*. Paris: International Energy Agency.
4. Strategic Petroleum Reserve. 2019. Accessed 28 Jan 2019. https://www.energy.gov/fe/services/petroleum-reserves/strategic-petroleum-reserve.
5. EIA. 2020. *Monthly Energy Review (March 2020)*. Washington, DC: U.S. Energy Information Administration.
6. DOE. 2016. Long-term Strategic Review of the U.S. Strategic Petroleum Reserve (Report to Congress). Washington, D.C.: United States Department of Energy.
7. Ogden Jr., D.M. 1978. Protecting energy turf: The Department of Energy Organization Act. *Natural Resources Journal* 18 (4): 845–857.
8. History of SPR releases. Accessed 01 Feb 2019. https://www.energy.gov/fe/services/petroleum-reserves/strategic-petroleum-reserve/releasing-oil-spr.
9. BP. 2018. *BP Statistical Review of World Energy 2018*. London: BP.
10. JOGMEC. 2018. *Annual report 2018*. Tokyo: Japan Oil, Gas and Metal National Corporation.
11. JOGMEC. 2016. *Petroleum Stockpiling: A tool for national energy security*. Tokyo: Japan Oil, Gas and Metals National Corporation.
12. Yin, Xiaoliang. 2016. Experience and lesson: Re-recognizing petroleum reserve strategy of Japan. *Contemporary Economy of Japan* 01: 22–31. (in Chinese).
13. OPEC. 2018. *OPEC Annual Statistical Bulletin 2018*. Vienna, Austria: Organization of the Petroleum Exporting Countries.

14. EBV. 2008. *Mineral oil duty storage in the Federal Republic of Germany.* Berlin: Erdölbevorratungsverband.
15. EBV. 2018. *Annual Report for the business year of 2017/2018.* Berlin: Erdölbevorratungsverband.
16. EBV. The intoduction of the Erdölbevorratungsverband. Accessed 20 Mar 2019. https://www.ebv-oil.org/cmse/cms2.asp?sid=57&nid=&cof=57.
17. Giles, Harry N. 1991. Petroleum stockpiling projects—A worldwide survey. Paper presented at the 4th International Conference on Stability and Handling of Liquid Fuels, Orlando, Florida, USA.
18. MEST. 2016. Energy and climate panorama, 2016 edition: Ministry of Ecological and Solidarity Transition (MEST).
19. MEST. 2016. Security of oil supply. Accessed 6 Dec 2016. https://www.ecologique-solidaire.gouv.fr/securite-dapprovisionnement-en-petrole.
20. IEA. 2014. *Energy Supply Security: Emergency Response of IEA Countries 2014.* Paris, France: Internatinal Energy Agency.
21. BP. 2019. *BP Statistical Review of World Energy 2019.* London: BP.
22. BEIS. 2019. *Energy trends:September 2019.* London: Department for Businiess, Energy & Industrial Strategy.
23. Azarbarzin, Azin. 2019. Diversity of supply for oil and oil products in OECD countries in 2018. London: Oil and Gas Statistics, Department for Business, Energy & Industrial Strategy.
24. Liu, Chaoquan, and Xuefeng Jiang. 2019. *2018 oil and gas industry development in China and the world.* Beijing: CNPC Economics & Technology Research Institute. (in Chinese).
25. Yang, Zijian, and Li Wei. 2015. Development situation and needs of China's petroleum reserve system. *International Petroleum Economics* 23 (9): 69–77. (in Chinese).
26. Significant progress has been made in the construction of national oil reserves. http://www.nea.gov.cn/2017-12/29/c_136859895.htm. Accessed 29 Dec 2017.
27. China Energy News. 2010. Private oil companies officially get the access to national oil reserve market in China (14 June 2010).
28. "Regulations on National Petroleum Reserve (Exposure Draft)" for pubilic comment. 2016. http://www.nea.gov.cn/2016-05/31/c_135402100.htm. Accessed 31 May 2016.
29. Liang Changxin: Significant progress has been made in five aspects of energy legislation in recent years. http://www.nea.gov.cn/2019-04/29/c_138021567.htm. Accessed 29 Apr 2019.
30. Tao, L.Y.U., and F.U. Li. 2017. Analysis of the activity recognition and structural of oil emergency management system. *China Mining Magazine* 26 (7): 1–6. (in Chinese).
31. NDRC. 2016. *Energy production and consumption revolution strategy (2016–2030).* Beijing: National Development and Reform Commission.

Chapter 6
Joint Oil Stockpiling Between Middle East Exporters and Northeast Asian Importers: A Winning Formula?

Tilak Doshi and Sammy Six

The previous chapter summarizes the development of the oil reserves of major countries around the world and points out the importance of oil reserves. This chapter will focus on the feasibility of establishing joint oil stockpiling between major Middle East oil exporters and Northeast Asia importers.

6.1 Introduction

'Joint oil stockpiling' in this paper refers to stored oil located in an importing country owned and commercially traded by an exporting country in exchange for first drawing rights by the host country in times of emergency. Joint oil stockpiling can therefore be classified as both commercial and strategic storage. The distinctive attributes of the joint oil stockpiling agreements can serve the perceived energy security needs of net oil-importing countries by enhancing their respective Strategic Petroleum Reserves (SPRs) at lower cost while at the same time it can work as a channel for downstream integration by the national oil companies (NOCs) of the oil exporting countries in their objectives of ensuring market share (at competitive prices) for their crude exports in the large oil importing regions. Our focus is on joint crude oil stockpiling

Tilak K Doshi was Director of Industry & Markets division, and Sammy Six was Research Analyst at King Abdullah Petroleum Studies and Research Center (KAPSARC) when this paper was written. The original paper can be accessed in full at https://www.kapsarc.org/research/public ations/joint-oil-stockpiling-between-middle-east-exporters-and-northeast-asian-importers-a-win ning-formula/.

T. Doshi (✉) · S. Six
Middle East Institute, National University of Singapore, Singapore, Singapore
e-mail: meitkd@nus.edu.sg

S. Six
e-mail: sammysix646@gmail.com

© Shanghai Jiao Tong University Press 2021
T. Zhang and D. Wang (eds.), *China-Gulf Oil Cooperation Under the Belt and Road Initiative*, https://doi.org/10.1007/978-981-15-9283-6_6

agreements between the Middle Eastern crude oil exporters and Northeast Asian importers.

An early agreement by Statoil with Korea in 1999 was probably the first actual example of a joint oil stockpiling agreement between a net crude exporting country and a net importer. According to the state-owned Korea National Oil (KNOC), Statoil payed $ 8.6 million to stockpile 8 million barrels of North Sea oil at its Yeosu and Ulsan storage plants.[1] Under the agreement, Statoil delivered the oil over a three-year period, beginning July 1, 1999. KNOC retained the right in this agreement to have a 'pre-emptive' choice to buy the stored oil in an 'emergency'. According to press reports, the agreement was the first of what Korea hoped would be several similar arrangements with crude suppliers including those in the Middle East aimed at increasing its SPR volumes. Since 1999, there have been a number of similar joint oil stockpiling arrangements between leading Middle East National Oil Companies (ME NOCs) and the large Northeast Asian (NEA) oil importers, specifically Japan and South Korea. News reports over the past decade have also noted the high level talks between Chinese energy officials and Middle East oil producers regarding similar joint oil stockpiling arrangements but these have not yet led to fruition.

It should be noted that joint oil stockpiling agreements discussed in this paper are an entirely different practice to the case where oil-importing countries stockpile oil as part of their SPR requirements in a multilateral framework of cooperation for oil emergencies. This was among the fundamental motivations that led the OECD to establish the International Energy Agency (IEA), in response to the events associated by the Arab oil embargo in 1973. Proposals for other regionally-based joint stockpiling agreements have also been discussed on and off since the oil price shocks of the 1970s. For instance, ASEAN member countries have long discussed a regional stockpiling agreement for the group of Southeast Asian countries but no binding treaty has been ratified by the group's member countries.[2] To date, the IEA remains the sole multilateral agency with an oil emergency agreement among its members.

For Japan and South Korea, among the world's largest oil importers and as members of the OECD/IEA, the question of building up and maintaining their SPR has long been part of their energy policy. The emergence of China, and more recently India, as very large Asian net crude oil importers has been accompanied with ambitious SPR plans as part of their national defence strategies. In the context of heightened concern over energy security as the Middle East region's turmoil continues unabated after the Arab Spring erupted in December 2010, the potential gains to trade presented by joint oil stockpiling agreements have become of increasing interest to the NOCs of both regions. To the extent that ME crude oil stored in host country facilities enhances the host country's definition of SPR (despite the MENOC retaining

---

[1] Alexander's Oil and Gas Connections, "Statoil is stockpiling North Sea oil in Korea", June 24, 1999. Accessed at http://www.gasandoil.com/news/south_east_asia/108376c212b466a62d57ef2a 2800d464.

[2] The ASEAN Petroleum Security Agreement was signed by the member countries in March 2009 but not ratified by all; the agreement in any case calls for member countries to "help" other members in case of an oil emergency on a "best endeavour" basis. Accessed at http://www.jus.uio.no/eng lish/services/library/treaties/09/9-06/asean_petroleum_security.xml.

title until the event of an oil supply emergency), there are potential gains to trade. The carrying cost to the ME NOC is a fraction of the cost that host country would bear if it were to buy the crude up-front for its SPR. On the other hand, the availability of storage facilities close to destination markets provides an oil producer significant advantages: it offers logistical flexibility and the ability to supply oil cargoes on a prompt basis and deliveries can be made within days rather than the three weeks or more it takes to transport oil from the Arabian Gulf to Northeast Asia.

From the adoption of formula pricing in 1987 through the extended commodity boom and high oil prices period since 2002 (ending emphatically in the second half of 2014), the focus of oil producers has been on maximizing long term contracts (within the OPEC or country quota targets if any) with standard pricing terms for large buyers who would pick up FOB Arabian Gulf cargoes in large crude carriers. Their customers in Asia are typically the large NOCs or privately-owned conglomerates with their own shipping arms. Joint oil stockpiling agreements were seen by the ME NOCs as advantageous logistical investments which provided added flexibility to serve regular clients in Asia. However, in the context of low oil prices after the second half 2014 price collapse, joint oil stockpiling agreements have regained significant attention, although this time with different bargaining dynamics between the ME exporters and NEA importers. The new environment in oil markets has led to increased competition in the Asian crude oil market and Asian buyers have been adding greater weight to spot markets in their crude oil purchase portfolios. The increased use of spot markets by Asian importers and the willingness to have a greater percentage of their crude purchases via spot rather than term deals have led even the most conservative ME NOCs to engage in spot market sales albeit intermittently. The ME NOCs who have long preferred to sell their oil under long term crude oil sales agreements (COSA) have begun to engage opportunistically in spot market sales in order to protect or grow their market share while minimizing price discounts in their formula pricing.

As the ME NOCs see the need to engage in spot markets to access new market niches in a context of heightened competition, the commercial options provided by the lease of storage facilities in NEA markets have gained in importance. Even though it is far more efficient to move crude in large crude carriers direct to the delivery ports of the large NEA NOC refining facilities, reaching smaller customers located at or near ports that cannot handle large vessels has become an important option (breaking bulk) available to ME NOC trading practices. The intermittent engagement in spot sales by the ME NOCs can be seen as attempts to convert new customers into clients with long term COSAs. It is hard to imagine the ME NOCs having any intention to "cannibalize" their own term contract COSAs that account for the vast majority of crude oil exports with spot sales in weak markets.

The case for SPRs in enhancing energy security remains much debated in the literature. Nevertheless, governments of the large Asian importers such as India and China are going to go ahead and build SPRs. Oil supply security is high on the national agendas of these countries despite the uncertainties related to the economic benefits of building and maintaining large SPRs which impose significant financial costs on these countries. The fact that a storage facility can be used for commercial purposes by the owner of the stored crude oil while simultaneously being credibly committed to an enhancement of the host country's SPR program provides the basis for mutual gains between the country hosting the storage facility and the owner of the stored crude oil. Unlike international investments in oil refining and marketing (R&M) by the NOCs, where returns may have been at best modest, the storing of crude oil in key destination markets such as the NEA countries may prove to be significantly cheaper and more effective in the marketing of ME crude oil. Joint oil stockpiling agreements could become a more common and important mode of business cooperation with mutual gains for the ME NOCs and their partner NEA host countries.

In this chapter, we (1) describe the existing and proposed joint oil stockpiling agreements and their commercial and strategic benefits for both the exporter and the importer, and (2) examine in detail the relevance of joint oil stockpiling to host country SPR programs and its potential cost savings. We finish by providing some concluding remarks.

6.2 Necessity of Joint Oil Stockpiling and IEA Emergency Agreement

The section below provides a definition of Joint Oil Stockpiling, and details the emergency agreement under the IEA mechanism.

6.2.1 The Definition of Joint Oil Reserve

In response to the oil crisis of 1973, the Organization for Economic Cooperation and Development (OECD) launched the International Energy Agency (IEA) in 1974. IEA is committed to the prevention of oil supply disruption and provides statistical information on the international oil market and other energy sectors. In 1975, the United States adopted legislation to establish strategic petroleum reserves (US Strategic Petroleum Reserves). Joint oil stockpiling' in this paper refers to stored oil located in an importing country owned and commercially traded by an exporting country in exchange for first drawing rights by the host country in times of emergency. Joint oil stockpiling can therefore be classified as both commercial and strategic storage. The distinctive attributes of the joint oil stockpiling agreements can serve the perceived energy security needs of net oil-importing countries by enhancing their respective Strategic Petroleum Reserves (SPRs) at lower cost while at the same time it can work as a channel for downstream integration by the national oil companies (NOCs) of the oil exporting countries in their objectives of ensuring market share (at competitive prices) for their crude exports in the large oil importing regions. Our focus is on joint crude oil stockpiling agreements between the Middle Eastern crude oil exporters and Northeast Asian (NEA) importers.

It should be noted that joint oil stockpiling agreements discussed in this paper are an entirely different practice to the case where oil-importing countries stockpile oil as part of their SPR requirements in a multilateral framework of cooperation for oil emergencies. This was among the fundamental motivations that led the OECD to establish the International Energy Agency (IEA), in response to the events associated by the Arab oil embargo in 1973. Proposals for other regionally-based joint stockpiling agreements have also been discussed on and off since the oil price shocks of the 1970s. For instance, ASEAN member countries have long discussed a regional stockpiling agreement for the group of Southeast Asian countries but no binding treaty has been ratified by the group's member countries.[3] To date, the IEA remains the sole multilateral agency with an oil emergency agreement among its members.

6.2.2 The 'Joint Oil Stockpiling' and Strategic Petroleum Reserves (SPR)

An early agreement by Statoil with Korea in 1999 was probably the first actual example of a joint oil stockpiling agreement between a net crude exporting country and a net importer. According to the state-owned Korea National Oil (KNOC), Statoil payed $ 8.6 million to stockpile 8 million barrels of North Sea oil at its Yeosu and Ulsan storage plants.[4] Under the agreement, Statoil delivered the oil over a three-year period, beginning July 1, 1999. KNOC retained the right in this agreement to have a 'pre-emptive' choice to buy the stored oil in an 'emergency'. According to press reports, the agreement was the first of what Korea hoped would be several similar arrangements with crude suppliers including those in the Middle East aimed at increasing its SPR volumes. Since 1999, there have been a number of similar joint oil stockpiling arrangements between leading Middle East National Oil Companies (ME NOCs) and the large Northeast Asian (NEA) oil importers, specifically Japan and South Korea. News reports over the past decade have also noted the high level talks between Chinese energy officials and Middle East oil producers regarding similar joint oil stockpiling arrangements but these have not yet led to fruition.

For Japan and South Korea, among the world's largest oil importers and as members of the OECD/IEA, the question of building up and maintaining their SPR has long been part of their energy policy. The emergence of China, and more recently India, as very large Asian net crude oil importers has been accompanied with ambitious SPR plans as part of their national defence strategies. In the context of heightened concern over energy security as the Middle East region's turmoil continues

---

[3] The ASEAN Petroleum Security Agreement was signed by the member countries in March 2009 but not ratified by all; the agreement in any case calls for member countries to "help" other members in case of an oil emergency on a "best endeavour" basis. Accessed at http://www.jus.uio.no/english/services/library/treaties/09/9-06/asean_petroleum_security.xml.

[4] Alexander's Oil and Gas Connections, "Statoil is stockpiling North Sea oil in Korea", June 24, 1999. Accessed at http://www.gasandoil.com/news/south_east_asia/108376c212b466a62d57ef2a2800d464.

unabated after the Arab Spring erupted in December 2010, the potential gains to trade presented by joint oil stockpiling agreements have become of increasing interest to the NOCs of both regions. To the extent that ME crude oil stored in host country facilities enhances the host country's definition of SPR (despite the ME NOC retaining title until the event of an oil supply emergency), there are potential gains to trade. The carrying cost to the ME NOC is a fraction of the cost that host country would bear if it were to buy the crude up-front for its SPR. On the other hand, the availability of storage facilities close to destination markets provides an oil producer significant advantages: it offers logistical flexibility and the ability to supply oil cargoes on a prompt basis and deliveries can be made within days rather than the three weeks or more it takes to transport oil from the Arabian Gulf to Northeast Asia.

From the adoption of formula pricing in 1987 through the extended commodity boom and high oil prices period since 2002 (ending emphatically in the second half of 2014), the focus of oil producers has been on maximizing long term contracts (within the OPEC or country quota targets if any) with standard pricing terms for large buyers who would pick up FOB Arabian Gulf cargoes in large crude carriers. Their customers in Asia are typically the large NOCs or privately-owned conglomerates with their own shipping arms. Joint oil stockpiling agreements were seen by the ME NOCs as advantageous logistical investments which provided added flexibility to serve regular clients in Asia. However, in the context of low oil prices after the second half 2014 price collapse, joint oil stockpiling agreements have regained significant attention, although this time with different bargaining dynamics between the ME exporters and NEA importers. The new environment in oil markets has led to increased competition in the Asian crude oil market and Asian buyers have been adding greater weight to spot markets in their crude oil purchase portfolios. The increased use of spot markets by Asian importers and the willingness to have a greater percentage of their crude purchases via spot rather than term deals have led even the most conservative ME NOCs to engage in spot market sales albeit intermittently. The ME NOCs who have long preferred to sell their oil under long term crude oil sales agreements (COSA) have begun to engage opportunistically in spot market sales in order to protect or grow their market share while minimizing price discounts in their formula pricing.

As the ME NOCs see the need to engage in spot markets to access new market niches in a context of heightened competition, the commercial options provided by the lease of storage facilities in NEA markets have gained in importance. Even though it is far more efficient to move crude in large crude carriers direct to the delivery ports of the large NEA NOC refining facilities, reaching smaller customers located at or near ports that cannot handle large vessels (breaking bulk) has become an important option available to ME NOC trading practices. The intermittent engagement in spot sales by the ME NOCs can be seen as attempts to convert new customers into clients with long term COSAs. It is hard to imagine the ME NOCs having any intention to "cannibalize" their own term contract COSAs that account for the vast majority of crude oil exports with spot sales in weak markets.

The case for SPRs in enhancing energy security remains much debated in the literature. Nevertheless, governments of the large Asian importers such as India and China are going to go ahead and build SPRs. Oil supply security is high on the national agendas of these countries despite the uncertainties related to the economic benefits of building and maintaining large SPRs which impose significant financial costs on these countries. The fact that a storage facility can be used for commercial purposes by the owner of the stored crude oil while simultaneously being credibly committed to an enhancement of the host country's SPR program provides the basis for mutual gains between the country hosting the storage facility and the owner of the stored crude oil. Unlike international investments in oil refining and marketing (R&M) by the NOCs, where returns may have been at best modest, the storing of crude oil in key destination markets such as the NEA countries may prove to be significantly cheaper and more effective in the marketing of ME crude oil. Joint oil stockpiling agreements could become a more common and important mode of business cooperation with mutual gains for the ME NOCs and their partner NEA host countries.

6.2.3 The IEA Emergency Agreement: Governance and Performance

The efficacy of oil stocks as a policy tool depends not only on the nature of the instrument but also on how it is used. The focus of much of the applied economics literature has been on modeling the link between oil price shocks and economic activity, and the role oil stock releases can or should play on alleviating such oil price shocks. However, the institutional and governance aspects of the IEA's oil emergency management program and of the US' SPR have also received significant attention in research and policy circles.

The IEA was founded in 1974, in the immediate aftermath of the 1973 Arab oil embargo, to help OECD members coordinate a collective response to major disruptions in the supply of oil. Outside of the OECD/IEA agreement on oil emergencies, there are no other institutional mechanisms in the world for coordinated government responses to oil supply disruption. Oil stock obligations for its member countries and emergency response to oil supply disruptions have been core missions of the International Energy Agency since its founding. To gain from the benefits of collective action to such immediate threats to oil supply, the IEA legally requires each member country to have oil stock levels that equate to no less than ninety days of net imports.[5] The obligation is based on net imports of oil, including crude oil and refined products. The 90-day commitment of each IEA member country is based on an average of daily net imports of the previous calendar year. This commitment can be met through stocks held exclusively for emergency purposes and stocks held for commercial or operational use, including stocks held at refineries, at port facilities, and in tankers.

---

[5] See International Energy Agency (IEA), "Topic: Oil Stocks" http://www.iea.org/topics/oil/oilsto cks/ .

6.2.3.1 IEA Administrative Structure and Constraints to Stock Release Consensus

According to the IEA, "by temporarily replacing disrupted supplies, the action is intended to help oil markets re-establish the supply/demand balance at a lower price level than would otherwise have been the case".[6] If any of the IEA's 29 member countries experience a drop in crude oil supply exceeding 7%, then other members are obligated to share. If and when an IEA analysis were to identify a significant supply disruption "or the likelihood of one in the very near future", the Executive Director would inform member countries through the Governing Board. The Board is made up of representatives of all 29 member countries, and in the case of a "significant supply disruption", the Executive Director would specify whether or not activation of emergency response measures is desirable. If action is recommended, the Executive Director would suggest the amount of oil-equivalent stocks should be made available to the market. Each country's share in the action is based on its share of total IEA oil consumption. The agency asserts that "it takes most member countries two to seven days to implement the necessary approvals for the release, after which actual physical delivery to markets can take as little as one day or as long as three weeks, depending on the emergency stocks structure".[7]

There are thus three levels of administrative strata governing IEA action in ordering a release of stocks and in coordinating emergency oil sharing: the IEA Secretariat, the Management Committee (made up of representatives of member countries) and the Governing Board (consisting of oil or energy ministers of member countries). There is a complicated distribution of voting rights, with at least 14 member countries (out of 28)[8] needed to vote in favour of activation.[9] And, within negotiating rooms, it can be reasonably assumed that US concurrence would be a requirement given its dominating position as both a large crude oil producer and as the stockholder of the largest single SPR in the world. Countries such as Germany, France, Japan and the UK also have large voting weights, and most likely could block consensus on any activation decision.

The description of how the IEA should work in theory is at variance with actual accounts of IEA actions related to oil disruption emergencies. Blake Clayton (2012) describes the behind-the-scenes negotiations and bureaucratic hurdles within the IEA to activate the emergency response in 2011 with the loss of Libya's oil exports from the market.[10] His account indicates the extent of the inherent bargaining and coordination problems within the IEA on joint action.

---

[6]See IEA, "How does the IEA respond to energy security emergencies?", accessed at https://www.iea.org/topics/energysecurity/subtopics/energy_security_emergency_response/.

[7]Ibid.

[8]In 2011, there were 28 members; the 29th member Estonia joined in 2014 (see https://www.iea.org/aboutus/faqs/membership/).

[9]Bohi and Toman [1].

[10]Clayton, B. (2012). Lessons Learned From the 2011 Strategic Petroleum Reserve Release. http://www.cfr.org/world/lessons-learned-2011-strategic-petroleum-reserve-release/p28953. Accessed August 22, 2016.

The IEA announced plans on June 23, 2011, to coordinate the release of emergency oil stockpiles to offset the loss of crude oil production in Libya. Over the previous 6 months or so, oil prices had jumped more than 20%, as political upheaval in Libya had prevented oil exports from loading. Policymakers feared that high oil prices would subvert a nascent global economic recovery, in the aftermath of the 2009 financial crisis. In the event, twelve IEA member countries released around sixty million barrels of crude oil, diesel and gasoline.[11] The "Libya collective action" release took place from July 23, 2011 to September 15, 2011.[12] However, it was as early as March 2011 that the US officials began lobbying their IEA peers for a release. In other words, it took about four months for the IEA to reach a decision. According to Clayton (2012).

> The Obama administration's early attempts at persuasion were met with "nothing but resistance." By late April, talks among the twenty-eight IEA nations had begun. On May 6, President Barack Obama called King Abdullah of Saudi Arabia and Kuwaiti Emir Sheikh Sabah al-Ahmad al-Sabah to discuss a possible release. The president then sent a secret delegation of senior administration officials to Saudi Arabia, the United Arab Emirates (UAE), and Kuwait. By May 19, after a meeting of the IEA's governing board, international buy-in for a release was strong enough for the agency to publicly announce that member nations were ready to use "all tools" at their disposal to settle the market. Later that month, President Obama pressed his peers at a G8 summit in France to take joint action. After the OPEC meeting in June ended without an agreement to raise production quotas, IEA member countries made a final decision to intervene, announcing their intention two weeks later. (pp. 12–13).

Not only did getting a consensus take time but also internal dissensions among negotiators were leaked to the press.[13] Reporters cited anonymous official sources as stating that France, Italy and Germany were already hesitant with the first release announced by the IEA, and that these top European holders of SPR stocks were opposed to any talk of a 2nd release. This was despite the IEA having announced that its governing board would "review the impact of [its] coordinated action and decide on possible future steps" within thirty days" which suggested that the Board was ready to instruct a 2nd release if required. What oil analysts thought was a clear signal by the IEA to squash further speculative activity with the threat of further releases "as required" turned out to be followed by press leaks showing that key IEA members were in fact disunited and that there was little likelihood of a 2nd release if prices continued in an upward trajectory. As Clayton (2012) concluded, "Any power the IEA may have to tamp down short-term oil prices by threatening to draw down emergency stocks [was] undercut by the appearance of divisions among IEA member countries.".

---

[11]"IEA Makes 60 million Barrels of Oil available to Market to Offset Libyan Disruption," International Energy Agency press release, June 23, 2011.

[12]It was the third time in its nearly thirty-year history that the IEA activated a coordinated release; the United States has unilaterally released strategic stocks on several occasions for raising revenue or countering refined product price spikes due to bad weather.

[13]See for instance, Muriel Boselli, "Exclusive: Germany, Italy May Resist Second IEA Oil Release," Reuters, July 15, 2011; Javier Blas, "Italian and German Resistance on IEA Release Sends Oil Higher," Financial Times, July 20, 2011.

Perhaps most fundamental to the potential shortcomings of the IEA's oil emergency program are the problems of public goods provision and the incentives to free-ride facing its member countries. Given the intrinsic fungibility of oil in today's integrated world oil markets, the release of oil stocks anywhere affects supply everywhere; in other words, an oil stockpile is a global public good.[14] As any net oil-importing country's decision to release oil stockpiles will lead it to lower oil imports than would otherwise have been the case, this would lead to greater oil supply availability to other importers. Yet each country that builds and maintains oil stockpiles does so at its own costs. Hence, each country incurs the costs of building and maintaining an oil stockpile while international externalities of a global oil market (where traded crude oil is efficiently arbitraged and priced according to the quality of the crude oil, its location, and time of delivery) mean that the release of oil stocks allows all other countries to also benefit from the lower priced crude oil resulting from the increased supply. Given the positive global externalities of an oil stock release, there would therefore be a natural reluctance to build large oil reserves in the first place unless other strategic policy objectives such as energy security were given higher priority.

Given the international public goods aspect of oil stockpiles, the IEA agreement was a result of each member country negotiating for its "fair share" of the burden in which each had an incentive to overstate its contribution and to free ride on the efforts of other members. Inflating a contribution by including private working inventories as part of the strategic reserves was part of the negotiating strategies of its members. Reflecting the frictions in bargaining for equitable burdens in the provision of a global public good, the US Energy Secretary warned other IEA members that the US might not share its stocks with the group if others drew heavily on their own stocks to avoid purchasing oil at higher prices.[15] There are also differences in approach between its European members who see demand constraint as the first priority in facing oil emergencies, and stock release only as a second, and the US which sees SPR as the first step in policy response.

Given that participants to an international alliance are sovereign nation-states, and given the absence of a supranational judicial institution with enforcement powers, the incentives to free ride would be strong for all participants.[16] Given free ride incentives, countries will see advantages in being the last to commit to policy targets,

---

[14]Hogan [2].

[15]According to the New York Times, June 16, 1981, "Secretary of Energy James B. Edwards warned other nations in the International Energy Agency that the United States might not share oil with them during a shortage if they draw heavily upon stockpiles now to avoid buying while the dollar is strong." This example is cited by Hogan [2].

[16]The free rider problem is defined as the difficulty of undertaking group efforts in which all individuals (or individual nations) in the group share in the benefits from the effort regardless of how much (or little) each has contributed to it, because each selfishly rational individual in the group tends to refuse to contribute to the effort, and instead each tends to hope that others in the group will contribute to the effort.

hence risking coordination failure in negotiating agreements.[17] In a relatively large group (such as the OECD), the incentives to free ride make the existence of a tightly-defined universal agreement with credible commitments by all member participants, of net benefit to all countries and in stable equilibrium, rather unlikely.

The IEA oil sharing agreement, in reflecting the complexity of strategic interactions within any alliance of sovereign states providing global public goods, has complex formulas to calculate the burden sharing program. Nevertheless, it is straightforward in its basics: if disruption occurs to the supply of oil to any country beyond a threshold (of 7%) of pre-disruption supply, then those member countries affected more than proportionately relative to the pre-disruption period are entitled in principle to transfers from less affected members.[18] The application of this principle would thus cause the burden to fall more heavily on crude oil-producing members such as the US, UK, Australia and Canada than other countries in the grouping which are almost wholly reliant on imports.[19] In order that the oil-sharing plan does not lead to unintended wealth transfers among its members during an emergency, oil sharing is to occur "at prices prevailing on comparable international transactions". Only under market prices could government authorities of net donor countries expect private oil companies to participate in the oil-sharing program. Only by agreeing to oil sharing under market prices could governments claim to their various constituencies that the stockpiling program did not impose a differential burden on them relative to their fellow member countries that were recipients of oil transfers.

But as observed by Bohi and Toman [1], this leads to a conundrum in that, if the IEA emergency sharing mechanism was to emulate allocations on the basis of market prices, then how would this appreciably differ from the allocation that would occur in any case as a result of autonomous market forces? If contemporary markets are highly competitive, and if markets adjust rapidly to allocate supplies during periods of supply disruption according to willingness to pay, then any oil sharing plan based on transfers at market price would differ little from free market oil supply allocations in any case—why have the oil sharing plan in the first place? "Without market pricing, the oil sharing plan seems highly unlikely to be viable. On the other hand, given recent changes in the structure and performance of the oil market, the sharing plan with market pricing seems to offer little (if any) discernible gain to IEA members over the market outcome".[20]

A case may be made that if the IEA oil-sharing plan were perceived by its members to be robust and credible, then such an agreement would serve to the members' collective benefit by avoiding panic buying and oil price spirals during supply disruptions. Transactions costs that occur in disrupted markets, such as the necessity to rapidly

---

[17]Coordination failure in a game-theoretic context is a state of affairs in which agents' inability to coordinate their behaviour (choices) leads to an equilibrium outcome that leaves all agents worse off than in an alternative situation that is also an equilibrium. This can occur due to lack of information, strategic miscalculation in negotiating strategies, or differing expectations.

[18]Bohi and Toman [1].

[19]Norway is a not party to the sharing agreement.

[20]Bohi and Toman [1].

switch to new sources of oil supply and arrange new transportation arrangements, and the need to test and handle different grades of crude oil that might not be efficiently refined in less complex refineries can lead to escalating willingness to pay by the most vulnerable participants. Panic buying will be amplified as long term contracts are reneged by oil suppliers who can command higher premiums in spot markets which set the price of marginal barrels offered for prompt sale.

6.2.3.2 IEA Cooperation with the Large Non-OECD Asian Oil Importers

National security concerns of governments of the large Asian oil importing countries such as India and China suggest that these governments are committed to building up their SPRs. Energy security issues are not just within the jurisdiction of each country's energy and trade ministries but are subjects of primary interest to both defence and foreign ministry agendas as well. Despite the ambiguity apparent in empirical studies of the costs and benefits of SPRs (as covered in Annex 1), it is clear that China, India and other significant Asian crude oil importers will follow through on all or at least some of their announced SPR plans.

China has now emerged as one of the world's largest holders of SPRs in the world, after the US and Japan. In recent years, oil purchases by the Chinese state-owned oil companies have become a significant factor in the global market. China's intensified efforts to fill their newly built SPR facilities since 2012 increased the country's crude oil imports and is one of the factors analysts identify as having contributed to the escalation in oil prices in that period. Little or no regular data is available on China's inventories of crude oil and refined products and hence this precludes definitive statements.

Nevertheless, according to some reports it was widely believed by oil market traders and observers that China was often accounting for anywhere between a quarter to half a million barrels per day during the trading year to fill up their stockpiles.[21] The scale of China's SPR build-up was such that it was of real concern to IEA officials that their plans in 2011 to implement an oil stock release would be simply negated by China's buying of crude oil to increase their SPR stock levels. An IEA stock draw countered by China's large volume build-up of its SPR would not only have neutralized any impact the IEA members would have hoped to achieve in global oil markets, but would have been detrimental to the credibility of the international institution in handling any future oil supply emergency. While details of the liaison talks between IEA and Chinese officials that occurred prior to the 2011 release are not publically accessible, China officials were quoted as supportive of the IEA announcement of the stock release.[22]

---

[21] Javier Blas, "Fears Over Conflict Fueling Oil Hoarding," Financial Times, March 22, 2012.

[22] Clayton, B. (2012). Lessons Learned From the 2011 Strategic Petroleum Reserve Release. http://www.cfr.org/world/lessons-learned-2011-strategic-petroleum-reserve-release/p28953. Accessed August 22, 2016.

It is clear that one of the IEA's highest priorities would be to be able to have high-level coordination with Chinese officials as well as other large Asian importers such as India to make emergency stock release plans viable. As non-OECD countries increasingly dominate global oil demand growth, this priority of the IEA for some sort of global coordination with non-OECD members in the event of oil supply disruption will only grow more critical. Given the common interest in avoiding market disruptions and oil price spikes among the large net-oil importing countries, there is a strong case for the IEA and the leading Asian oil consumers to attempt to coordinate stock releases, or at least to credibly committing to avoid filling their SPR reserves during oil supply crisis episodes. As a global public good, such coordination would be critical for stock release actions to attenuate oil price shocks. Nevertheless, as we have seen, while the aims of global cooperation are laudable, the actual implementation of coordinated oil stock releases are fraught with problems of negotiations and bargaining among members of the IEA, let alone among a larger group comprising both IEA and large non-OECD consumers such as China and India. While talks between IEA officials and the large Asian oil importers will continue, it is too early to say whether credible international agreements on coordinated oil stockpile will be achieved in the near future.

6.3 Existing and Proposed Joint Oil Stockpiling Agreements

In 2005, David Nissen and David Knapp of the Energy Intelligence Group described "forward commercial storage" as an arrangement whereby OPEC producers could utilize storage facilities located in consuming regions as part of their normal commercial operations; the stored oil would remain under the producer's ownership but with priority purchase rights possessed by the consuming country in case of an oil disruption crisis.[23] According to the proponents of this "forward commercial storage", such joint stockpiling arrangements would benefit the consuming country hosting the storage facility by enhancing its SPR availability while it would signal the producing country's standing as a "preferred and secure" supplier of crude oil to its large customers in Northeast Asia. It should be assumed that a joint stockpiling agreement would have a clause stipulating that the owner of the crude (i.e. the ME exporter) should assure a certain level of crude in the tanks at any given time. Were this clause not stipulated, the host country would face the real risk of empty storage tanks during a supply emergency (Table 6.1).

---

[23]Nissen, D. and Knapp, D. (2005). "Oil Market Reliability: A Commercial Proposal," Geopolitics of Energy.

Table 6.1 Joint oil stockpiling agreements between Middle East producers and Asian consumers as of 2016

Year of initial deal	Middle Eastern country	Asian country	Location of stockpile	Current volume (in million barrels of stored crude oil)
2006	Kuwait	South Korea	n/a	2
2009	UAE	Japan	Kiire	6.3
2010	Saudi Arabia	Japan	Okinawa	6.3
2012	UAE	South Korea	Yeosu	6
2016*	UAE	India	Mangalore	6
2016*	Iran	South Korea	Seosan	2

*Agreement yet to be finalized. *Source* various (see footnotes)

6.3.1 Joint Oil Stockpiling in South Korea

The first Middle East—Northeast Asia joint stockpiling deal was concluded in 2006 between Kuwait and Korea, and involved a 2 million barrels joint crude oil stockpile at KNOC facilities in South Korea.[24] In exchange for storing Kuwaiti oil and allowing KPC to trade from their depot in Korea, the host country receives a lease fee and is able to access those 2 million barrels on a primary basis within 90 days of it requesting should an emergency take place.[25] Since the deal was concluded in 2006, the two countries have been in talks about adding two more storage terminals under the same conditions.[26] Prior to the agreement with Kuwait, Korea also concluded similar deals with a variety of other companies, such as Algeria's Sonatrach, Norway's Statoil, Chinaoil, Shell, Total and Western traders such as Glencore and Trafigura.[27] All these agreements share the same basic principles: the exporting country or company remains the owner of the oil and can freely trade its crude in the region from the storage facility in exchange for giving Korea pre-emptive rights to buy the oil in times of emergency.[28] As part of its International Joint Stockpile (IJS) Project, which was

---

[24]KNOC (2006). Joint Stockpiling with Kuwait. http://www.knoc.co.kr/ENG/sub04/sub04_1_5.jsp. Accessed August 17, 2016.

[25]Korea Joongang Daily (2006). Kuwait will rent storage for 2 million barrels here. http://koreaj oongangdaily.joins.com/news/article/Article.aspx?aid=2836387. Accessed August 17, 2016.

[26]Al Arabiya (2013). Kuwait, South Korea discuss oil refinery, future projects. http://english.alarab iya.net/en/business/energy/2013/09/14/Kuwait-South-Korea-discuss-oil-refinery-future-projects.html. Accessed August 17, 2016.

[27]Reuters (2009). Korea aims for 40 mln bbls joint stockpiling by '10. http://fr.reuters.com/article/idUKSEO1121920090521. Accessed August 17, 2016.

[28]SHANA (2006). S. Korea to Triple Joint Oil Stockpiling with Algeria. http://www.shana.ir/en/new sagency/83381/S-Korea-to-Triple-Joint-Oil-Stockpiling-with-Algeria. Accessed August 17, 2016.

launched back in 1999, South Korea reserves around 40 million of its total 146 million barrels of storage capacity for leases to oil producers, majors, investment banks, etc.[29]

Korea signed another joint oil stockpiling deal with the UAE's ADNOC in 2012.[30] ADNOC agreed with KNOC to lease 6 million barrels of crude in Korea's oil storage depot at Yeosu, which Korea is trying to develop as a regional oil hub. Contrary to the stockpiling deal with Kuwait, Korea agreed to forego leasing fees in exchange for participation rights in developing three oil fields in Abu Dhabi.[31] The agreement was reached as part of high-levels talks between the South Korean President and the Crown Prince of Abu Dhabi. In 2016, Iran and South Korea, following the lifting of sanctions, have agreed to expand cooperation on oil and gas, specifically mentioning joint stockpiling of Iranian oil in Korea.[32] It is believed that the future stockpile will consist of 2 million barrels of crude and condensates and will be located in Seosan.[33]

6.3.2   Joint Oil Stockpiling in Japan

Japan has concluded similar deals with Middle Eastern producers. In 2009, JX Nippon agreed with ADNOC to establish a joint oil stockpile at the Kiire oil terminal at Kagoshima.[34] The agreement has been renewed twice since (in 2012 and 2014) and total stored volumes by ADNOC in Kiire have grown to 6.3 million barrels.[35] Only one year after the deal with ADNOC, Japan's JOGMEC, the agency responsible for managing the country's strategic storage, signed a similar deal with Saudi Aramco.[36] In exchange for providing free storage capacity of 3.8 million barrels to Saudi Aramco on the island of Okinawa, Japan receives priority to purchase crude from that stockpile

---

[29]Gulf News (2012). Adnoc to store crude in S. Korean facility for 3 years. http://gulfnews.com/business/sectors/energy/adnoc-to-store-crude-in-s-korean-facility-for-3-years-1.1108746.   Accessed August 17, 2016.

[30]Gulf News (2012). Adnoc to store crude in S. Korean facility for 3 years. http://gulfnews.com/business/sectors/energy/adnoc-to-store-crude-in-s-korean-facility-for-3-years-1.1108746.   Accessed August 17, 2016.

[31]Platts (2013). First UAE crude shipment for joint storage in S Korea to arrive Wednesday. http://www.platts.com/latest-news/oil/seoul/first-uae-crude-shipment-for-joint-storage-in-27438119. Accessed August 17, 2016.

[32]Koreanet (2016). Korea-Iran joint statement supports denuclearization, peaceful unification. http://www.korea.net/NewsFocus/Policies/view?articleId=135939. Accessed August 17, 2016.

[33]Platts (2016). South Korea, Iran in talks over 2 million barrel joint crude oil storage deal. http://www.platts.com/latest-news/oil/seoul/south-korea-iran-in-talks-over-2-million-barrel-26431823. Accessed August 17, 2016.

[34]JX Nippon (2009). Agreement Reached with Abu Dhabi National Oil Company for Crude Oil Reserves. http://www.noe.jx-group.co.jp/english/press/noc/2009/e71_enpr_091214.html. Accessed August 17, 2016.

[35]RIM (2014). ADNOC agrees to more crude oil storage in Japan. https://eng.rim-intelligence.co.jp/default/news/print-article/id/119423. Accessed August 17, 2016.

[36]The National (2010). Japan agrees to store Saudi crude. http://www.thenational.ae/business/energy/japan-agrees-to-store-saudi-crude. Accessed August 17, 2016.

in the event of an oil supply shortage.[37] This contract has since been extended and storage capacity was increased in 2013 to 6.3 million barrels.[38] By storing oil in Okinawa, Saudi Aramco wants to obtain easier access to the greater East Asian market, China in particular. By then, it had already given up on leasing storage capacity in the Caribbean amid slowing exports to the US.[39]

6.3.3 Joint Oil Stockpiling in India

In 2016, ADNOC proposed to store oil in India's maiden strategic storage in Mangalore.[40] Under the proposed agreement, ADNOC would occupy 6 out of the storage facility's total capacity of 12 million barrels. Contrary to local media reports, this oil is not given to India "for free"[41]; rather the agreement would operate on similar terms to the other joint stockpiling deals. ADNOC would be able to commercially trade its crude from the storage and in exchange India will be able to access that oil on a preferential basis in times of emergency at prevailing market prices. India is also looking at inviting other exporting NOCs from the Middle East such as Saudi Aramco, KPC and Qatar Petroleum to store oil at underground caverns in Visakhapatnam, Mangalore and Padur along the country's west coast.[42,43] In order to achieve this, India will first need to liberalize its policy so that the producing country NOCs would be able to export their oil from storage depots in India to third countries if it was commercial profitable to do so. At the moment, crude oil stored in India is barred from export.[44]

---

[37]METI (2010). Japan and Saudi Arabia Signed a Renewal Contract for the Japan-Saudi Arabia Joint Petroleum Stockpiling Base Project. http://www.meti.go.jp/english/press/2013/1217_01.html. Accessed August 17, 2016.

[38]Saudi Aramco (2014). Okinawa storage agreement renewed. http://www.saudiaramco.com/en/home/news-media/news/okinawa-storage-agreement-renewed.html. Accessed August 17, 2016.

[39]Argus (2010). Japan to store Saudi crude. http://www.argusmedia.com/pages/NewsBody.aspx?id=711205&menu=yes. Accessed August 17, 2016.

[40]Hindustan Times (2016). Store our oil and take 2/3rd for free: UAE's offer to India. http://www.hindustantimes.com/business/store-our-oil-and-take-2-3rd-for-free-uae-s-offer-to-india/story-fiSZwbJh6abWWM3NfpEveI.html. Accessed August 17, 2016.

[41]Ibid.

[42]First Post (2016). National oil firms in Middle East keen to hire storage in India. http://www.firstpost.com/business/national-oil-firms-in-middle-east-keen-to-hire-storage-in-india-2420034.html. Accessed August 17, 2016.

[43]Energy Intelligence (2016). India Courts Qatar for Stockpile Plan. http://www.energyintel.com/pages/eig_article.aspx?mail=PA_TEXT_31_3629&DocId=926764&utm_campaign=website&utm_source=sendgrid.com&utm_medium=email. Accessed August 17, 2016.

[44]Reuters (2016). India's Mistake Over Crude Oil Exports: Oil Isn't Entirely Fungible. http://www.forbes.com/sites/timworstall/2016/05/08/indias-mistake-over-crude-oil-exports-oil-isnt-entirely-fungible/#20dfc1aa59bd. Accessed August 17, 2016.

6.3.4   Joint Oil Stockpiling Negotiations in China

Although China has not yet formalized any joint oil stockpiling deals, it has been involved in negotiations from at least a decade ago. In 2006, for instance, Chinese president Hu Jintao's visit to Saudi Arabia included talks about a proposal for China to host Saudi crude oil in Chinese storage facilities along the lines of a joint stockpile arrangement.[45] The agreement, however, failed to materialize and Saudi Aramco chose to stockpile its crude in Okinawa instead.[46] During President Xi Jinping's visit to Riyadh in 2016, the topic of joint stockpiling between Saudi Arabia and China was again discussed and agreed upon in principle as part of the two countries' bilateral cooperation plans involving energy.[47] Iran, meanwhile, has effectively leased storage capacity at Dalian, China since 2014[48], although it is not reported that this also includes a clause stating that China can access the oil on a first-refusal basis. Due to western sanctions affecting its oil exports which led to a shortage of storage capacity, Iran used the port at Dalian to make deliveries into China, India and South Korea. Most of these exports consisted of surplus NGLs, condensates and heavy oil.

6.4   Commercial and Strategic Benefits of Joint Oil Stockpiling

As an oil reserve model of joint operation, risk sharing and benefit sharing, joint oil stockpiling can bring benefits to both the oil exporting countries and the oil importing parties.

6.4.1   Benefits for the Middle East

Joint stockpiling of crude oil in Asia can help Middle Eastern exporters satisfy security of demand concerns by defending and/or gaining market share: it allows them to better compete against other regional short haul crudes, it can function as a low-cost trading hub to serve other nearby markets, and it provides customers in Asia with a sense of "credible commitment" which Gulf exporters can use to invest in their image as reliable crude suppliers of choice.

---

[45]BBC (2006). Chinese leader ends Saudi visit. http://news.bbc.co.uk/2/hi/middle_east/493847 4.stm. Accessed August 17, 2016.

[46]Al-Tamimi [3].

[47]While no explicit reference is made to joint stockpiling in publically accessible sources, the authors were informed by a source within a Chinese national oil company that joint stockpiling was indeed discussed as part of bilateral cooperation between the two countries.

[48]Reuters (2014). Iran leases oil storage in China, ships crude to India from there. http://www.reu ters.com/article/us-iran-china-storage-idUSKCN0J40VI20141120. Accessed August 17, 2016.

6.4.1.1   Competition with Short-Haul Flows

Middle Eastern exporters are seeing their market share in Asia challenged because of the latter region's increased accessibility of non-traditional long- and short haul flows. Long haul flows include imports from Latin America and West Africa that were reoriented from the Atlantic basin, while Russia's ESPO crude provides Asian refiners with a nearby alternative. ESPO cargoes are attractive not only because they help Asian refiners in diversifying from their heavy dependence on Middle Eastern imports, but also because they ① are only 2–4 days away in terms of sailing distance and can be delivered on board smaller Aframax tankers, ② are generally sold on a spot basis, ③ have less sulphur content and are therefore easier to refine by less complex refineries and ④ can be hauled by rail to refineries that do not have access to pipelines.[49,50] Because of these characteristics, but predominantly because of its higher quality, ESPO usually fetches a significant premium over the Dubai benchmark.

The characteristics of Russian Pacific crude are proving especially attractive to Chinese customers, the smaller so-called "teapots" operated by independents in particular. Since July 2015, these teapot refineries have been granted licenses and quotas to import crude oil by themselves without having to purchase their feedstock from China's NOCs.[51] Teapot refiners, which are now also allowed to export refined products, have been aggressively sourcing the most competitive barrels off spot markets and collectively account for 1.2 mbpd, or 15% of China's total crude imports. Beijing's relaxation of import rules for independent refineries—as well as the expansion of the Skovorodino-Mohe pipeline into China—has contributed to Russia's rise as China's largest import source, overtaking Saudi Arabia.[52] In April 2016, Russia exported 1.17 mbpd to China—up 52.4 percent year-on-year, while Saudi exports to China declined by 21.8%.[53] ESPO crude will, however, most likely not be able to fundamentally challenge Middle Eastern imports as base load feedstock in Asia, because of two 'handicaps': limited liquidity and a late release of shipping schedules.[54] Rival Middle Eastern and African crudes are usually sold two or three months before the loading date, while ESPO cargoes are sold only six weeks before the loading date—at a time when Asian refineries have already satisfied the bulk of

---

[49]Bloomberg (2015). Oil Sails From Russia to Asia Faster on Smaller Ships. http://www.bloomb erg.com/news/articles/2015-02-26/oil-sails-from-russia-to-asia-faster-on-smaller-ships. Accessed August 17, 2016.

[50]Energy Intelligence (2016). China's Oil Demand Disconnect Widens.

[51]Wall Street Journal (2016). 'Teapot' Refineries Shore Up China's Demand for Crude. http://www. wsj.com/articles/teapot-refineries-shore-up-chinas-demand-for-crude-1464616123.   Accessed August 17, 2016.

[52]Bloomberg (2015). Russia Races Past Saudi Arabia in Tussle for Chinese Oil Market. http:// www.bloomberg.com/news/articles/2015-10-21/russia-races-past-saudi-arabia-in-tussle-for-chi nese-oil-market. Accessed August 17, 2016.

[53]Energy Intelligence (2016). China's Oil Demand Disconnect Widens.

[54]Reuters (2015). Russia's ESPO Blend crude still struggles in Asia-Pacific. http://www.reuters. com/article/us-espo-sales-idUSKBN0UD1LE20151230. Accessed August 17, 2016.

their demand. As a result, the number of ESPO buyers has fallen and deliveries are now mainly concentrated to China and Japan. Russia is actively looking at eliciting term contract customers in the Far East.[55]

Joint stockpiling in Asia can be an effective way for Middle Eastern exporters to better compete against these short haul flows. Crude in leased storage facilities in Asia has the following competitive advantages:

(1)   Shorter voyage times

Taking Saudi Aramco's leased storage at Okinawa in the East China Sea as an example, we can see that cargoes need only a fraction of time to arrive in Northeast Asian refining centres as compared to their usual loading location in the Gulf. A VLCC travelling at a speed at 10 knots (nautical miles per hour) from Ras Tanura arrives in China (Qingdao), Japan (Yokohama) and Korea (Yeosu) in 26 to 27 days.[56] The same vessel can deliver a cargo from Okinawa to the same ports in China, Japan and Korea in 2 to 4 days. That is a significant reduction in travel time and corresponds almost exactly with Russian shipment times from Kozmino to Northeast Asia. Shorter voyage times evidently represent substantial savings in shipping and insurance costs for the customer. It should be noted, however, that supplying crude oil from Okinawa involves double handling and cargoes sold ex-Okinawa will incorporate freight costs for moving the crude from the Arabian Gulf in the first place (Table 6.2).

(2)   Spot pricing

Middle Eastern NOCs have been reported to have sold cargoes of crude on the spot market intermittently. This is a radical departure for the NOCs' preference for term contracts. These one-off sales are being experimented with by Gulf exporters as customers in the Far East are increasingly willing to consider purchasing cargoes in the spot market. China's teapot refineries, located mainly in the Shandong province, are a good example of commercial entities who are new to the global oil market and see spot purchases as a way to test the market value of crudes and compare the reliability of competing exporters. Gulf NOCs can most easily reach these new customers by selling them spot cargoes from their joint storage facilities in Asia. Saudi Aramco, for example, in 2016 sold a cargo of crude from its Okinawa storage depot to a Chinese independent refiner, Chambroad Petrochemical, on a spot basis.[57] Saudi Aramco has reportedly priced this cargo on a FOB Okinawa basis, instead of quoting an official selling price. Saudi Aramco is purported by a source to have sold the cargo at a discount to the Dubai benchmark, rather than at a "prompt" premium.[58] Saudi

---

[55]Platts (2016). Indonesia seeks term ESPO contract.

[56]Sea Distances website. www.sea-distances.org.

[57]Platts (2016). First cargo of Saudi crude sold to independent refiner arrives in China. http://www.platts.com/latest-news/oil/singapore/first-cargo-of-saudi-crude-sold-to-independent-21502265. Accessed August 21, 2016.

[58]Forbes (2016). Saudi Russia Fight For China Market Make Oil Price A Sham. http://www.forbes.com/sites/kenrapoza/2016/05/01/saudi-russia-fight-for-china-market-make-oil-price-a-sham/#4c20dcfe111e. Accessed August 22, 2016.

Table 6.2 Shipping distances between major ports, expressed in days

	China (Qingdao)	Japan (Yokohama)	Korea (Yeosu)
Gulf			
Saudi Arabia (Ras Tanura)	26	27	26
Kuwait (Mina Al-Ahmadi)	26	28	26
UAE (Jebel Dhanna)	25	27	25
Iraq (Basrah)	26	28	26
Iran (Kharg Island)	25	27	26
Oman (Mina Al-Fahal)	23	25	23
Qatar (Halul Island)	25	26	25
West Africa			
Nigeria (Qua Iboe)	43	45	43
Angola (Cabinda)	40	42	40
Americas			
Venezuela (Puerto Miranda)	39	35	37
Ecuador (Balao)	36	32	34
Mexico (Salina Cruz)	31	27	29
FSU			
Russia (Kozmino)	4	4	2
Okinawa	3	4	2

Source Sea Distances website. Based on a VLCC travelling at a speed of 10 knots and shortest possible route

Aramco had sold spot from Okinawa before, for example in 2012, when it shipped a cargo to Japanese refiner Cosmo Oil.[59] A discussion of spot price discovery in Northeast Asia is provided in Sect. 6.4.4.

---

[59]Reuters (2012). Japan's Cosmo Oil buys Saudi crude from Okinawa storage. http://www.reuters.com/article/saudi-crude-idUSL3E8FB4BN20120411. Accessed August 22, 2016.

(3) Volume flexibility

Oil from a leased storage depot can be delivered in smaller or custom-made quantities on board smaller vessels, which suits many refining centres and ports in Asia that only have limited offload capacity. Saudi Aramco's cargo to Chambroad Petrochemical, for example, consisted of 730,000 barrels loaded on an Aframax sized tanker.[60] Standard sized VLCCs travelling the route between the Gulf and Asia usually ship fixed volumes of two million barrels. This volume and contract flexibility is much wanted by financially and capacity restricted simple refineries in Asia, which is a major reason Arabian crude is now better able to directly compete with ESPO deliveries given that the latter ones are usually also shipped in smaller lots.

6.4.1.2 Creation of Low-Cost Trading Hubs

Crude oil from leased storage in a particular country is not necessarily sold by the exporter to that same host country. Instead the storage depot can emerge as a trading hub with cargoes being sold to a wide variety of customers in the region. Okinawa therefore can act as Saudi Aramco's "mini-Ras Tanura" conveniently located in the Northeast Asian region. ADNOC can similarly use Kiire as an Asian satellite of its main loading terminals in the Arabian Gulf. Tankers loading from joint stockpiling tanks mainly sail to Asian countries although Okinawa in the past has also been a source of oil cargoes heading to US West Coast customers. Location is key here, which can significantly reduce the exporters' trading risk. New players in the crude market, for example, such as the Chinese teapot refiners, often have unfamiliar credit profiles which bears a clear risk to the exporter. However, if a spot contract is reneged upon, it would be easier for the seller to reach alternative customers given shorter voyage times and smaller cargo volumes.[61]

Apart from minimizing trading risk, joint stockpiling incurs lower costs on the exporter. This is because in most bilateral storage agreements, the host country may cover the storage leasing costs either fully or to a large extent. Japan for example, is providing Saudi Aramco with free storage space in exchange for first drawing rights in times of emergency or unexpected supply shortages.[62] Japan likely agreed to this given that the Okinawa storage terminal was underutilized and represented a sunk cost. Storage capacity in Japan is generally available at competitive rates given the country's decreasing oil consumption and gradually declining refining capacity.[63] Similarly, ADNOC also does not pay a fee for leasing storage at the

---

[60] Platts (2016). Saudi Crude Set to Sail for Shandong From Japan.

[61] Platts (2016). Saudi Aramco Courts China's Independents.

[62] Reuters (2013). Japan agrees to extend Saudi Aramco crude storage deal. http://www.reuters.com/article/japan-saudi-crude-idUSL4N0FH1U620130711. Accessed August 18, 2016.

[63] The National (2010). Japan agrees to store Saudi crude. http://www.thenational.ae/business/energy/japan-agrees-to-store-saudi-crude. Accessed August 18, 2016.

Kiire oil terminal.[64] Korea also does not charge ADNOC a leasing fee in Yeosu, in exchange for participating rights in some of Abu Dhabi's oil fields.[65]

6.4.1.3 "Credible Commitments"

The Middle East has traditionally been Asia's supplier of choice owing to its relative proximity, reliability of term contracts and general crude quality which is appropriate to many of the Asian refineries built with Middle East sour crude as their ideal slate. Asian importers, therefore, have for a long time been dependent for a majority of their demand on Gulf crude—especially Japan and Korea which source over 80% of their imports from the Middle East.[66] China is less dependent on Middle East crude due to its large domestic production, pipeline connectivity to Russia and Kazakhstan and the fact that its simpler refineries often require higher-quality oil which predominantly comes from West Africa. As a result, Chinese imports of crude are significantly more diversified than Japan and Korea. China's current crude imports originate from the Middle East (52%), Africa (22%), FSU (13%) and the Americas (11%).[67]

Stockpiling substantial volumes of Middle Eastern crude near consuming centres in Asia can underscore that region's long-held image as a reliable supplier of crude oil to the world's fastest growing oil market. Committing assets close to the buyer can be seen as a risk-sharing strategy designed to safeguard commercial and strategic relationships. Joint stockpiling is a "credible commitment" in the words of economist Oliver Williamson.[68] By placing commercial oil in storage in Asia which can become part of the host' country's SPR in times of emergency or supply disruption, the Middle East is actively supporting alliances and promoting mutually beneficial exchanges with their Northeast Asian customers. As noted by Mitchell, "It is in the interest of oil-exporting countries and companies to demonstrate their commitments to importing markets by contribution to arrangements for securing supply in the event of a disruption".[69]

---

[64]Reuters (2014). Japan agrees to extend UAE crude storage deal. http://af.reuters.com/article/ene rgyOilNews/idAFL3N0T01TH20141110. Accessed August 18, 2016.

[65]Platts (2013). First UAE crude shipment for joint storage in S Korea to arrive Wednesday. http://www.platts.com/latest-news/oil/seoul/first-uae-crude-shipment-for-joint-storage-in-27438119. Accessed August 18, 2016.

[66]EIA (2014). Country profiles.

[67]EIA (2014). China country profile.

[68]See Williamson, O. (1983). Credible Commitments: Using Hostages to Support Exchange.

[69]John Mitchell, 2014, "Asia's Oil Supply: Risks and Pragmatic Remedies", Research Paper, Chatham House.

6.4.2   Benefits for Northeast Asia

By making it attractive to Middle Eastern exporters to stockpile crude close to their main refining and distribution centres, Asian importers perceive benefits in their energy security and commercial objectives. In reference to the Okinawa deal with Saudi Aramco, for example, METI stated that "this project will fortify the relationship between Japan and the oil-producing country, Saudi Arabia, as well as represent Japan's enhanced ability to respond to any emergency situation".[70] METI again stated after closing the joint stockpiling deal with ADNOC that "this project contributes to enhancing the relationship between Japan and Abu Dhabi, on which Japan depends for about 23% of its imports of crude oil, and also strengthens Japan's ability to respond to crises".[71]

6.4.2.1   Security of Supply and Strategic Petroleum Reserves

A crucial part of any joint stockpiling deal is that it allows the host country first or preferential access to the crude in storage in case there is an oil supply disruption. By having a joint oil stockpiling agreement with a crude oil producer, the host country would save on capital costs by not having to pay upfront for oil to fill its SPR. The hypothetical cost savings implicit in a joint oil stockpiling agreement is examined further in Sect. 6.4.3. Such potential cost savings are an important reason why joint stockpiling deals are seen as an attractive supplement to the unilateral filling of a national SPR. This is especially the case in China, as its national oil companies are reluctant to pay for SPR programs given that their shareholders do not want to finance a public good at their expense.[72] Building a national stockpile, it is argued by the NOCs, should be financed by the government. Currently, the NOCs are obliged by central planning authorities to stock up on oil reserves to ensure they hold a certain amount of barrels in storage beyond their own commercial requirements as a complement to China's SPR.[73,74]

Given that joint oil stockpiling agreements are confidential to the parties involved, it is unclear under what terms oil can be bought by the host country on a first access basis. An 'emergency' is likely defined as an unexpected loss of crude supplies

---

[70]METI (2013). Japan and Saudi Arabia Signed a Renewal Contract for the Japan-Saudi Arabia Joint Petroleum Stockpiling Base Project. http://www.meti.go.jp/english/press/2013/1217_01.html. Accessed August 18, 2016.

[71]METI (2014). Continuation of the Joint Oil Storage Project between Japan and Abu Dhabi. http://www.meti.go.jp/english/press/2014/1110_03.html. Accessed August 18, 2016.

[72]OIES (2016). The structure of China's oil industry: past trends and future prospects. https://www.oxfordenergy.org/wpcms/wp-content/uploads/2016/05/The-structure-of-Chinas-oil-industry-past-trends-and-future-prospects-WPM-66.pdf. Accessed August 17, 2016.

[73]Energy Intelligence (2016). Chinese NOCs Told to Ship Equity Oil Home.

[74]China SME (2016). As world's largest oil importer and key pricing power, China plans new system for oil stocks. http://www.sme.gov.cn/cms/news/100000/0000000381/2016/6/7/02d772cab6cf423aba0ac8cb0393739c.shtml. Accessed August 18, 2016.

beyond a certain threshold.[75] If such a situation arises, it will have to be clear to both parties what 'preferential access' means.

There is disagreement about whether stored oil in a joint stockpile can officially be considered as part of the host country's SPR. This is not an issue for non-OECD Asian countries which determine their own stockpiling policies. For OECD member states such as Japan and South Korea, however, the IEA does not consider oil stored in joint stockpiles as part of their obligations to hold ninety days of net imports of oil in storage. Since 2014, METI has counted half of the crude stored by Saudi Aramco and ADNOC as part of the secondary SPR of Japan.[76] South Korea does not consider joint stockpiled crude as part of its national SPR.

6.4.2.2 "De-Risked Barrels"

Oil tankers delivering cargoes from the Middle East to Asia are exposed to transit risk, crossing the world's two most critical chokepoints: the Straits of Hormuz and the Straits of Malacca. The most vital shipping lane is the Straits of Hormuz, which connects the Arabian Gulf with the Arabian Sea via the Gulf of Oman. About 17 million barrels are carried through this narrow sea-lane each day, which represents roughly 30% of all seaborne traded oil.[77] Of those 17 million barrels, more than 85% goes to Asia.[78] Over 15 million barrels of crude per day pass through the Straits of Malacca, which stretches between the Malay Peninsula and the Indonesian island of Sumatra, connecting the Indian with the Pacific Ocean. Both Straits are vulnerable to a variety of threats, ranging from piracy and terrorist attacks to shipping accidents and geopolitical hostilities which all could result in a significant dislocation of the global oil trade. Because of this, shipping rates between the Gulf and Asia often include additional insurance premiums. Stockpiled oil in Asia held by Gulf exporters can therefore be seen as 'de-risked' barrels—an attractive feature for importing countries occupied with security of supply considerations. Having an alternative storage location is also seen as important to Middle Eastern exporters' energy security, especially for producers who cannot diversify away from the Straits of Hormuz as their sole transport route to world markets. This has been cited as a major reason for Kuwait's interest in joint stockpiling ventures in Asia.[79]

---

[75]For instance, the IEA defines the threshold in loss of supplies as seven percent of the country's normal oil supply. IEA (2014). Energy Supply Security. https://www.iea.org/media/freepublicat ions/security/EnergySupplySecurity2014_PART1.pdf. Accessed August 21, 2016.

[76]Platts (2014). Abu Dhabi to store more crude in Japan. https://online.platts.com/PPS/P=m& e=1415751042637.4958837906244928967/PON_20141111.xml?artnum=c2705f4d8-2dc2-40b4-9b67-112bbaa3ccdd_4. Accessed August 18, 2016.

[77]EIA (2014). World Oil Transit Chokepoints.

[78]Tank World Expo (2016). Overview of the Middle East's Bulk Liquid Storage Sector. http://www. easyfairs.com/fileadmin/groups/8/TS_Middle_East_2015/Petroleum_Review_-_Middle_East_M arket.pdf. Accessed August 18, 2016.

[79]Reuters (2008). Kuwait mulls oil storage plans to allay Iran threat. http://uk.reuters.com/article/ businessproind-kuwait-oil-iran-dc-idUKL338301620080804. Accessed August 18, 2016.

6.4.2.3 Commercial Objectives

Joint stockpiling allows Asian importers to achieve several commercial goals, besides improving their perceived "security of supply". The advantage of having Middle Eastern crude oil stored nearby or within their own jurisdictions is the ability to access cargoes at short notice when needed due to unforeseen circumstances. This can help regional refineries optimize their crude slates more efficiently when circumstances dictate. The existing joint oil stockpiling facilities in Japan and South Korea are within two to three days from Northeast Asian oil loading ports in China, South Korea, Japan and Taiwan, China. In terms of sailing time for crude oil carriers, this compares to the three weeks or so required to transport oil from the Gulf.

If unused for want of commercial bids by privately-held companies, government-owned storage tanks can be leased out free or at low marginal costs for the SPR programs. Lease charges have been waived by the host country in most joint oil stockpiling agreements. South Korea's KNOC has described its "dynamic stockpiling" approach through which it manages the Korean public oil stockpiles with flexibility in order to alleviate the expense associated with building and maintaining SPR stocks. Apart from earning storage fees (if not waived) from renting out spare storage space under the joint stockpiling program, it also occasionally offers "time swaps." Invitations are sent to Korean refiners and sometimes international oil purchasers to bid on a quantity of stockpiled oil with the winning bidder having to return the oil within a stipulated time period and pay the bid premium. It is unclear whether these time swap exercises have been of net benefit to the agency. While KNOC's innovative system may have"broadened the concept of strategic oil stockpiling by showing that stockpiled oil need not be dead oil",[80] the use of strategic oil stockpiles to engage with oil market transactions as a means of raising revenue for sustaining SPR programs is not likely to be seen as strictly operating within the guidelines of the IEA's SPR "best practice".

Crude oil storage by Middle East NOCs in Asia could provide momentum to those countries that are looking into developing an oil trading hub in the Far East. South Korea has invested the most in this policy objective, building up large storage capacities along its southern coast.[81] South Korea, with its deep-water ports and expansive logistics infrastructure around Yeosu and Ulsan, is geographically and logistically well positioned to deliver cargoes further north, especially to the Chinese teapot refineries clustered around Qingdao, and so become a distribution centre for Northeast Asia. Japan's joint stockpiling depots are mostly utilized for supplying crude to China, South Korea and Taiwan, China rather than Japan due to laws requiring intra-Japanese shipping to use Japanese ships. This makes shipping crude from Okinawa

---

[80]Daniel Nieh, 2006, "The People's Republic of China's Development of Strategic Petroleum Stockpiles" University of Pennsylvania Global Commons, accessed at http://repository.upenn.edu/cgi/viewcontent.cgi?article=1037&context=curej.

[81]Bloomberg (2016). South Korea to Add Oil Storage as Traders Eye China Teapots. http://www.bloomberg.com/news/articles/2016-05-05/south-korea-to-add-oil-storage-as-china-teapot-refiners-buy-more. Accessed August 18, 2016.

to other parts of Japan expensive (similar to the Jones Act in the US).[82] Asian oil companies are more willing to purchase crude oil in the spot market for a larger share of their total purchase portfolios based on arbitrage and benchmark spread differences and the limits of their technical capabilities in refining different grades of crude oil. Storage capacity and ancillary port infrastructure in strategic locations are key to competitively source their spot cargo import requirements.

Joint oil stockpiling agreements have reportedly been linked to Asian NOC acquisitions of equity stakes in Middle East upstream fields.[83] The storage agreement between Japan and Abu Dhabi was reported as part of a larger arrangement consistent with Japanese government objectives to secure extensions for Japanese upstream concessions in Abu Dhabi's ADMA block due to expire in 2018.[84] When KNOC signed its storage deal with ADNOC in 2012, it reportedly agreed to forgo leasing fees in return for equity stakes in some of Abu Dhabi's oil fields.[85] Indian oil companies have also been cited as being interested in acquiring stakes in the ADCO concessions, with negotiations that include the Indian government's proposed stockpiling agreement with ADNOC reported in early 2016.[86]

6.4.3 Northeast Asian SPR Cost Savings

As mentioned in the introduction, the unique character of the joint oil stockpiling agreements between Middle Eastern exporters and the Northeast Asian importers can serve two objectives simultaneously. The first is the perceived energy security needs of net oil-importing countries and their objectives of enhancing their respective SPR volumes at low cost. The second is downstream integration ventures by the Middle Eastern NOCs in their objectives of competing for market share for their crude exports in the large oil importing regions such as Northeast Asia. The idea of saving costs in the building up of SPRs is not new. The US Department of Energy asked Congress for authority to lease foreign oil to continue filling the US SPR reserves in 1990.[87] This was preceded by discussions between the US DOE and Hisham Nazer, the Saudi oil

[82]Based on personal correspondence between KAPSARC and energy analysts in Asia.

[83]Gulf News (2016). India's tie up with Adnoc on oil storage to give energy security. http://gulfnews.com/business/sectors/energy/india-s-tie-up-with-adnoc-on-oil-storage-to-give-energy-security-1.1671049. Accessed August 18, 2016.

[84]Platts (2014). Japan's crude oil storage leases with producers: scope to do more with strategic stocks. http://blogs.platts.com/2014/11/25/japan-strategic-oil-stocks/. Accessed August 18, 2016.

[85]Bunker Ports News (2013). First UAE crude shipment for joint storage in S Korea to arrive Wednesday. http://www.bunkerportsnews.com/News.aspx?ElementId=23b1d210-1ee1-44a8-aa5f-9437e6780b00. Accessed August 18, 2016.

[86]Gulf News (2016). India's tie up with Adnoc on oil storage to give energy security. http://gulfnews.com/business/sectors/energy/india-s-tie-up-with-adnoc-on-oil-storage-to-give-energy-security-1.1671049. Accessed August 18, 2016.

[87]Lipmann, Thomas. "Energy Dept. Seeks to Lease Foreign Oil", The Washington Post, February 3, 1990.

minister. The proposal did not get adopted due to a number of complicating factors that emerged in the negotiations such as applicable taxes and risk-sharing.

In this and the next section below we attempt to provide indicative economics underlying the two dimensions of joint oil stockpiling: cost savings for host-country SPR programs and commercial benefits for crude oil exporters. For Middle East NOCs, if the production, movement and international storage of crude oil is not additional to the OPEC quota, then working capital tied up in "forward commercial storage" would be production cost plus freight.[88] In its accounts, it could be itemized as "cost of doing business". The working capital requirement for ME NOCs would be much lower than the carrying costs of the importing country if the importing country were to purchase the crude up-front for its strategic reserves. The table below poses the two cases:

1. A NEA country purchases ME crude for its SPR, then stores it until required under emergency or crisis conditions, at assumed cost of $41/bbl and cost of freight at $1/bbl. At a total cost of owning and transporting the crude of $42/bbl, its interest cost at 5% would be $2.10/bbl.
2. A ME NOC retains title to crude oil stored in NEA, and assures the host country the pre-emptive right to buy the oil at prevailing market price if an emergency situation is proclaimed. At a total production and freight cost of $6.00/bbl, its interest cost is only $0.30/bbl, or cheaper than the NEA interest cost incurred by $1.80/bbl.

In both cases, the construction and maintenance of the oil storage facilities for SPR purposes is borne by the host country. It should be noted that the acquisition costs of oil accounts for the largest share in overall costs related to emergency oil stockpiles. The operating costs of storing crude oil vary widely, but estimates suggest $3/barrel per year in underground salt caverns (as in the US Gulf Coast SPR), $6–$9/barrel per year in land-based tanks with marine docking facilities and $9–$18/barrel in chartered large crude-carrier vessels (Table 6.3).[89]

The comparison of the two scenarios in the table above rests on the assumption that even though the ME NOC retains title to the oil until an agreed protocol of emergency proclamation is invoked, this is an acceptable substitute to the case where the NEA host country buys and stores its own crude oil under the joint oil stockpiling

---

[88]That is, the supply of crude oil for storage is not counted against the OPEC quota (if any) or the exporting country's own target supply level since a net increase of volume into markets would cause a fall in prices. Note that this applies primarily to Saudi Arabia which is large enough to unilaterally alter global supply levels (for most of the past three decades, only Saudi Arabia has had spare crude production capacity of any appreciable magnitude in any case). It should also be naturally assumed that Saudi Aramco would not want to "cannibalize" its own sales such that it gains volumes on spot markets while losing sales in the long term market which accounts for the vast majority of their crude oil sales.

[89]In mid-2016, for example, storage cost for chartered very large crude carriers ranged from $1.00 to $1.20/barrel per month or $12–$14.50/barrel per year. See Gary Shilling, "Oil Is Still Heading to $10 a Barrel", June 28, 2016, Bloomberg View (accessed at https://www.bloomberg.com/view/articles/2016-06-28/why-oil-is-still-headed-as-low-as-10-a-barrel).

Table 6.3 Indicative benefits to joint oil stockpiling between ME NOC and NEA NOC

$/bbl	Scenario 1 NEA buys SPR crude	Scenario 2 ME stores and retains title to crude	Difference/Benefit
Cost of purchase/Production	41	5	36
Freight (ME—NEA)	1	1	0
Total cost of storing in NEA*	42	6	36
Interest cost (@ 5%)	−2.1	−0.3	1.8
Security premium (split benefit 50/50)	–	0.9	–
Net gain	+2.1	+0.6	–
For 15–30 MMB ($mn/yr)	31.5–63	9–18	–

*Excluding costs of construction and maintenance of storage facilities

agreement. The economic rationale for the ME NOC in the second scenario rests on the assumption that the stored crude oil would be linked to the amount of crude purchased under the usual term contracts for crude oil exports. By storing the crude, the ME NOC would aim to both protect and increase its market share for term crude oil sales in the country. In exchange for elimination of the considerable working capital requirement, the NEA country or NOC would thus expect to sign a term contract (standard COSA terms) to lift ME crude with the crude oil purchasers in the host country, since the commercial objective of ME NOCs would be to maximize their long term contracts under standard terms and formula prices. It could also be the case that given the location of the joint oil stockpiling facility within close proximity to large consuming countries allows the ME NOC to take advantage of the flexibility provided by effectively having short-haul crude on offer to both, their customary clients who have signed term contracts and to other crude oil refiners who are not term clients. From the point of view of the ME NOC, the consuming country could be expected to provide free storage.[90] In an equal division of the carrying cost savings, the ME NOC could in fact claim a stockpiling "security premium" to be paid by the host country. If it stores 15–30 MMB, it can gain $9–$18 million a year if it enjoyed 50% of the cost savings.

From the point of view of a large Asian net crude oil importing country, if the storage of crude oil by the ME NOCs within their territory allows them to reduce the costs of the overall SPR program, then the economic rationale would favour scenario 2 in which the ME NOC retains title to the oil since it could perform a similar function to SPR expenditures at a much lower cost. The host NEA country saves the $2.10/bbl carrying costs while retaining the essential SPR character of the

---

[90] As is indeed the case with the joint oil stockpile in Okinawa, Japan does not charge Saudi Aramco for the storage lease. It should be noted that Japan's storage facilities in Okinawa were reported as unused or "idle" when its first joint oil stockpiling deal with Saudi Aramco was announced.

oil stockpile. If 15–30 MMB are stored, the NEA country would save an estimated $31.5 to $63 million per year.

As mentioned above, the two scenarios compared above is based on the assumption that the pre-emptive right to buy the ME NOC-owned crude oil under emergency conditions by the host country gives it the same benefits as owning its own crude oil and stored in its SPR (i.e. they are substitutes). However, from the host NEA country's point of view, the lack of title to stored crude also means that it faces the uncertainty of the purchase price of crude held in storage as the price of the crude oil is only determined when the crude is lifted (at prevailing market price). The pre-emptive right to purchase (declared after the host government invokes an oil supply disruption emergency) means that the right can be exercised only on payment of the market price at the time of lifting. If the NEA country were to own the oil it would, as the owner, benefit from the uplift in crude oil prices attendant upon the supply disruption event. Against the uncertain benefit of ownership (since one cannot forecast oil supply crises with certainty), of course, is the onerous certain cost of carrying for the host country, amounting to over $2/barrel, assuming a crude purchase price of just over $40/barrel as illustrated in the example above.

The question of the prevailing "market price" during a supply disruption is fundamental, in that there must be an agreed clause expressing a mutual understanding between the NEA country and the ME owner of crude on what the market price is at the time of lifting. What is a fair assessment of the market price for a Saudi Aramco or ADNOC crude oil cargo available for sale FOB Okinawa at relatively short notice? The most direct indicator would be the "best alternative offer" that the crude oil owner can prove exists for the stored crude oil (that is, they have an open bid for their stored oil at hand), so that any government purchase on a pre-emptive basis would need to at least match this offer. Alternatively, there could be clauses in the joint oil stockpiling agreement that specify a particular formula that reflects the market price. The issue of market price is further discussed in the section below.

In a 2005 article published in the industry journal Petroleum Intelligence Weekly, two oil analysts published a proposal for "forward commercial storage" where OPEC producers utilise storage facilities located in consuming regions under the producer's commercial control, but with a call option sold to the consuming country as part of its SPR program.[91] A call option is defined as an agreement that gives the owner the right, but not the obligation, to buy a stock, bond, commodity or other asset at a specified price within a specific time period. However, in the case of the joint oil stockpiling agreements, the option carrying the right to buy does not have a specified price; instead it is the option to buy at "prevailing market prices".[92] In normally-operating liquid markets, this option would carry a zero or negligible value, as anyone has the opportunity to buy the commodity at the market price (as long as the buyer has credit

---

[91] PIW (2005). Oil Market Reliability: A Commercial Proposal.

[92] The specified time period would be the period for which the lease is agreed in the joint oil stockpiling contract. Nissen and Knapp's option value is a US option (the option can be exercised at any time to the termination of the contract) not a European one (which can only be exercised at termination date).

lines and other perquisites such as the ability to charter a vessel that meets the crude seller's specifications for delivery at the specified port). A "pre-emptive" right only grants the host country the preference in the case where it matches the best alternative bid. In a context of a supply disruption event when panic buying and price spirals can occur (and have occurred, as during the 1970s price shocks), the pre-emptive right to buy at the "prevailing market price" can be problematic: when prices can spike wildly day to day or over hours and minutes, the agreement to supply oil in an emergency to the host government would need to be very precise regarding the mode of price discovery. Any ambiguity could result in requirements to arbitrate or litigate, leading to potentially large losses on either or both parties to the joint oil stockpiling agreement. Large economic losses can lead to a failure in commercial reputations with possible spill-overs into diplomatic relations between the parties concerned.

In the event of a global crude oil supply disruption marked by panic buying and price spikes, the right of the government to invoke an official oil supply emergency and gain the preferential right to buy the crude in the joint oil stockpiling facilities located in their jurisdiction could be valuable even if only exercisable at the prevailing market price. If the government correctly predicts that a price spike is due to intensify, proclaiming an oil emergency and exercising the pre-emptive right to buy the stored crude oil would save the government from even higher prices further into the oil disruption period. Of course, in the reverse case, if the government gets it wrong, and what is expected to be a continued spike ends up shortly being a reversal, then the government would stand to lose money, having bought at a peak (in hindsight).

As joint oil stockpiling agreements are commercial and confidential to the parties to the agreement, it is not clear whether the existing joint oil stockpiling agreements in Japan and South Korea obliges the host government to provide proof of loss of supply beyond a particular threshold in order to invoke an "oil emergency". However, it is very likely that the host NEA government would find it in its own interest to exercise an emergency call on the joint oil stockpiling only when required and demonstrably justifiable. The expected reputational damage of calling an oil supply emergency when there isn't one, at least in the eyes of the international community, would militate against any strategic "gaming" over the emergency proclamation. Governments are likely to proclaim an oil emergency only in real emergencies and not use discretionary powers for short term market advantage. The latter would be a move that would damage the "relational" contract such as a joint oil stockpiling agreement where continued trust and good faith are critical.[93] Similarly, the risk of nationalization of crude oil stored in joint oil stockpiling facilities by the host government, while non-trivial, would also be expected to be remote. Nonetheless, the expropriation risk, however remote, of large-scale placement of assets by any government within another government's jurisdiction would be a factor of consideration in an oil producers' decision to participate in joint oil stockpiling agreements.

---

[93] A relational contract is one whose effect is based upon a relationship of trust between the parties. Relational contract theory is characterized by a view of contracts as relations rather than as discrete transactions. See for instance Ian MacNeil, "Reflections on Relational Contract", Journal of Institutional and Theoretical Economics, Vol 144, pp. 541–546.

6.4.4 Middle East NOC Pricing Norms

"Forward commercial storage" in or near large consuming markets has provided crude oil exporters logistical flexibility (in terms of breaking bulk and proximity to final delivery points) and improved freight economics in their downstream integration ventures. Leased or owned storage facilities in Rotterdam, Latin America and the Caribbean and elsewhere have been an established feature of the downstream investment ventures in or near large oil consuming markets by the ME NOCs since the 1980s. Joint oil stockpiling agreements however are distinctive in that they are not part of a larger downstream integration program that would include investing in R&M assets. In that sense, joint oil stockpiling ventures for the ME NOC are a pure logistics play.

The surge in oil supplies that prompted the fall in oil prices in the second half of 2014 has prompted key Asian refiners to buy more crude on the spot market that can be delivered immediately rather than at some future date under the typical term contracts offered by the ME crude sellers. As competition in Asian crude markets have intensified, and with a volatile trading environment, opportunistic buying of crude oil cargoes in spot markets have become more common. Even conservative Asian crude oil importers in Japan and South Korea, known for their concern with securing stable supplies under term contracts, are increasingly turning to spot markets to source increasing volumes of crude oil. For instance, Japan's JX Nippon Oil & Energy Corp. and South Korea's SK Innovation Co. are among the refiners aiming to enhance profits by purchasing more in the spot market while shrinking what they buy under long-term contracts which typical charge higher prices during periods of crude glut.[94] Short-term deals accounted for about 10% of purchases by the nation's refiners; now they reportedly account for as much as a fifth to a quarter of total imports.

Refiners in China and India have emerged as increasingly important buyers in the Asian crude oil market as both countries' crude oil imports grow rapidly. China and India's estimated combined daily net crude imports exceed 10 million barrels, or some 3 million bpd more than the United States, the world's largest single crude oil importer. As China and India play an increasingly dominant role in Asia's crude oil market, a growing share of trading is done on a spot basis as "buyers prioritize cost and delivery flexibility over fixed shipment schedules".[95] In China, state-owned oil giants have been joined by nearly 20 independent refiners which have been granted crude oil import licenses and buy their crude oil supplies exclusively from spot markets. According to a managing director at Mangalore Refinery and Petrochemicals Ltd., an Indian refiner, "there's a "perceptible shift" from term contracts to spot purchases; another source with a Korean refiner said, "It's become less important for us to secure

---

[94]Bloomberg (2015). Asian Oil Refiners Display Animal Spirits as Crude Glut Persists. http://www.bloomberg.com/news/articles/2015-06-11/asian-oil-refiners-display-animal-spirits-as-crude-glut-persists. Accessed August 22, 2016.

[95]Reuters (2016). Asia's Oil Markets in Upheaval as China, India Change the Game. http://www.reuters.com/article/us-asia-oil-markets-idUSKCN0VX075. Accessed August 22, 2016.

stable volumes under term contracts because there is a lot of crude available…we now think in terms of profitability and that's why we're buying more spot crude this year.".[96]

In an environment where spot sales are increasing as a percentage of total crude sales, the rationale for a ME NOC to participate in joint oil stockpiling would include gaining access to parts of the crude oil market that are not served by the larger Asian term crude oil buyers who have their own shipping arms to transport crude from the ME in VLCCs/ULCCs. For instance, the Saudi Aramco spot sale to an independent Chinese refiner with much weaker financial credit lines than the usual large Chinese NOCs that the company deals with was much reported by industry news sources. The "break bulk" capability offered by storage in Okinawa widens the range of refiners—namely, refiners with smaller receiving facilities that cannot handle direct imports from the Middle East which are typically transported in VLCCs or ULCCs—interested in purchasing ME crude.

For the joint oil stockpiling agreement to be profitable for the crude oil seller, the price at which it would sell its stored crude oil in NEA should at least cover the FOB price of the crude oil at the port of loading in the Arabian Gulf, the cost of freight for moving the oil from the Gulf to storage in the joint oil stockpiling facility in NEA, and any costs related to the leased storage fees (if any) and crude oil handling charges due to the owner or operator of the oil storage facility.[97]

ME NOC crude oil sales to international buyers are long-term crude oil sales agreements (COSAs), usually "evergreen" contracts renewable annually on mutual agreement between buyer and seller. The pricing formula generally has four components: point of sale, a market-related base price, an adjustment factor that is reflective of crude oil quality and the point of sale, and a timing mechanism that stipulates when the value of the formula is to be calculated.[98] For buyers of Saudi crude in Asia, the FOB crude oil price is linked to the monthly average spot price of Oman and Dubai crude oils (O/D) during the month t in which the crude is loaded at a Saudi port for delivery to the Asian market.[99] The base price for crude lifted at Ras Tanura or other

---

[96]Bloomberg (2015). Asian Oil Refiners Display Animal Spirits as Crude Glut Persists. http://www.bloomberg.com/news/articles/2015-06-11/asian-oil-refiners-display-animal-spirits-as-crude-glut-persists. Accessed August 22, 2016.

[97]As already noted, crude oil stored in Okinawa by Saudi Aramco for instance does not incur storage lease costs (as the storage is provided for free by JOGMEC, the Japanese agency responsible for SPR management.

[98]Kuwait, Iran, Qatar and Abu Dhabi are among the other Gulf oil producers using some form of formula prices for long term contracts. Among the few Gulf crudes sold on the "spot" market (i.e. not based on term contracts with end-user and re-sale restrictions) are Oman and Dubai. For a full if dated description of Middle East crude exports and pricing in Asia, see Paul Horsnell, "Oil in Asia: Markets, Trading, Refining and Deregulation" (OUP 1997).

[99]The sales invoice prices in Crude Oil Sales Agreements use quotes provided by the price reporting agency Platts, a division of Standard and Poors.. This is unlike the situation in the Atlantic markets of Europe and North America which have liquid exchange traded futures in West Texas Intermediate and Brent contracts which serve as the reference prices for Saudi and other GCC producers which export to the two major regions.

Table 6.4   Saudi OSP FOB gulf for Arab Light (Official Selling Price)

Saudi selling price formulate				
Oct	Nov	Dec	Jan	Feb
t-2	t-1	t	t + 1	T + 2

Saudi ports [100] is then adjusted by adding or subtracting an "offset" or adjustment factor.

$$AL_t = \frac{O}{D_t} + offset$$

The adjustment factor takes into account the quality differential between the given Saudi crude grade and the reference crude it is being priced off. The quality differential is measured as the difference in Gross Product Worth (GPW) of the Saudi crude relative to the reference crude.[101] The other two factors that determine the value of a commodity (i.e. apart from its quality differential) is its location and time of delivery; since AL, Oman and Dubai all originate in the Arabian Gulf, the freight differentials are marginal.[102] And the time of delivery (on FOB basis at an Arabian Gulf port) are for the same month of lifting for all the three crudes (Table 6.4).

In the case of Arab Light for instance, the offset for AL_t (Arab Light loading in month t, which is December in this example) are announced in the first week of t − 1 (November). At the time of the announcement of the December offset, the latest historical market data available is from month t − 2 (October). So, in determining the value of the offset for AL_t, the GPW difference between AL and the reference crude (O/D) is calculated for the most recently available data in month t − 2.

In Asia, the crude oil spot market trades two months ahead of delivery into Asian destinations, and Platts quotes for front-month Dubai in December are for February deliveries of 500,000 barrels cargo sizes.[103] That is, when loading occurs in month t (December), the front month quotes for Oman and Dubai crudes are for t + 2 (February). It is during t-2 (October) that front month quotes for Oman and Dubai refer to the month of loading t (December) and 3rd month quotes refer to month t + 2 (February).

Since December loading cargoes in the AG use the front month Platts quotes (which are for pricing February deliveries in Asia), the time structure of the reference

---

[100] The ports of Ras Tanura and Ras al-Ju'aymah on the Persian Gulf handles most of Saudi Arabia's crude oil exports from the Gulf. Most of the remaining volumes are exported from the Yanbu terminal on the Red Sea.

[101] The GPW measures the total value of all the refined product processed from the crude and determines the crude oil's refining value. In Asia, refined product prices quoted as Mean of Platts Singapore are taken as the reference prices for calculating the GPW of the crude oil.

[102] Cruel oil delivered from the Saudi port of Yanbu on the Red Sea would be an exception.

[103] For a full description of how Platts assesses Dubai and Oman physical crude oil prices, see Platts website at http://www.platts.com/IM.Platts.Content/MethodologyReferences/MethodologySpecs/Crude-oil-methodology.pdf.

crude prices impacts on the invoice price for the crude sale. That is, if the price of the reference crude Dubai in the month when AL is loaded exceeds the two-month forward price (i.e. the Dubai front month quote), it loses by that amount of backwardation. Hence a backwardation premium is added to reflect the value of December loading AL term contract FOB cargoes in the AG.

$$\text{offset} = \left(AL_{GPW(t-2)} - OD_{GPW(t-2)}\right) + \left(D_{M1(t-2)} - D_{M3(t-2)}\right)$$

In selling a cargo from a joint oil stockpiling facility to nearby refiners in NEA, one would presume that the general instruction guiding the ME NOC crude sales department would be to sell it at a price that would at least match the price (adjusted for freight) it would have got if it sold the cargo FOB Arabian Gulf. In other words, it would want to avoid incurring a loss relative to what it would have sold under the usual ME term contracts.

Consider the case where an existing term customer needed oil at shorter notice than the usual FOB nomination procedure for loading in the Arabian Gulf and which would take about 3 weeks or more of sailing time to arrive at its NEA destination. A term contract customer facing the urgent need for a spot cargo due to unforeseen circumstances could request oil from a nearby joint oil stockpiling facility. For the crude seller, acceding to this request from a long term contract client of good standing would be good business practice, provided that it does not cause the seller to incur a lower price realization compared to the normal FOB Arabian Gulf sale. Thus, if the crude oil seller received a request in December from a term client for a crude oil cargo for delivery in January, the crude oil seller could compare this to cargoes loaded in December in the AG, and charge the same price plus the cost of freight and loading/offloading and other applicable handling charges (plus the cost of storage at the joint oil stockpiling facility if any).

Middle Eastern NOCs have typically shunned selling crude oil in spot markets, preferring long term formula price contracts as the means to dispose of the bulk of their crude oil exports. However, ME NOCs have occasionally sold crude oil in the Asian spot market. According to press reports, Saudi Aramco sold its first cargo (to Japanese refiner Cosmo Oil) from the joint oil stockpiling facility in Okinawa in April 2012 (for May delivery) in the spot market.[104] In the post-2nd half 2014 environment of low prices and intense competition in the Asian crude oil market, the pressure for the ME NOCs to protect market share has increasingly led to engagements in spot markets with non-traditional customers. The recent Saudi Aramco sale of a spot cargo to a small, independent Chinese refiner sparked the attention of oil industry observers.[105] According to veteran oil observer Ed Morse of Citibank, "News that Saudi Arabia is selling a cargo on the spot market to Asia may mark the turning of a dramatic new chapter in the Saudi playbook...What is unusual is that the sale is

---

[104]Reuters, "Saudi Aramco is said to have sold the crude to an Asian refiner in the spot market", April 11, 2012.

[105]Henning Gloystein and Florence Tan, "Saudis open new phase in Asia oil market turf war with China spot sale", April 27, 2016.

spot rather than the initiation of a new term contract. Spot sales are about the only way the Kingdom can gain new market share in a world in which chunky buyers are interested in securing incremental purchases via spot rather than term arrangements."[106]

From the point of view of the ME NOC, one would assume that the sales of crude oil ex-Okinawa or some other NEA joint oil stockpiling facility would occur so long as it does not lead to a revenue loss relative to what the crude seller would have realized were it to have sold the cargo FOB Arab Gulf under its usual term contract arrangements. Furthermore, the sales of the spot cargo would be with the intention of converting at least some of the spot market buyers to "regular customers" under conventional term contracts preferred by the ME NOCs.

From the point of view of crude oil customer in NEA, the "market price" of the ME crude sold ex-Okinawa or some other joint oil stockpiling facility in Japan or Korea should be comparable to other similar crudes available in the region. A refiner in NEA would naturally assess the spot market for crude oil in the region, and buy the most competitively-priced crude oil adjusted for its relative quality and freight cost. As the spot market for crude oil in Asia is active two months forward, if a NEA refiner wanted to procure a prompt cargo from a nearby joint oil stockpiling facility one month ahead it would have to assess the month ahead market value of the reference crudes such as Dubai or Brent. As the front month Dubai crude contract is quoted for two months ahead, a NEA crude oil buyer would have to use quotes in the "over-the-counter" or derivatives market instead. The Dubai swap contract, quoted for one month ahead, is often used to hedge typical medium or heavy sour crude from the Middle East and Russia's Far East. Other spot crudes available to the NEA buyer from West Africa, Latin America and the US West Coast are priced off Brent, the other global benchmark crude used for the global crude oil trade. A buyer of prompt crude in NEA would have to consider the quality and freight cost of crude cargoes on offer as well as its price relative to the two global benchmarks.

Dubai swaps are settled against the average of Platts' front-month spot Dubai crude assessments. The cash-settled Dubai paper assessment reflects paper transactions of a minimum of 50,000 barrels. The relationship between Dubai swap and Brent prices is given by the following equivalences described in the table below, all reported for a time stamp of Singapore 4.30 pm ("Asia close"). A NEA crude oil buyer wanting to buy a cargo in December for a January loading off a nearby joint oil stockpiling facility would assess offers with the following price relationships in mind. Whether the buyer hedges his purchases or not, these pricing relationships present the context in which offers for prompt delivery by crude sellers would be assessed. In order to assess the theoretical value of a January delivered physical cargo in December, one would start with ICE January Brent futures and go through a derivation process as outlined in the Table 6.5.

---

[106] Sharon Cho, "Saudi Spot Oil Deal In China Seen By Citi A 'Dramatic' Shift", Bloomberg, April 26, 2016 (accessed at http://www.rigzone.com/news/oil_gas/a/144194/Saudi_Spot_Oil_Deal_In_China_Seen_By_Citi_A_Dramatic_Shift).

Table 6.5 Relationship between Dubai and Brent, swaps and physical contracts (Asia close time-stamp)

ICE Jan Brent Futures	−	ICE January Brent EFP*	=	ICE January Brent Physical
ICE Jan Brent Physical	±	ICE Jan Brent-Dubai EFS**	=	Jan Dubai swap
Jan Dubai swap	±	Dec/Jan Dubai swap spread	=	Dec Dubai swap
Dec Dubai swap	±	Jan/Feb Dubai physical spread	=	Jan Dubai physical

*Exchange of futures for physical; **Exchange of futures for swaps

It should be noted that the price of crude oil at any particular point in time in the NEA spot market is not necessarily higher than the opportunity cost facing ME NOCs which sell the vast majority of their crudes via term contracts on an FOB Arabian Gulf basis. That is, the spot market price for any particular grade of crude oil prevailing at any particular time may be lower than the cost of crude oil of a similar grade purchased under term contracts with the ME NOCs. In weak markets, the tendency is for spot prices to be lower than term contract prices, and vice versa. This is the case even though formula prices for crude oil purchased under term contract are typically referenced to spot crude prices, since term contract price movements lag spot price movements.

A final note is in order regarding the relatively small volumes of crude oil stored under the various joint oil stockpiling agreements in South Korea and Japan compared to the volume of exports by the ME NOCs to the NEA region. For instance, the 6.3 million barrels stored by Saudi Aramco in Okinawa pales in comparison to the approximately 1.1 million barrels per day imported by China from Saudi Arabia in the first half of 2016.[107] However, storage throughput rates can work out to a full turnover once a month, or about 12 times the total storage capacity annually. For the Okinawa facility, for example, this turns out to be 74.4 million barrels a year, or over 200,000 b/d. Thus, the Okinawa joint oil stockpiling facility utilized by Saudi Aramco could theoretically account for almost a fifth of all Chinese imports from Saudi Arabia were it to sell all its cargoes from the Okinawa storage to China alone with a full turnover once month.

6.5 Conclusion

The practice of oil exporting and importing countries jointly stockpiling crude oil in destination markets, first pioneered by South Korea and later adopted by Japan, has gained policy interest across other parts of Asia. Large non-OECD countries such as China and India, which are becoming increasingly dependent on growing volumes

---

[107]Chen Aizhu, "Saudi Arabia regains top ranking in China crude supply", Reuters, July 21, 2016.

of imported crude, are currently negotiating joint oil stockpiling deals with various Middle Eastern exporters. As the large Asian oil importing countries are in the process of building up their own sizeable SPR's, joint stockpiling could prove to be a cost-effective enhancement to their emergency oil reserves. As pointed out in the introduction, joint oil stockpiles can be classified as both commercial and strategic storage. This provides the importing country with access to crude oil reserves in times of emergency without incurring the costs of buying crude oil outright for SPR purposes. Joint oil stockpiling agreements can also be a concrete step in furthering deeper economic relations between exporting and importing countries. Indeed, jointly stockpiling crude is often discussed at the diplomatic level, as observed at several high-level meetings between Middle Eastern and Asian governments over the past years.

Middle Eastern exporters, by storing their oil closer to the large Asian demand centres, are better able to compete against other short haul crudes in the region. Stored Middle East crude oil in joint stockpiles offers the exporters a convenience yield given the close proximity of the storage facilities to the major markets in Northeast Asia.[108] Given the security concerns of Northeast Asian countries, Middle East oil stored in Northeast Asian locations offers buyers oil that has been "de-risked", in that the stored oil has already transited the critical chokepoints of the Straits of Hormuz and Malacca. Joint stockpiling agreements offer crude oil sellers and buyers the flexibility to nominate smaller cargo sizes and allowing break-bulk options. The joint stockpiling agreements have also offered the Middle East NOCs a platform to opportunistically access spot markets, an important consideration in the current low oil price environment. The joint oil stockpiling agreements between the Middle East producers and the large Asian importers can be expected to become an important feature of the oil trading relationships between the two regions and indeed, prove to be a "winning formula".

References

1. Bohi, D., and M. Toman. 1986. Oil supply disruptions and the role of the international energy agency. *The Energy Journal* 7 (2): 37–50.
2. Hogan, W. 1983. Oil stockpiling: Help thy neighbours. *The Energy Journal* 4 (3): 49–71.
3. Al-Tamimi, N. 2014. *China-Saudi Arabia Relations, 1990–2012*. New York: Routledge.

---

[108] Convenience yield was defined by Nicholas Kaldor as "a yield, qua stocks, by enabling a producer to lay hands on them the moment they are wanted and thus saving the cost and trouble of ordering frequent deliveries, or waiting for deliveries" (Kaldor, N., 1939, "A note on the theory of the forward market", Review of Economic Studies, 8, 196–201).

Chapter 7
Analysis of Sino-GCC Energy Cooperation Riskin Perspective of Geopolitics

Dehua Wang

The Energy cooperation between China and the GCC countries is faced with not only economic issues but two geopolitical risks: South China Sea and the tense situation of the Middle East. In view of the GCC's special status along with B&R and change of domestic and overseas situations, the Sino-GCC energy cooperation risk is closely linked to risk of the B&R construction. Covering many countries, the B&R is confronted with risks in economy, politics, finance, safety, law and infrastructure. The Economist Intelligence Unit (EIU) evaluated the overall risks of the B&R countries and the result showed that different operational risk levels and anti-risk capabilities posed severe challenges to BRI [1]. From a geopolitic perspective, the international community upholds a positive attitude towards BRI, however, some experts are skeptical about it and even think the BRI may be disrupted. For example, National Security Strategy Report issued by the White House on December 18, 2017 overtly and covertly imagined China as "a strategic competitor" and rendered threats and challenges in politics, economy, military and diplomacy [2], which not only had a negative impact on the international image of China, but also put pressure on the implementation of the BRI and energy cooperation between China and the GCC States. From the author's point of view, energy cooperation between China and the GCC States is faced with three risks, gambling and contest among great powers in the Middle East, competition and scramble among intra-territorial powers in the Middle East and competition among more extraterritorial powers arising from South China Sea.

D. Wang (✉)
Institute of South and Central Asia Studies, Shanghai Municipal Center for International Studies, Shanghai, China
e-mail: dehuawangz@126.com

© Shanghai Jiao Tong University Press 2021
T. Zhang and D. Wang (eds.), *China-Gulf Oil Cooperation Under the Belt and Road Initiative*, https://doi.org/10.1007/978-981-15-9283-6_7

7.1 Definition of Energy Geopolitics and Chinese Energy Safety

There is a need for a deep analysis of the risks faced by the Sino-GCC energy cooperation to know the origin of geopolitics, since the aforesaid understanding of the BRI is based on the thinking model of western geopolitics for more than a century, namely a complete set of thinking model and epistemology on geopolitics. The theory of such thinking model and epistemology is originated from classical geopolitics arising in the late nineteenth century [3].

7.1.1 Origin of Classical Geopolitics

Geopolitics is a theory analyzing and predicting global or regional strategic situations and political behaviors of relevant countries according to geographic elements and geographical characteristics of political pattern and a theory on the basis of political geography. Since geopolitics was proposed in the beginning of the twentieth century, it has gained extensive attention of the academic circles and derived many influential theories such as "Sea Power Theory", "Land Power Theory", "Rimland Theory" and "Air Power Theory" [4]. Western geopolitics, also called "western geopolitical imagination", has obvious regional features. Geopolitics shows some modern characteristics after years of development. Geopolitics: Re-visioning World Politics summarizes five characteristics of the modern geopolitical imagination: visualizing the world as a whole; the definition of geographical areas as "advanced" or "primitive"; the notion of the state being the highest form of political organization; the pursuit of primacy by competing states; and the necessity for hierarchy [5]. The crux of the modern geopolitics was discussed by Adhikari S. due to the spatialization of the world politics through spatial practices and representations of space, which is now being greatly challenged/frayed by the informational technological revolutions. This leads to a new concept—Post-Modern Geopolitics—which is characterized by the growing significance of informationalization and the telemetrical visualization of the world politics, with geo-graphing being replaced by info-graphing [6].

"Sea Power Theory", "Land Power Theory", "National Organism Theory" and "Rimland Theory" are typical examples of early classical geopolitics theories [7]. An U.S. naval officer, Alfred Thayer Mahan, who is the founder of "Sea Power Theory". Since its emergence, it has drawn extensive attention around the world and has been honored as the cornerstone of modern theories of sea supremacy. "Sea Power Theory" consists of trilogies. In Effect of Sea Power on the History (1660–1783) Mahan mentioned that sea supremacy played a critical role in national power especially the control over narrow channels with strategic significance, which indirectly explained why great powers engaged in fierce naval rivalries before World War I. The viewpoint that contending for maritime hegemony dominates the fate of a state and even the world has prevailed for more than 100 years and was adopted by the USA, Japan,

Germany and the Soviet Union successively to direct their development strategies. For example, Holmes J. examined the link between Mahanian sea-power theory and the German concept of a place in the sun prior to the First World War in his article, and contended that the use and misuse of Mahan helped propel Germany into zero-sum competition with Great Britain [8]. It seems that "Sea Power Theory" selectively introduced the history of sea power, actually it intended to popularize a complete set of naval strategic thinking customized for the USA. The analysis system created by Mahan was an important basis for "western geopolitical imagination" which divided the world into sea power and land power.

Halford John Mackinder, a British geopolitician, is the founder of "Land Power Theory". *The Geographical Pivot of History* proposed by Mackinder was read out to the British Royal Geographical Society on 25 January 1904. It interpreted and introduced geopolitics called Land Power Theory which opposite to Sea Power Theory [9]. According to Land Power Theory, "the 'heartland' of Eurasia is the most important strategic area with the development of land vehicle" and "the history of the world is fundamentally the history of the unremitting struggle between continental countries and maritime countries". Thus, "Land Power Theory" can be concluded as three sentences, "anyone who gets commands of Eastern Europe controls the heartland; anyone who gets command of the heartland controls the world island; anyone who gets command of the world island controls the world" [10], which is also called "Heartland Theory" and has a profound impact on world politics. Mackinder's view of geography is interpreted as a combination of a geographical longue duree and a theatre of military action [11].

With the development of international situation, the U.S. scholar Nicholas Spykman modified Mackinder's "Heartland Theory". In his opinion, great powers contend not for the "heartland" of Eurasia but a resourceful area, the "edge district" between land and sea. To be specific, "edge district" refers to European coastal areas, deserts of Arabia and Middle East and Asian monsoon regions. Spykman's theory can be summarized as the Mackinder dictum, "'Who controls eastern Europe rules the Heartland; who rules the Heartland rules the World Island; and who rules the World Island rules the World,' is false. If there is to be a slogan for the power politics of the Old World, it must be 'Who controls the Rimland rules Eurasia; who rules Eurasia controls the destinies of the world.'" [12], called "Rimland Theory". The reason why Spykman put forward the "Rimland Theory" is attributed to the background differences, the spatial distribution of national interest and the inter-state conflicts at that time. After the World War II, the US exclusively dominated the world, surpassed the Britain, and considered as the maritime hegemonic power. Therefore, it was inappropriate to continue with the sea power theory. The US took part in the two World Wars in order to prevent the great powers of Eurasia from controlling the rim lands. At that time, the U.S.'s national interests and inter-state conflicts extended all over Eurasia [7].

Classical geopolitical theories described by Mahan, Mackinder and Spykman constitute the base framework of current western geopolitics and become the main guiding ideology for policy makers of western countries. Particularly, the dualistic theory on the struggle between land power and sea power still dominates the attitude of western countries towards the world and it identifies western countries' struggle for the "rim lands" as a permanent interest. Besides, it's the reason why geopolitical strategy of the USA and other great powers has always stressed the importance of sea power and rim lands. Therefore, western countries represented by the USA will never and can never allow any continental country to possess sea power and pose a threat to them.

7.1.2 Overview of Energy Geopolitics

The "Energy geopolitics" was first proposed in *The Geopolitics of Energy* by Melvin A. Conant and Fern Racine Gold from the USA in 1978 [13] and then it was driven by scholars to further develop. Till now, the energy geopolitics is a new research trend of geopolitics closely connecting energy and geopolitics and a major issue concerned by energy policy makers, presidents of large oil companies and geopoliticians. In essence, the energy geopolitics is the correlation among different international actors and a strategy relating to significant international politics and international relations as well as occupation, utilization, control and transaction of energy in international politics arising from geographical distribution and critical geographical factors [14].

The "World energy heartland" is a very important concept in energy geopolitics consisting of world energy supply heartland and world energy consumption heartland [4]. The former refers to large areas covering Maghrib, the Persian Gulf, Caspian Sea, Russia, Siberia and the Far East and harboring abundant oil and gas resources and it is the main supply place of oil and gas resources. Other areas than "world energy supply heartland" are called world energy consumption heartland, which mainly consists of "inner demand zone" including East Asia, Southeast Asia, South Asia and Continental Europe and "outer demand zone" including North America, Sub-saharan Africa and South Pacific. The world energy supply heartland and the world energy consumption heartland plus energy channels make up the layout of energy geopolitics.

The energy producing place, consuming place and channels constantly change with times, so does the layout of energy geopolitics. The layout of world energy evolved from "era of the Mexico Gulf" to "era of the Persian Gulf" from the end of World War II to the 1980s and modern oil industry mushroomed in the middle of the nineteenth century. The USA took the lead in developing oil using steam drill in 1859, which opened up the development of oil industry. Afterwards, transnational and interstate oil trade emerged. The USA exported a great amount of oil to Europe and became the core energy supplier. In the middle of the twentieth century, The USA began to import oil from South America and the Middle East with the increase in oil consumption, as a result, the oil geopolitical layout changed. In 1972, the total crude output of the Middle East exceeded that of North America and became the oil producing and exporting center in place of Mexico. The world energy layout turned from "balanced" to "imbalanced" from the 1980s to the beginning of the twenty-first century and took on two features: the oil producing center focused more on the Middle

East, Latin America, Russia and Africa; proven oil reserves of oil consuming areas decreased and the imbalance between supply and demand stood out increasingly. As a result, the global energy market was severely impacted and the international energy pattern was challenged by energy cooperation, energy competition and even energy contradiction. In recent years, the rise of unconventional energy represented by shale gas, shale oil, oil sand and compact oil and gas rebuilt the international energy layout and benefiting from technical breakthrough of shale gas the USA was the best interpretation. Major economies are contending and will certainly contend largely for the layout of world energy geopolitics.

7.1.3 Strategic Characteristics of Energy Are Important Parts of Current International Geopolitics

The energy is the material basis for national economic development; while oil supply safety is the key of energy safety strategy of every country since oil is a major form of energy. Imbalanced distribution, scarcity and non-renewal endow energy with a strong geopolitical color; the energy producing place and transit transport area become a hotspot of international energy geopolitics and the target of geopolitical competition among great powers. To maximum the interest, all countries, especially some major energy importing countries and exporting countries, locate energy geopolitics according to their resource superiorities and geopolitical features and with strategic objectives of economic and social development as the starting point.

The USA, as the world's largest economy, aims to become the empire of energy. That is, to control energy supply and transportation channels so as to maintain strategic interests of a superpower. Geopolitists consider some important geographic positions such as the Strait of Hormuz, Strait of Malacca and the Nansha Islands as "epicenters of geopolitical upheaval"; while the USA see them as highly sensitive zones threatening its critical interests. Thus, it covets the absolute control and will take any necessary actions including military means once such zones are threatened. For instance, during Iranian Revolution and the Soviet invasion of Afghanistan in the 1970s–1980s, The USA actively took military action and developed and utilized plenty of military installations in the Middle East with the aim of presiding over Middle East affairs and seeking own interests. Two Gulf Wars, War in Afghanistan, the latest Iran nuclear crisis and Syrian Civil War reveal the U.S.'s geopolitical scramble for protecting the dominant right.

Russia that adopts the Great Chauvinism and the sense of mission pursues energy geopolitical strategy to resume the great power status and oil weapon is an important way to fight against the USA and its allies. Located in the "world energy heartland",

Russia harbors abundant oil and gas resources and a solid energy industrial foundation. Russia adjusts energy geopolitical strategy against the new international environment [15], adjusting energy policy to CIS from political relation; targeting at "re-accessing to European" power and counterbalancing EU using "energy lever"; cooperating more than competing with OPEC countries for national interests; inclining energy export structure to Asia–Pacific nations for diversified oil–gas export. On the whole, Russian energy industry is highly sensitive to change of the geopolitical environment and thus Russia practices flexible and balanced external energy policy [16].

Due to high import dependence on oil and natural gas, Japan dreams to become a political power and gain safe and adequate energy supply. Japan is an island with developed economy, small land area and all-sided but scarce resources and its national strategy has long been affected by the identity as a maritime state or a continental state. Its national strategy is also affected by the geopolitical layout of East Asian continent and the maritime power—the USA [17]. After Cold War, Japan began to realize strategy transition and further strengthen Japan–US alliance so as to enhance the strategy for containing China and fulfill the dream of building "a normal state" [18]. In nature, the goal of "normalization" is to change from an economic power to a political power under the assistance of America. To fulfill the strategic target, the primary task is to ensure safe and adequate energy supply according to energy resources and utilization status.

Again, Iran, an oil supplier in the Middle East, also sets the energy geopolitic target. Rich in oil resources and due to close connection with the Strait of Hormuz and other key oil channels, these potentials have turned Iran into one the world's important energy hubs in the Middle East and the Persian Gulf region giving the country an exclusive geopolitical and geo-economic lever which can pave the way for its economic development [19]. Iran has always committed to maintaining security, promoting cooperation and increasing public interest, taking the Middle East as the first choice of geostrategy; expanding the living space and contending against the U.S.'s containment and economic blockade through energy diplomacy; enlarging and consolidating the status of a regional power by means of the Iranian Revolution and devoting to keeping order of the Islamic world; taking the promotion of scientific and technological development as the fundamental guarantee. A series of events such as Iranian release, Syrian Civil War and Yemeni Civil War in recent years show the chance of Iran to return to Central Asia and the rise in the Middle East.

Consequently, areas rich in energy resources become the focus of geopolitical competition among great powers and complex geopolitical factors give rise to potential geopolitical crises such as terrorist threat, Color Revolution, reinforcement of military deployment and gambling of oil–gas pipeline route. For example, enjoying a good geographical location, abundant oil resources, moderate reservoir and low oil cost, the Middle East has drawn great attention from major powers. The U.S.'s Government tries to overturn the anti—U.S. regime of the Middle East by "Color Revolution" and keep appropriate military presence so as to terrorize Iran and other countries and ensure safety of oil and natural gas supply. Meanwhile, it cautiously facilitates Arabia–Israel reconciliation to guarantee Israeli interests. Russia also keeps an eye on the situation of the Middle East through strengthening cooperation with Iran and other countries, consolidating energy cooperation with Turkey and gambling with the USA strategically. EU strengthens oil–gas cooperation with the Middle East so as to ensure safety and stability of oil–gas supply. Japan looks at differences between the USA and Saudi Arabia and gives aids to Saudi Arabia to gain oil and energy interests. It also resists the pressure from the USA and continues cooperating with Iran. Regardless of the pressure from the USA, India also acts in round cooperation with Iran through increasing energy trade and constructing energy transport network and port.

7.1.4 Chinese Energy Security is Essentially Geopolitical Security of the Middle East

The National energy security is an important topic of national security system and the research focus of geopolitics. With the aggravation of global energy geopolitical game and the rapid growth of Chinese energy demand, Chinese energy security becomes increasingly severe. Thus, it is necessary to study change of international energy geopolitics and China's energy strategy and countermeasures. The Middle East accounts for most of oil reserve and oil export and its geopolitical security affects all links of international energy supply chain. From the energy geopolitics layout, China is the pivot of energy supply and demand and the largest energy consuming country in East Asia connected to the heartland of the Middle East in the east and adjacent to East Asian energy consumer market where it resides in the west. In order to decentralize energy import risk, China has formed a diversified energy import system. However, energy is mainly from the Middle East. In other words, Chinese energy security is essentially geopolitical security of the Middle East. Therefore, change of geopolitical situation of the Middle East has a warning effect on international energy security and Chinese energy security.

First, security of the Middle East relates to security of Chinese energy import. The OPEC statistical data [20] shows that 5 of top 10 daily oil exporting countries in 2018 were distributed in the Middle East, they were Saudi Arabia, Iraq, UAE, Kuwait and Iran. Oman and Qatar also had a large oil export. However, these oil exporting countries were confronted with complicated and confusing situation. On the one hand, the Middle East policy introduced by Trump remained to be specified, because it upheld mutual conflicts and lacked internal logic. It was sure that Trump's personal independence of conduct cannot be divorced from restrictions of the Middle East situation and the U.S.'s politics. On the other hand, although "Islamic States" were heavily mauled, the risk of spillover and diffusion expanded continuously. As extremists and refugees from "Islamic States" were intertwined with each other and spilt over, terrorist attacks continued spreading and frequently occurring all around the world especially Europe and Islamic States, which made global governance difficult. The Chinese oil dependence on the Middle East deepened increasingly and

Chinese oil security was closely bond up with geopolitical security of the Middle East. In 2018, Chinese oil consumption was increased to 135.25 million barrels/day and oil putout was 3.798 million barrels/day. According to statistics, Chinese crude oil import was 464.5 million tonnes, daily import was increased to 9.328 million barrels and oil dependence rose to 69.8% in 2018 [21]. Moreover, the Middle East is also a key liquefied natural gas and fuel oil supplier of China. Statistical data showed that 17.3% of 73.5 billion m^3 of Chinese imported liquefied natural gas was from Qatar and 0.9% of LNG import was from Oman in 2018 [21]. Even though our energy supply diversification strategy achieved the preliminary result, China will still depend on the Middle East both in the short run and in the long run since the Middle East plays an important role in the international energy market. Maintaining geopolitics security of the Middle East is a must for ensuring Chinese energy safety.

Then, China has invested a lot in oil and gas of the Middle East. With China's further implementation of "Go Out" energy strategy, the Middle East becomes an important oil and gas investor of China involving in upstream, midstream and downstream of oil and gas and covering risk exploration, oil and gas exploitation, oil and gas refining, pipeline construction and harbor construction. China invests in oil and gas of the Middle East mainly in the form of joint venture and strives to guarantee market shares so as to avoid geopolitical risk of energy supply of the Middle East. China has invested in almost all major oil and gas producing countries in the Middle East. Mid-large oil and gas fields such as Saudi Arabia Rub Al Khal Desert B block gas field, Iran Yadavaran oil field and Iraq Rumaila oil field as well as oil refining companies such as Red Sea Oil Refining Company, Greater Nile Petroleum Co., Ltd. and Khartoum Refinery are typical projects [22]. With the promotion of the "Belt and Road", Chinese investment in oil and gas of the Middle East further increased. In January, 2016, Yanbu Aramco Sinopec Refining Company Ltd. (YASREF) was put into production and among the total investment of USD 9.15 billion Sinopec and Saudi Aramco held 37.5–62.5% of shares respectively [23]. It is the largest investment project of China in Saudi Arabia. Built to handle 400,000 barrels per day, the site is geared to produce premium transportation fuels and high-value refined products for domestic and international markets. In November, 2016, a deal was signed by the National Iranian Oil Company and a consortium involving CNPC, France's Total and Iran's Petropars to develop Iran's South Pars (SP11) gas field which is the world's largest gas field [24]. According to the agreement, Total will operate the SP11 project with a 50.1 interest alongside CNPC with 30% and PetroPars with 19.9% [24]. However, it is reported that the share of this project is 100% shifted to PetroPars due to the successive withdrawals of Total and CNPC in 2017 and 2019 [25]. In February, 2017, the CNPC and CEFC China Energy company, a private enterprise, acquired 12% stake in the onshore concession of state-owned Abu Dhabi National Oil Company (ADNOC) Group by USD 2.7 billion, among which CNPC and CEFC China Energy held 8–4% of shares respectively [12, 26]. On 9 December 2018, the onshore stake held by CEFC China was transferred to North Petroleum International Company Ltd, a subsidiary of China ZhenHua Oil Co. Ltd. under the approval of Abu Dhabi's Supreme Petroleum Council [27]. Considering high geopolitical risks of the Middle East, Chinese enterprises are badly in need of establishing steady investment strategy and solution, strengthening political risk analysis and deploying practical risk prevention measures.

Finally, the Middle East involves in interests of many countries and the rise of China impacts existing geopolitical layout. The 19th National Congress of CPC reported that "socialism with Chinese characteristics has entered a new era" and "opened up a new journey to build a great modern socialist country in an all-around way". At the present stage, China needs to "transform the development mode, optimize the economic structure and change the growth momentum". The development of China requires a relatively peaceful international environment and China adheres to peaceful coexistence and not to expand and scramble for supremacy with great powers. Smooth implementation of "Belt & Road" highlights the rise of China in the international community, but it also arouses public concern. For example, western developed countries represented by the USA could hardly adapt to and accept the rise of China after making use of global resources for continuous expansion and entering the post-industrial age. The USA regards China as a strategic competitor and considers the rise of China a challenge and threat to its hegemony. Japan, as an ally of the USA, is reluctant to be with a powerful neighbor. India, an emerging developing country, is also jealousy of Chinese strength. In addition, some Southeast Asian countries conflicting against China for the South China Sea dispute fear its rise. Thus, once there is a chance to impede the development of China, for example, to impede China's access to energy resources, they will seize the opportunity to contain and even crack down on China.

To sum up, guaranteeing Chinese energy safety largely is to guarantee geopolitical stability of the Middle East. China cannot underestimate the risks in the Middle East. Under the complicated international situation, many Middle East countries are experiencing political, economic and social transition and facing many external disturbances, internal disorders and conflicts as well as the possibility of energy supply failure. With China's further oil dependence on the Middle East, the Middle East policy will be increasingly partial to its political stability. Now China still had limited political influence on the Arab world. China needs to reflect on how to promote political stability of Arab countries and other countries in the Middle East using limited strength.

7.2   The Middle East is Contested by Great Powers

The Middle East has always been a place contested by all strategists and the storm center of world politics. The situation of the Middle East over the years can be summarized as "disordered" and many forces have long fought openly and secretly there. In view of abundant oil and gas resources of the Middle East plus above 1/3 of Chinese oil and gas import from the Middle East, once the Middle East is out of control, it is quite possible to interrupt stable oil and gas supply of China. Therefore, geopolitical risks of the Middle East from great powers should be thoroughly analyzed for energy cooperation between China and the Middle East represented by the GCC.

7.2.1 The USA Seeks a Strategic Target to Maintain Its Hegemony in the Middle East

The USA has established relations with the Middle East for nearly 300 years. The USA did not set foot in the Middle East deeply before World War II, but during World War II, it began to cultivate pro-American forces in the Middle East, transport political, economic and military forces on a large scale and expand its influence on Saudi Arabia, Iran, Turkey, Syria and Lebanon, which pushed US-Middle East relations into a new stage of comprehensive development. It can be easily discovered that the U.S.'s Middle East policies in different stages strived to maintain its global hegemony and core benefits in the Middle East.

During Cold War, the U.S.'s Middle East policy aimed to resist against the Soviet Union. The Middle East is both the cradle of US–Soviet Cold War and an important battlefield. The USA resisted against the Soviet Union to observe and handle the Middle East affairs and its Middle East policy was to obey and serve the strategic need for contending for hegemony with the Soviet Union. Based on this, the USA presented two ideas: taking the Middle East as the strategic base and making it a forward position between the USA and the Soviet Union; Scrambling for the control over petroleum and other resources of the Middle East so as to obtain more economic benefits and strategic benefits [28]. During that period of time, the USA also acted in cooperation and even allied with Turkey, Saudi Arabia and Iran during the Pahlavi Dynasty. To urge more allies to resist against the Soviet Union, the USA also allied with and utilized Islamic Movement.

After Cold War, the U.S.'s Middle East policy aimed at seeking global hegemony and its benefits in the Middle East changed dramatically due to the Soviet Union's withdrawal. Petroleum of the Middle East became the core benefit of the USA. Nevertheless, growing mightiness of the Middle East and Iraq and expansion of Saddam's regime threatened economic benefits of western countries such as the USA in the Middle East. For this reason, the US Government adjusted the basic framework of the Middle East policy after Cold War with the aim of building a new order of the Middle East in line with the U.S. interests. By the excuse of facilitating post-war reconstruction, the USA opened up a new era of strengthening its dominant right in the Middle East affairs through a series of events such as Gulf crisis and Gulf War. After that, the USA continued strengthening its influence on the Middle East and making the Middle East a testing ground of the next "American century". As a result, the Middle East turned out to be one of the important strategic focus for the USA.

The U.S.'s Middle East policy was adjusted to seek stability of the Middle East in a "democratic" way after "9/11". Objectively, "9/11" compelled the USA to re-examine relations with many countries, concentrate on threats which may be aroused by internal problems of the Middle East Countries and to achieve opportunity and prosperity through upholding freedom and democracy in the Middle East. The core Middle East policies of successive governments such as "new order of the Middle East" of the previous Bush Administration, "Containing Iran and Iraq in the east and promoting peace negotiations in the west" of the Clinton Administration and "detachment" of the Bush Administration showed little essential changes, during which the Middle East took on the USA-oriented "peace and stability".

During the Obama Administration, the U.S.'s Middle East policy focused on strategic contraction, avoidance of war and stability. On account of the Middle East predicament, financial crisis and financial deficit of the Bush Administration, the Obama Administration tightened the Middle East policy and transferred global strategy and economic center to Asia. In the matter of Middle East Affairs, the Obama Administration put more emphasis on cooperation with allies and international orga-nization as well as negotiation and conciliation, advocated carefully using military power in the Middle East and actively improved relations with the Islamic world. The Middle East policy of the Obama Administration was proved to be successful in main aspects. Not only did it reduce the U.S.'s resource investments and armed forces in the Middle East and the casualties, but also it effectively cooperated with promoting "the Asia–Pacific rebalancing" strategy. However, the Middle East policy of the Obama Administration had bad consequences. It not only weakened the U.S.'s interests in the Middle East and the control over the Middle East, but also enlarged the gap of interests between America and allies and increased the influence of worldwide terrorist attack [29].

The Middle East policy was looming and extending with the change after Trump came into power. Trump addressed a campaign speech on diplomatic policy centered on "America first" which is also the diplomatic policy guide of the current American Government. As an important diplomatic effort of the USA, interweaved and linked old and new hot issues of the Middle East contain and impede its eastward global strategy. The Trump Administration is faced with hot potatoes such as the Syrian Civil War, Iraqi crisis, Pacification of Libya and its sequelae, Yemeni conflicts, Saudi Arabia's air attack on Houthis, striking ISIS, north–south Sudanese conflict, Israeli-Palestinian conflict and Kurdish issue [30]. In order to maintain and solidify the U.S.'s dominance over the Middle East, the Trump Administration breaks the first visit habit of the previous administrations, pays the first foreign visit to Saudi Arabia and redefines the main purpose of the Middle East Policy [31, 32]: First, to repair the relations with allies; second, to contain Iran; third, to reconcile Israeli-Palestinian conflict. In the aspect of repairing the relations with Saudi Arabia and Israel, the Trump Administration acts in cooperation in addressing the Syria crisis, striking extremist groups of ISIS and other hot issues so as to regain its influence on the Middle East affairs. In the matter of Iranian nuclear issue, the Trump Administration denies diplomatic policy of the Obama Administration and asserts Iranian support for terrorism so as to sharpen a new round of Saudi Arabia–Iran conflict. Furthermore, the USA peddles military equipment valued 110 billion USD to Saudi Arabia, which further worsens Saudi Arabia–Iran relations. In the aspect of reconciling Israeli–Palestinian conflict, the Trump Administration does not adopt concrete actions even if it voices support for reinitiating peace negotiations, which demonstrates that the Trump Administration upholds an ambiguous attitude towards "two-state solution" for Saudi Arabia and Iran and is partial to Israel.

Till now, there are a whole bunch of policies toward the Middle East made by the Trump administration: rebuild the close ties with Israel and Saudi Arabia that become frayed in the Obama administration (e.g. moving the embassy to Jerusalem and closing the PLO office and ceasing the abide by the JCPOA, paying his first foreign visit to Saudi.), harden the attitude towards Iran, emphasize on anti-terrorism against ISIS [33]. Nevertheless, it is widely discussed that there are two Trump administration polies toward the Middle East and barely figure out which one it really is, given the recent behavior of Trump made, such as twitted the decision of pulling out of Syria.

In all, US will keep his eyes closely on the Middle East since the USA still have major interests there. But it is hard to tell that the current Middle East policy made by the U.S. administration can make things better or worse, given the Middle East today is going through a set of convulsions.

7.2.2 Russia Has National Interests Which Cannot Be Ignored

The Middle East policy of Russia (the Soviet Union) takes on different era characteristics. As a whole, it is formulated under the international strategic pattern to maintain national interests in the Middle East which cannot be ignored.

The Soviet Union and the USA were at a stalemate from 1917 to 1956. The October Revolution burst on 7 November 1917 in Russia, during which the diplomatic policy focused on promoting world revolution and breaking through capitalism. In 1921, Russia adjusted the diplomatic policy to peacefully coexist with capitalist countries, concluded treaties of friendship and cooperation with Turkey, Iran and Afghanistan and established normal diplomatic relations. Until before World War II, the Soviet Union still concentrated on Turkey, Iran and Afghanistan and had limited influence on the Arab states. During World War II, the Soviet Union attempted to build "a buffer zone" in three countries to ensure safety of southern frontier, actively developed relations with the Arab States and established diplomatic relations with Egypt, Syria, Lebanon and Iraq. Since then, the Soviet Union stepped into the Arab world. The relationship between the Soviet Union and Middle East countries changed dramatically during the Suez Canal War from the end of World War II to 1956. First, conflicts between the Soviet Union and Turkey and Iran were intensified and Turkey and Iran allied with the USA. Second, in the matter of Arabian–Israeli issue, the Soviet Union shifted its support to Arab States represented by Egypt. Third, as to total strategy, the Soviet Union changed the tune from anti-UK to anti-US. The

Soviet Union established diplomatic relations with all other Arab States than gulf Arab monarchies after World War II, which indicated that the Soviet Union took a step deep into the Middle East. After the Suez Canal War, the Middle East was divided into the U.S.'s camp and the Soviet Union camp and the US-Soviet rivalries surfaced in the Middle East.

From 1956 to 1991, US-Soviet rivalries turned into fiery struggle. Within two decades from 1956 to 1976, the Soviet Middle East policy served US-Soviet rivalries and strived to become the only ally and backer of the Arab states through strong military and economic aid and to weaken or eliminate western countries' power in the Arab world. At that time, the Soviet Union took Arab republics as major partners by offering military aid to Syria, recognizing the Republic of Yemen, acknowledging the provisional government of Algeria and the establishment of diplomatic relations and regarding Egypt as the backbone of the Middle East policy. But eventually Egypt broke up with the Soviet Union in 1976. After Gorbachev came into power (from 1976 to 1985), the Soviet influence on the Middle East gradually shrank due to weakening of national strength and failure in the Middle East policy. The Soviet Union faced a lot of problems during that period. First, although the Soviet Union enlarged influence on Syria, South Yemen, Libya and the Red Sea, its influence on the Gulf area and southeast bank of the Mediterranean Sea was poor and gradually turned from the Middle East to peripheral countries. Second, the "rejectionist front" made up by the Arab States backed by the Soviet Union and opposed to Peace-process between Egypt and Israel neither isolated Egypt, nor weakened Israel. Third, the Soviet invasion of Afghanistan in December, 1979 severely deteriorated the relations between the Soviet Union and the Middle East and Islamic states. Fourth, after the Iranian Revolution and the Iran–Iraq war, the Soviet Union tried to seek a balance between Iran and Iraq, but in vain. Gorbachev fundamentally adjusted the Middle East policy to change the US-Soviet rivalries into US-Soviet cooperation so as to improve the relations with pro-American Middle East countries and maintain the relations with traditional allies. But eventually Gorbachev's diplomatic policy adjustment brought little effect and resulted in collapse of existing Soviet Middle East policy.

Since the collapse of the Soviet Union in 1991, the Russian Middle East policy roughly experienced Yeltsin period, Putin period, Medvedev period and Putin period. At the beginning of Russian independence, Russia went through an upheaval and its comprehensive strength dropped sharply. Meanwhile, Russia comprehensively contracted diplomatic maneuvers. Just after Yeltsin took power, the Russian Government pursued "one-sided" policy of western countries and the Middle East policy was ill-considered. As a result, Russian influence on the Middle East diminished continuously. Russia began to adjust "one-sided" policy of western countries to "double-headed eagle" policy of both eastern and western countries. From then on, Russia has revalued the Middle East and intended to enlarge its influence there. After Putin took power in 2000, Russia further adjusted diplomatic policy and established the principle that diplomacy serves domestic affairs and of national interest first. The Russian Middle East policy was intended to ensure national security. Russia and Middle East countries are separated by sea, two factors which influenced safety of the Russian hinterland were that the USA triggered the Afghanistan War and the Iraq War successively and infiltrated its military power into Central Asia and Islamic extremists posed potential threats. For this purpose, immediately after taking power Putin set about strengthening relations with Iran, conducted economic diplomacy with Middle East countries and intensified energy cooperation with oil producing countries in the Middle East. After Medvedev came into power in 2008, the Russian Government almost carried on Putin's diplomatic policy. As to the Middle East policy, Russia further strengthened economic and trade cooperation with the Middle East countries and the dominant right of the Middle East affairs. Relative to Putin, Medvedev attached importance to cooperation with western countries especially the USA. He stressed on keeping in good contact with western countries and avoiding rivalries with western countries especially the USA under the premise of not damaging Russian interests.

Putin regained the power in 2012 and the Middle East policy still aimed to maintain Russian status and influence in global politics. At the beginning of the "Arab Spring", Russian power over the Middle East was heavily compressed and thus Russia adopted a series of measures for the re-access to the Middle East [34]. First, by the excuse of striking terrorist organizations Russia dispatched troops to Syria, protected safety of Assad regime and Russian military base, rebuilt Mediterranean fleet and cruised as usual. Then, it strengthened the dependence of countries such as Egypt, Iran and Algeria on Russia through arms sale and nuclear energy cooperation. Third, it used the breakdown of the relationships between the USA and its allies to boost the relationship with countries such as Saudi Arabia and Israel. Researchers pointed out that the re-access to the Middle East was primarily aimed at containing and obstructing enlargement of North Atlantic Treaty Organization (NATO), then recovering Russian soft power in the Middle East and finally maintaining Russian influence on the Commonwealth of the Independent States, Central Asia and Caspian Sea [35]. The USA has been the biggest competitor of Russia in the Middle East for a long time. As the USA was caught in a dilemma for withdrawing from the Middle East and Europe, Russia, with an ingenious layout in the Middle East and Syria, voiced support for Assad regime and Kurdish forces in the north of Syria and even its independence in order to scramble for the dominant right of the Middle East. In general, Russian influence extended in the Middle East.

On 23 February, 2016, Russian and the USA issued a joint declaration on a ceasefire agreement in respect of the Syria War, which proved irreplaceability of Russia in the Middle East affairs and after which Russian Middle East policy during "New Cold War" became increasingly tough. Russia had an absolute control over the sphere of influence. Russia counted the Middle East as an important strategic measure to contain western countries as long as the USA and its NATO allies tried to make a big fuss about Ukraine. The core of Russian Middle East policy in 2016 was to clench the Syria crisis and stabilize the Bashar Administration. The Russian military campaign in Syria in 2017 could be regarded as a major military-political success in a sort of way, but the exit strategy remains a challenge [36].

On the whole, Russian Middle East policy of the Putin Administration during "New Cold War" was intended for economic interests and to contain the USA so as to relieve stress from Europe and enable Russia to regain the influence on great powers.

7.2.3 The Focus of European "Three Carriages" Was Different

Several European countries were concerned about the Middle East early at the beginning of the EEC. Since the founding of the European Economic Community (EEC), Europe had participated in regional and international affairs as an economic community. The contents and framework of its diplomatic policy not only were closely related to integration degree, but also was restricted by the US-Soviet rivalries. The EEC gradually formulated and presented its Middle East policy until 1972. Confined to US-Soviet rivalries for the Middle East, the EEC felt helpless. In summary, the EEC's Middle East policy consisted of economic policy and political policy. The former was the most successful policy. Since the EEC just initiated political integration in 1973, it needed to make a uniform response of diplomacy and security. At that time, economic policy was the top priority and member countries carried out foreign trade activities mainly in system construction, bilateral trade, mutual investment, development assistance and arms trade. The EEC's Middle East policy changed with further growth of the EEC and change of the world pattern from 1973 to 1990. Politically, it not only aired its opinions, but also took practical action. Besides, it no longer passively reacted to international affairs but actively proposed solutions. In short, the EEC's Middle East policy considers close contact with the U.S. Middle East policy economically and it was almost a supplement and attachment to the U.S. Middle East policy. As to political policy, the EEC extended the relations only with Israel to with all regional countries. However, member countries upheld different attitudes towards the Middle East policy. For instance, France and Germany took different attitudes towards the relations with Israel. For one thing, in consideration of international strategy, they developed friendly relations and cooperation with Arab States and acted distant to Israel. For the other, they did to keep good contact with the USA. Such differences among member countries laterally reflected weakness and dilemmatic political diplomacy and security of the EEC's Middle East policy.

Upheaval of Eastern Europe, collapse of the Soviet Union, German reunification and Gulf War before and after the end of Cold War pushed the EEC to the EU. Later on, the EU set the target of "Common Foreign and Security Policy", which symbolized a progress of political integration. During this time, the international security situation changed as traditional security threats of the Soviet Union diminished to the lowest and the dependence on the USA gradually weakened. With continuous internal integration and expansion, the EU had intentionally adjusted the Middle East policy different from America's since 1991. The EU's Middle East policy had three outstanding features: First, recognition of the Middle East affairs was deepened. Second, the Middle East policy turned more independent and strategic. Third, diversified and tridimensional measured were adopted. First, the EU no longer made a passive response but actively took actions, expanded simple economic and trade relations to all-around political, economic and cultural relations and observed and analyzed the Middle East affairs at a global level instead of at a national level. Second, it opened the distance from the Middle East policy of member countries and the USA. Third, it developed systematic means such as cooperative agreement and partnership and attached importance to giving play to international organizations, multilateral forces and soft powers and solving the problems using regionalism. As a whole, the EU's Middle East policy during the post-cold war not only maintained stability of the southern EU partly and guaranteed its energy safety, but also consolidated and expanded its market share of the Middle East.

After the "Arab Spring" burst, the EU intended to promote democratization process of the Middle East, rebuild order of the Middle East and enlarged it's speaking right and influence using more radical policy. To this end, the EU countries dispatched troops to overturn the Gaddafi regime, conspicuously intervened with the Syria issues and voiced support for overturning the Gaddafi regime, appointed the ambassador of the "Arab Spring" area and gave much stronger aid to the Middle East, but in vain. With flooding and overflow of the Middle East terrorism and involvement of embattled Syria and Syrian refugees, the "Islamic world" and other terrorist organizations launched terrorist attacks one after another in Europe. As a result, Europe was no longer the paradise of security but a victim of the turbulent Middle East [34]. Moreover, differences of the EU countries in the Middle East affairs exacerbated the imbalance of EU's Middle East policy and had complex negative effect on the unity of the EU. For example, the U.K., France and Germany expressed different interest appeals to the Middle East affairs.

In the matter of upheaval of the Middle East especially the Libya issue, France and the U.K. were main forces of striking Libya and formed "a new military alliance". France practiced more radical policy. Analysis showed that France aimed to gain the dominant right of the Middle East and establish the leadership inside the EU and the status of a great power [37]. The mastery of Libyan energy was an important factor of French policy as well the U.K. engaged in the Middle East affairs as the foremost EU partner of America and for its own interest: rebuilding the dominant right in the Middle East just like France and managing diplomatic and security affairs of EU jointly with France. "Brexit" publically voted and announced by the U.K. on 24 June 2016 undoubtedly diluted the EU's influence and position in the Middle East. In Europe where terrorist attacks took place frequently in recent years, "Brexit" seemed to keep out of trouble, but it undoubtedly made anti-terrorism of the EU more difficult [38]. Relative to the U.K. and France, Germany had different purposes of the Libya issue and military strike on "the Islamic state". In the matter of the Libya issue, Germany refused to take part in military strike and upheld a distinct attitude from other western powers, which displayed the contradictions between the EU and western countries. The same was true of military strike on "the Islamic state". Some thought Germany seemed to send troops outside Europe for the first time to strike terrorism and assist French military action. As a matter of fact, there was deeper meaning. In other words, Germany intended to build an isolation area on the border of Turkey and Syria so as to solve the refugee problem of Europe [35].

Above all, the EU was confronted with tough surroundings and deep internal differences. With the addition of massive outbreak of "Brexit", Syrian refugee problem and extreme terrorist attack in Europe, the EU's Middle East policy appeared feeble and futile.

7.2.4 Disputes of the Middle East Resulted in US–Russian Rivalries

The Middle East has always been the cradle of international hotspots. Other than complex situation, gambling among great powers especially US–Russian rivalries were a major driving force of the disorder of the Middle East. Jin Canrong, an International Relations specialist, said: "Whether the USA concentrates or not, it's destined to be a major player based on comprehensive national strength. Due to geographical advantages and historical reasons, Russia is also a very important player." It's visible that US–Russian rivalries were hidden behind disputes of the Middle East.

After Cold War, due to differences in strength of great powers, US–Russian Middle East policy was regulated. The U.S.'s Middle East policy aimed to seek absolute dominant right in the Middle Right: pursuing absolute security and absolute interest and containing the development potential great powers in the Middle East, especially compressing Russian strategic space in the Middle East. In order to guarantee geopolitics security and maintain economic interests and oil interests, Russia practiced distinct policy and stood for fair, reasonable and peaceful solutions for the disputes of the Middle East with the aim of strengthening the relations with traditional allies in the Middle East and maintaining a positive image in the Middle East and its international influence and standing. Specifically, The USA and Russia gambled each other for strategic interests of the Middle East mainly in Arab–Israeli conflict, the Iraq issue and the Syria issue. US–Russian rivalries highlighted the contradictions of interests in the Middle East.

Take the Syria issue as an example. Since the Syria crisis burst in 2011, social and political conflicts have evolved into a gamble among great powers. For this, the USA intended to resist and contain Iranian influence on the Middle East, protect the interests of Israel, a loyal ally of the USA, guard against employing and diffusing chemical weapons and prevent Islamic jihadists from building new activity bases or refuges using the Syria crisis. Russia also performed actively in the Syria crisis: in consideration of geopolitics, guaranteeing safety of the "backyard"; preventing other countries from interfering or restraining Syria through the use of force; in consideration of military and economic interests, accelerating economic rehabilitation and resuming international standing; relieving pressure from Europe and subsequent effect of the Syria crisis. The USA and Russia gambled each other for the Syria crisis at different levels and in many aspects, including chemical weapon crisis and

Bashar regime [39]. Chemical weapon crisis occurred more than a year after the Syria crisis. The U.S.'s Government accused the Syrian government of using sarin gas on civilians; while Russia denied and stressed that Syrian opposition used chemical weapons. Thereafter, the war of words became increasingly fierce between the USA and Russia. The USA played hardball and even intended to solve the problem of chemical weapon through the use of force; while Russia advocated amicable settlement. After repeated arguments, Moscow and Washington eventually reached an agreement on destroying chemical weapons. The infighting between the USA and Russia was further exacerbated. Although "the Islamic state" was defected in 2017, military strike on extremists in Syria and Iraq gained a decisive victory and America and Russia seized the chance to expand their forces there, which cast a shadow over post-war reconstruction. The U.S.'s and Russian warcrafts resisted each other in the territorial air of Syria immediately after Russia declared to retreat from Syria on December 13, 2017, Russia, which suggested the possibility of a fire. Generally speaking, the USA and Russia transferred the Syria issue to the conference table.

In the matter of "anti-terrorism", both the USA and Russia aimed to strike "the Islamic state" despite of their own wishful thinking. Since upheaval of the Middle East, "the Islamic state" has indulged in wanton massacre in Iraq and Syria; some western countries and Gulf monarchies strived to overthrow the Bashar regime, but touched the bottom line of Russia. Then, the Syria conflict developed from a fight of Russian and the U.S.'s agencies into a complex gamble among government force, opposition and "the Islamic state". Confronted with such a complex situation, America and Russia could hardly control change of the situation and strive for their own interests. As a result, they had to compromise and cooperate in common issues. For example, both stroke "the Islamic state" jointly and Russia was an important strike force of "the Islamic state because it concerned its interest in the Middle East. The Assad regime was an important ally of Russia after the "Arab Spring". Russia stroke "the Islamic state" for the purpose of maintain the interests of allies, causing a substantial impact on western countries and "the Islamic state" and distracting the attention of western countries to the Ukraine issue. For the USA, the rise of "the Islamic state" threatened its interests and it hated to see it. After Iraq War, the USA began to implement and push "the Asia–Pacific rebalancing" strategy and contracted the Middle East strategy. However, the outbreak of the Syria crisis and the rise of "the Islamic state" stumbled eastward expansion and the USA had to turn around again and again. For this reason, the USA and Russia acted in limited cooperation in striking "the Islamic state" [44]. Russia intended to reach a win–win situation of strongly supporting the Assad regime and not joining the western anti-terrorism alliance against "the Islamic state". With a good feeling to Putin, Trump strengthened its strategic coordination in the Middle East affairs and consequently the—Russian diplomatic relations seemed to have been improved. Both countries agreed with ceasefire in February 2016, opening up the peace process of Syria. Trump and Putin make a joint declaration on the Middle East affairs on 11 November, 2017 during the APEC summit with the attempt to smooth their diplomatic relations by virtue of Syria and strike on "the Islamic state" [40].

So far, the relations between Russia and the USA seems to be strained and irreconcilable. Competition among great powers headed by the USAand Russia tensed the situation of the Middle East and its development was deeply affected by US–Russian bilateral relations. The Syria crisis has lasted for over 8 years and the gamble between America and Russia related to the course of political settlement and future political pattern of Syria. Furthermore, more scattered and "fissile" terrorist attacks may happen and it's difficult to eliminate terrorism and extremism, even if "the Islamic state" has been defeated. Thus, the U.S.'s and Russian Middle East policies still will face multiple challenges.

7.3   Regional Great Powers Engaged in Fierce Battle of the Middle East

Except for inseparable interests of great powers in the Middle East, regional countries expect things to turn out as they wish. For example, Turkey, Saudi Arabia and Iran embarked upon a political venture; Syria seems to fall apart; will Israel be able to stand out in the Middle East?

7.3.1   Turkey Intends to Dominate the Middle East

Located in the Eurasia, Turkey enjoys a good geographical location. From 1919 to 1922, Turkey went through "Kemal's Revolution", ended feudalism and thearchy ruled by the Ottoman Empire for over 6 decades and established a democratic republic. After that, Turkey got rid of national crisis and embarked on the independent modernization road. Its social, political and living conditions changed drastically and Turkey stood out starkly in the politically turbulent Middle East. Hence, Turkey tended to build the image of a regional great power and strive for the dominant right and speaking right of the Middle East.

Since the Republic of Turkey was founded in 1923, it has experienced four political stages. The first stage was the radical secularization stage (1923–1959). Since its establishment, the Turkish government has carried out a radical secularization reform on politics, economy, culture, education, law and custom. As to polistics, Kemal abolished the Abbasid Caliphate on behalf of Islam. As to law, the Constitution as well as Civil Law, Criminal Law, Commercial Law and Marine Law with laws of European countries as the blueprint were enacted. As to education, religious forces were eliminated and decrees on secularization and modernization of education were enacted. As to culture, the writing system was reformed. Besides, Turkey also embarked on drastic reform of social custom. The purpose of such reforms of secularization was to eliminate the effect of religious theocracy on national construction and nationalism. Soon afterwards, turkey practiced a multi-party system. Despite of hardships, heads of the Turkish Government were determined to "marching west" and developing into a western country. The second stage was the stage of party struggle and military intervention (1960–1980). Superficially, the founding of the multi-party system seemed to open up the democratic era of Turkey, but the subsequent three military coups interrupted the process of democratization. Complex party struggles were arisen from military coups and military coups were partly arisen from a strong desire for Muslim. Consequently, Turkey began to treat its political development from Muslim's perspective and seeking a foothold of national culture and national identification instead of blindly following western countries. The third stage is the stage of recognition and gambling (1981–2001). Turkey has ushered in the flourishment of the multi-party system and identity politics since the 1980s. In the 1990s, identify politics further developed, but Turkey was challenged by the Islamic fundamentalism and the Kurd issue. It's just based on the continuously deepened differences between innovationists and traditionalists that Turkish political model developed rapidly and the relationship between government and citizens changed. The fourth stage was the stage when the Conservatives held power (since 2002). The Justice and Development Party led the evolution of the political model after 2002. During that time, Democratization reform of the Erdogan Administration and re-interpretation of "secularization" and "democracy" were the biggest political achievements of Turkey and accomplished moderate Turkish Islamism based on secular democracy. Moderate Islamism was mainly benefited from the establishment of democracy and in turn democracy accelerated the development of moderate Islamism.

As a Middle East country with unique political form, Turkey has its own Middle East policy. In early times, the Turkish government did not put the Middle East affairs in mind but wholeheartedly got closer to the western world and focused on developing the relations with the USA and the EU. Nevertheless, this strategy did not work but embarrassed Turkey by hindering the access to EU and challenging "westward" policy. Then, the new party turned to eastern countries, especially Arab States. Since the Erdogan Administration took power in 2003, Turkey has launched such Middle East policies as good-neighbor policy, "zero problem diplomacy" and Arab–Israeli conflict coordination. Under the guidance of good-neighbor policy, the Erdogan Administration actively developed and improved the relations with the Islamic states such as Iran, Iraq and Syria, advocated cooperation in various fields and flattered them so as to rebuild the image in an active and friendly manner. Turkey also behaved actively in coordinating Arab–Israeli conflict. In terms of motive, Turkey and Israel were military alliances and political partners of the USA in the Middle East; Turkey and Arab States were similar in historical and cultural origin and Islam belief. As to diplomatic policy, Turkey launched "zero problem diplomacy", which was another diplomatic strategy after "the Justice and Development Party" came into power designed to reconcile differences from the Middle East countries and expand foreign cooperation. Under the guidance of "zero problem diplomacy", Turkey developed good economics and trade relations with Iraq and other Middle East countries. It has been proved by facts that "zero problem diplomacy" has made a lot of achievements.

After the upheaval of the Middle East in 2010, "zero problem diplomacy" faced severe challenges. The relationship between Turkey and some western countries underwent a subtle change with change of the situation in West Asia and North Africa and Turkey realized a limited upside potential in the western world. The Erdogan Administration sized up the new situation, broke constraints of zero problem and adjusted its Middle East policy. As an Islamic state, the Erdogan Administration used the common language-Islam belief to improve the friendship with the Middle East and Arab countries and then to elevate the status in the Arab world. Therefore, the Erdogan Administration adjusted Israel-oriented policy, launched "eastward" policy and expressed interest and support for the Arab world using the diplomatic policy of being close to Arab world and being distant from Israel. Turkey's economic boom and intimacy with western countries in recent years set "an example" for the development of some Arab states.

On 5 June 2017, Qatar suffered a diplomatic crisis from the Saudi Arabia countries and was accused of supporting terrorism activities and destroying regional security. The international community attached great attention to it and many countries actively helped to address the crisis, among which Turkey performed extremely actively. It not only called for a constructive summit meeting among related parties, but also carried out military exercise in Qatar and gave material assistance to it so as to enhance the strategic position in the Middle East, stabilize the situation of the Middle East and popularize the development pattern among Middle East countries. Besides, Turkey was deeply aware of the importance of controlling energy channels to Europe for the speaking right of the Middle East. "The Middle East-Turkey-Europe" oil–gas channel is of great significance for Europe and gulf oil producing countries. Lacking energy resources, Turkey will hold a decisive position in both the Islamic world and EU once the channel is opened. It's also an important reason why Turkey is determined to become a regional great power.

7.3.2   "New Cold War" Between Saudi Arabia and Iran During the Upheaval of the Middle East

As a great power in the Middle East, Saudi Arabia and Iran have similarities and differences. Both countries are similar in politics and religion as well as economic and strategic position. First, they are theocracies. Then, the petroleum industry is the economic pillar of both countries. Third, they reside vital communication lines of the Middle East and many great powers have scrambled for them over for years. They are different in religious sect and international relation. As to religious sect, Saudi Arabia is the core of Sunni and Iran is the core of Shia; they have been incompatible with each other. As to international relation, Saudi Arabia is a strategic alliance of the USA and Iran is a lonely anti-American country. Since the Iranian Revolution burst in 1979, Saudi Arabia and Iran has kept an instable relationship mainly in a hostile and opposed manner. For a long time, both countries have gambled fiercely for the Iraq War, the Syria crisis, Bahrain's unrest, Lebanon issues, Yemeni conflicts and other regional issues.

After the Iraq War took place in 2003, Saudi Arabia and Iran have exhausted their abilities for reconstruction of Iraq with the hope of playing a leading role. In addition to good location and abundant petroleum resources of Iraq, they pursued their own interests. Sharing a very long border line with Iraq, Saudi Arabia intervened with post-war construction of Iraq to contain the rise of Shia and guarantee domestic security and security of the Gulf area. Sharing a 1200 km long border line with Iraq, Iran got involved in the Iraqi affairs to pursue religious interest, strategies interest and economic interest and make strategic deployment for the Fertile Crescent of Shia. Iran had the upper hand in that battle and Iraq became a part of Shia. On the contrary, Saudi Arabia was marginalized and the speaking right of the Iraqi affairs gradually weakened.

Since the Syria crisis burst in 2011, Saudi Arabia and Iran also have contended for agencies. With a good location, Syria is located at the intersection of Europe, Asia and Africa. Based on common religious belief, historical origin and strategic significance, Iran kept long-term close partnership with Syria, which is the primary cause of its involvement in the Syria issue. Iran got involved in the Syria issue mainly through offering strong military support to the Syrian Government and boosting political dialogues. After the Iraq War, the USA carried out "Greater Middle East policy" and met with opposition of most countries, among which Iran and Syria took the toughest line and were considered as two rivals of the USA in the Middle East. As anti-American countries, Iran and Syria got increasingly closer. The affinity between Syria and Iran put great pressure on Saudi Arabia. Thus, Saudi Arabia strived to come into play in the Syria crisis so as to strike Iran, destroy Shia alliances in the Fertile Crescent and ensure domestic safety. Saudi Arabia stepped in the Syria affairs mainly through giving military support for Syrian opposition and dominating Arab League decisions. Both Iran and Saudi Arabia endeavored to control and exert influence on Syria. With the addition of great power's involvement in the Syria affairs, the situation turned incredibly complex. In February, 2016, the Syrian Government and Syrian opposition were forced by the USA and Russia to declare a ceasefire successively, but it turned out to be a mere scrap of paper. Even though Trump and Putin announced a ceasefire of southwestern Syria during G20 summit on 7 July, 2017 in Hamburg, there is still a long way to solve the Syria issue. In the matter of the Syria affairs, Iran had the upper hand than Saudi Arabia.

Saudi Arabia and Iran also struggled for Yemeni conflicts. With an important location, Yemen is in the southernmost of Arabian Peninsula, borders on Saudi Arabia in the north, adjoins Oman in the east and guards the Red Sea and the Mandab Strait of Aden in the southwest. Affected by the "Arab Spring", Houthis of Shia invaded and disturbed Yemen. Saudi Arabia stepped in Yemeni conflicts for three reasons. First, its safety was threatened by Yemeni forces. Second, the growth of Houthis had a great effect on its core interests. Third, transportation safety was threatened. So Saudi Arabia put pressure on Yemen in the nane of the GCC and gave military support. For Iran, Yemen was a shield to resist Saudi Arabia and Houthis was a major force for expansion. So Iran also stepped in Yemeni conflicts by providing support for Houthis. The Yemen conflicts have warmed up since 2015, especially Saudi Arabia launched an air attack on Houthis in March, 2015, which upgraded the Yemen conflicts to regional conflicts. It was "a fight for agencies" between Saudi Arabia and Iran and the latest specimen of the Saudi Arabia "New Cold War" [53]. In the end, although Saudi Arabia inputted plenty of capital and energy in the Yemeni conflicts, the results were unsatisfactory. In contrast, Houthis was pushed to Iran and consequently Iran reaped the rewards and prevailed.

Iran and Saudi Arabia also competed with each other secretly for petroleum, since both are major oil producing countries and exporting countries in the Middle East. In 2018, crude oil output of Iran and Saudi Arabia was 3.553 million barrels/day and 10.317 million barrels/day respectively, and crude oil export was 1.850 million barrels/days and 7.372 million barrels/day respectively [20]. International oil prices have sharply fallen after risen since 2014 due to global economic downturn, the Shale Gas Revolution and oil consumption demand destruction. In 2017, the oil price hovered at 50–60 dollars/barrel, which undoubtedly hit Saudi Arabia and Iran with petroleum as the major income source hard. Therefore, OPEC planned to elevate oil prices through production reduction. In April, 2016, OPEC and non-OPEC oil producing countries called a meeting on production reduction in Doha, in which Iran objected to production reduction but Saudi Arabia backed up it. Eventually the production reduction agreement aborted. Having been sanctioned for many years, Iranian petroleum industry encountered a chilly winter. But with the re-access to the oil market, Iran advocated recovering the output so as to regain market share. On 30 November, 2016, Saudi Arabia finally made a concession and concluded the production reduction agreement with Iran "excluded". Iran was the only country which could increase the production. Obviously, Saudi Arabia lost out to Iran in respect of oil production reduction.

In short, the rise of Saudi Arabia and Iran has become a "new normal". The relationship trend between Saudi Arabia and Iran gets entwined with regional situation and interest of many countries and "New Cold War" between two countries will keep on and on.

7.3.3 Israel Strives for Stability in the Middle East

Israel is a great power in the Middle East different from other Arab states and it is strong in politics, economy, technology, religion and international relations. As to politics, Israel gangs up with European countries and the USA. As to economy, Israel, whose most civilians are Jews, is extremely intelligent on banking industry and other financial fields and accumulates a great deal of wealth. As to technology, Israel is one of the counties with nuclear weapons and its military technology comes out top in the world. As to religion, Israelis believe in Judaism and are highly united. As to international affairs, Israel not only is an alliance with European countries and the USA, but also acts in good cooperation with Russia and China.

Israel is a "pocket-size" country in the Middle East. After a few Middle East wars, the land area is about 25000 km^2 and the population is 8.55 million, including about 6.38 million Jews. After the upheaval of the Middle East, the Israeli security environment and security strategy faces multiple threats and challenges. Territorial security is a safety factor for Israel. Presently, the negotiation between Israel and Palestine is hampered by the Jewish settlement, Jerusalem issue and Palestinian refugees and all of them are "secondary territorial issues". The purpose of Israeli territorial security is to guarantee national security and control territory of Palestine as much as possible. It's just because of this that Israel is threatened by neighboring countries. First, Arab States are hostile and disallow the subsistence right of Israel. Then, Palestine resists Israel by force. Third, Hamas revolts and refuses to negotiate with Israel [41].

For this reason, Israel actively seeks "protection" from western great powers represented by the USA and the international community so as to satisfy the need for survival and security. For example, America "plays a special role in survival and security of Israel". First, as the leader of US–Israel relations, the USA makes adjustments according to different strategic needs. US–Israel relations changed from serving US-Soviet rivalries to impairing the power of great powers and radical nationalism after Cold War and focused on serving "the greater Middle East initiative" after "9/11". In need of economic and military aid from the USA, Israel most often had to yield to the USA. Second, Middle East peace talks are an important task of US–Israel relations and both counties cooperate and differ. As to Arab–Israeli conflict, the USA is partial to Israel and actively promotes the Middle East peace process and Israel actively cooperates with peace talks to some extent. However, Israel holds different opinions about the U.S.'s interest in this region. The USA and Israel put pressure on each other so as to achieve their own aims. Third, anti-terrorism and counter-proliferation became new tasks of strategic cooperation after Cold War. Since terrorism burst in the USA and Israel was trapped in terrorism, both countries reach a consensus on anti-terrorism, which lays a strategic foundation for maintaining special US–Israel relations. Although both countries differ for interest in different stages, their strategic partnership will remain sustainable and stable in future due to common interests and cooperation basis. In May, 2017, the President of the United States Trump while visiting Israel mentioned to promote Israeli-Palestinian peace talks. In December, 2017, Trump abandoned the neutral position and unilaterally alleged Jerusalem as the capital of Israel, which was another depth charge to the turbulent Middle East and undoubtedly another proof of the U.S.'s resolute support for Israel.

7.4 Impact of Geopolitics on the Middle East: Taking Saudi Arabia as an Example

For years, the political arena of the Middle East has gone through ups and downs and stricken hot discussions. With the addition of gambling among great powers represented by the USA and Russia, it's difficult to stabilize the political scene of the Middle East, which not only hits Middle East countries hard, but also scares of Europe and the USA. With Saudi Arabia, a GCC country, as an example, influences of the endless battle in the Middle East are discussed.

7.4.1 Simplex Oil-Dependent Economy Puts Pressure on Saudi's Social Stability

The Kingdom of Saudi Arabia is a country with the largest population (33.7 million in 2018) and the largest land area (about 2.25 million km^2) in Arabian Peninsula. For a long time, almost economic development, fiscal revenue and social stability of Saudi Arabia have depended on petroleum. In the second half of 2014, international oil prices dropped dramatically and consequently Saudi Arabia faced severe economic challenges. First, economic growth slowed down. Economic growth rate continuously declined from 4.1% in 2015 to 1.4% in 2016. With a continuing slowdown of oil prices, IMF predicted in July, 2017 that the economic growth rate of Saudi Arabia would be 0.1% in 2017. Second, financial deficit scaled up. The oil profits of Saudi Arabia fell with decrease in oil prices. Saudi Arabia has suffered from financial deficit since 2014 and it is scaling up. However, it scaled down relatively in 2017 due to a slight rise. Third, foreign exchange reserve decreased with decrease in oil prices. Thus, it's possible that Saudi Arabia would usher in a political unrest. Some analysts disagree. They think it's impossible that Saudi Arabia would suffer from a political unrest in the next few years. If oil prices continue to decline and Saudi Arabia fails to achieve the expected effect by reform measures, its social stability will be threatened. To solve the economic problems, the Saudi Government adopted a series of measures and practiced "boxing" combining short-term and long-term strategies. In the short term, it will raise funds and enlarge productive investment; in the long term, it will transform the simplex oil-dependent economic structure.

7.4.2 Saudi Arabia Is Trapped by Military Problems

For the need of safety protection, Saudi Arabia is a country with the strong military power in Arabian Peninsula and its military expenditure is ranked fourth in the world. In recent years, Saudi Arabia acted as the leader of Arab region. Inside the Gulf area, Saudi Arabia is responsible for safeguarding the GCC countries as the leader. Outside the Gulf area, it supports Syrian opposition to overturn the Bashar regime, strikes Houthis, organizes the establishment of Islamic military alliance, intervenes with the Syria crisis and gives military aid to Syrian opposition. However, well-equipped and militarily expensive Saudi Arabia fails to win a decisive victory in resisting Iran, overturning the Bashar regime and striking Houthis mainly because of incomplete military system and mutually constrained military departments. For example, lacking an industrial military system, Saudi Arabia imports most military equipment from different channels, so it is unable to effectively integrate military equipment. In spite of a complete chemical system, Saudi Arabia lacks a complete military system. As a result, Saudi Arabia has been long confined to the USA, Europe and other developed countries/economics and had no access to advanced and core military command system. Saudi Arabia purchases military equipment from the USA, U.K., Germany and Italy whose weapon systems can hardly be integrated. Therefore, Saudi military equipment was cast into the shade in a real combat. Moreover, Saudi armies lack practical experience and military departments are mutually constrained. Saudi Arabia has always sought a shelter from great powers; its armies have acted as a costar and rarely engaged in a war, so they are inexperienced in military training and actual combat. Meanwhile, Saudi armies can hardly be uniformally deployed due to strong tribal nature and diversification of factions. Such military problems cannot be solved in a short time and seriously restrict the influence of a great power on the Middle East.

7.4.3   Politics and Religion of Saudi Arabia Are Instable

Saudi Arabia adopts familial politics rooted from the special historical environment of Arabian Peninsula during the pre-petroleum era. With modernization of the economic society during the post-petroleum era, its familial politics took on the new features of legislation, authorizing and diversification. Through the control over petroleum economy, Saudi Arabia controls social change indirectly. In order to gain loyalty and obedience of civilians, the House of Saud practices high-welfare social policy and provides extensive social subsidies to ensure political stability and consolidate political hegemony. The mass movement that happened in the Middle East, North Africa and Arab states in 2011 overthrew the regime of Egypt, Tunisia and Libya, etc. Even if monarchies represented by Saudi Arabia remained relatively stable, Saudi Arabia also had a strong sense of survival crisis. For instance, an overlarge income gap aggravates the conflicts between the rich and the poor and underemployment also adversely affects social development. Again, monarchy is in favor of centralization of authority and political stability, but it can easily trigger power struggle and even internal contradictions among the heads. Culturally, differences between traditions and modern lifestyle give rise to more collisions and conflicts. Conservative and extreme cultural conflicts have potential impacts on the Saudi society in two aspects: conservatism restricts innovation and extremism fosters radicalization.

7.4.4   Saudi Arabia Is Besieged on All Sides Due to External Pressure

As stated above, Saudi Arabia is rich in oil resources but weak in military force, so it is seriously insecure when beset by enemies from within and without. In order to guarantee security and stability in the turbulent Middle East, Saudi Arabia has always turned for protection to western countries headed by the USA. As a US alliance in the Middle East, Saudi Arabia adopted a series of measures, for example, confronting Iran, leading the GCC to deeply intervene with Yemeni conflicts, dispatching troops to Bahrain to suppress Shia, supporting Syria opposition and dominating Qatar "breakoff". As a result, Saudi Arabia was bogged down deeper and deeper in the Middle East affairs. What's worse, due to shale oil revolution and the rise of new energy, the USA reduced oil import from Saudi Arabia, for which Saudi Arabia recognized the relationship with the United States. The solution for the nuclear issue of Iran laterally reflected the essence of Saudi–US relations. Besides, the Saudi government was caught in a dilemma in face of democratic reforms and improvements in human rights launched by the USA and other western countries. Plus security threats from such neighboring countries as Iran, Yemen and Bahrain, Saudi Arabia still faced a tough geopolitical environment.

In cope with changes of domestic and international situations, Saudi Arabia launched a series of significant reform measures in 2017. In the aspect of domestic affairs, the King of Saudi Arabia Salman "twice replaced" the crown prince and appointed his son Mohammed Bin Salman as the crown prince. Afterwards, the crown prince established the National Anti-Corruption Commission in November, 2017 and many corruption suspects including several princes, ministers and merchant princes were arrested. It was later reported that properties confiscated from such corruption suspects and fines will be granted to civilians as welfare allowances. In the aspect of economy, Mohammed proposed "the vision of 2030" early in 2016 of energetically developing science and technology, tourism, industrial engineering and service industry with the aim of getting rid of dependence on petroleum economy. Meanwhile, Saudi Arabia also planned for oil production reduction together with Russia and other oil producing countries so as to elevate oil prices and make preparations for listing of Saudi Aramco. In the aspect of society, Mohammed boldly practice religious reform: establishing entertainment institutions, enriching the life of young people, liberating women for driving, allowing women to watch football matches together with men in the stadium and reopening cinemas, etc. In the aspect of foreign matters, Saudi Arabia continued to consolidate the relationship with the USA and strived to develop the relationship with Russia. Even so, Saudi Arabia still faces many challenges. In the aspect of domestic affairs, massive reforms undoubtedly infringed on the interests of other groups and other domestic interest groups would probably plot a rebellion. Financial deficit and market depression are still economic problems caused by low oil prices and gambling with Iran is still a major diplomatic issue. In addition, Yemeni conflicts still will perplex Saudi Arabia.

7.5 Short Summary

In a word, disorder of the Middle East is the concurrent result of many sides. Both intra-territorial and extraterritorial powers hope to benefit from the Middle East situation, but it is hard to reconcile the differences of interests. Some scholars think "the current situation of the Middle East is a Pandora's box open to a terrible world. It is expanding restlessly and it is difficult to predict the result." Confronted with complex contradictions, the relationship between the Middle East countries, Arab countries and Islamic states is experiencing new changes. In the new pattern, the key to solve the Middle East issue is to unite Middle East countries, Arab countries and Islamic countries as one.

References

1. EIU. 2015. *Prospects and Challenges on China's 'One Belt, One Road': A Risk Assessment Report*. London: The Economist Intelligence Unit.
2. NSSC. 2017. National Security Strategy of the United States of America. Washington D.C.: National Security Strategy Archive.
3. Flint, Colin, and Xiaotong Zhang. 2016. Belt and Road" and Theoretical Innovation of Geopolitics. *Foreign Affairs Review* 3: 1–24.
4. Dong, Xiucheng, and Guanglin Pi. 2014. Energy geopolitics and China's energy strategy. *On Economic Problems* (2): 6–8+62. (in Chinese).
5. Agnew, John. 2003. *Geopolitics: Re-visioning World Politics*. London: Routledge.
6. Adhikari, S. 2013. Modern Geopolitics Versus Post-Modern Geopolitics: A Critical Review. *Transactions of the Institute of Indian Geographers* 35 (1): 35–48.
7. Hu, Zhiding, and Lu. Dadao. 2016. Re-interpretation of the Classical Geopolitical Theories in a Critical Geopolitical Perspective. *Journal of Geographical Sciences* 26 (12): 1769–1784. https://doi.org/10.1007/s11442-016-1357-1.
8. Holmes, J. 2004. Mahan, A Place in the Sun, and Germany's Quest for Sea Power. *Comparative Strategy* 23 (1): 27–61. https://doi.org/10.1080/01495930490274490.
9. Mackinder, H.J. 2004. The Geographical Pivot of History. *Geographical Journal* 170 (4): 298–321.
10. Nichols, Jeannette P. 1920. Democratic Ideals and Reality: A Study in the Politics of Reconstruction by Halford. *Journal Mackinder. American Journal of Sociology* 48: 552–554.
11. Sloan, G. 2014. *Sir Halford Mackinder: The Heartland Theory then and now*, 15–38. Geography and Strategy: In Geopolitics.
12. ADNOC awards China National Petroleum Corporation 8% stake in ADCO Onshore Concession. 2017. <https://adnoc.ae/en/news-and-media/press-releases/2017/adnoc-awards-china-national-petroleum-corporation-stake-in-adco-onshore-concession>. Accessed 19 Feb 2017.
13. Conant, Melvin A., and Fern Racine Gold. 1978. *The Geopolitics Of Energy*. New York: Taylor and Francis.
14. Fang, Yebing, Limao Wang, Qu. Qiushi, Yan Yang, and Chufu Mou. 2017. A Review of Research on Energy Geopolitics in China. *Resources Science* 39 (6): 1037–1047 ((in Chinese)).
15. Lang, Yihuan, and Limao Wang. 2007. Russian Energy Geopolitic Strategy and the Prospects of Sino-Russia Energy Cooperation. *Resources Science* 29 (5): 201–206 ((in Chinese)).
16. Chen, Xiaoqin. 2016. Russia's Foreign Energy Cooperation from the Perspective of New Geopolitics. *Russian, East European and Central Asian Studies* (6): 106–117+157–158. (in Chinese).

17. Li, Zhenfu, and Hongyi He. 2016. Study on Japan's National Ocean Strategy and Change of Arctic Geopolitical Structure. *Japanese Research* 03: 1–11 ((in chinese)).
18. Tian, Qingli. 2017. Japan's Strategic Transformation after the Cold War: The Domestic Backgraound, the International Environment and its Influence. *Theory Horizon* 01: 116–124 ((in Chinese)).
19. Babaei, M., E.T. Mehr, and A. Mousavibaladeh. 2017. Iran's Status on World Energy Security Geopolitics. *Astra Salvensis* 2017: 29–44.
20. OPEC. 2019. *OPEC Annual Statistical Bulletin 2019.* Vienna, Austria: Organization of the Petroleum Exporting Countries.
21. BP. 2019. *BP Statistical Review of World Energy 2019.* London: BP.
22. Wu, Lei. 2012. The Structural Contradictions of Energy in the Middle East and China-Middle East Oil Cooperation. *Arab World Studies* 06: 19–30 ((in Chinese)).
23. The heads of state of China and Saudi Arabia attended the launching ceremony of Yasref. <https://energy.people.com.cn/n1/2016/0121/c71661-28074055.html>. Accessed 21 Jan 2016.
24. Iran, China, France sign 4.8 billion USD gas deal 2017. <https://www.xinhuanet.com/english/2017-07/03/c_136414404.htm>. Accessed 03 July 2017.
25. CNPC withdraws from Iran's South Pars gas field project. 2019. <https://www.sohu.com/a/345424328_505855>. Accessed 07 Oct 2019.
26. ADNOC awards China's CEFC 4% interest in ADCO onshore concession. 2017. <https://adnoc.ae/en/news-and-media/press-releases/adnoc-onshore/2017/adnoc-awards-china-cefc-interest-in-adco-onshore-concession>. Accessed 21 Feb 2017.
27. ADNOC awards China ZhenHua Oil a 4% interest in its onshore concession 2018. <https://adnoc.ae/en/news-and-media/press-releases/2018/adnoc-awards-china-zhenhua-oil-a-4pc-int erest-in-its-onshore-concession>. Accessed 09 Dec 2018.
28. Zhou, Zhou. 2007. The Involvement of America's Middle East policy. *Journal of University of International Relations* 4: 11–16 ((in Chinese)).
29. Wang, Jin. 2016. An analysis of Obama's Middle East Policy. *Contemporary International Relations* (15–20+39+63. (in Chinese)).
30. Liu, Zhongmin. 2017. The Containment of Middle East Issue on Tramp Administration's Global Strategy. *the Contemporary World* 04: 20–23 ((in Chinese)).
31. WEN HUI BAO. 2017. Trump's first-ever foreign visit to the Middle East: Extraordinay Trump behavior. 18 May 2017.
32. Zhou, Ming. 2017. U.S. Influences on Saudi–Iranian Relations Since the Iraqi War. *Arab World Studies* (05): 45–57+119. (in Chinese).
33. Gordon, P.H., M. Doran, and J.B. Alterman. 2019. The Trump Administration's Middle East Policy: A Mid-term Assessment. *Middle East Policy* 26 (1): 5–30. https://doi.org/10.1111/mepo.12397.
34. Liu, Xinlu, and Gang Feng. 2016. The Trend of Evolvement of the Middle East Order and its Challenges and Opportunities for China. *International Forum* 18 (06): 61–65+79. (in Chinese).
35. Global Times. 2015. What are the various figures of main powers on Middle East issue?
36. Vasiliev, Alexey. 2018. *Russia's Middle East policy: From Lenin to Putin Russia's Middle East Policy.*
37. Liu, Zhongmin. 2012. The Middle East Upheaval and the Readjustment of Great Powers' Middle East Strategies. *West Asia and Africa* 02: 4–23 ((in Chinese)).
38. Yu, Guoqing. 2016. Britain's "Brexit" Shocks EU-Middle East Relations. *Contemporary World* 08: 52–55 ((in Chinese)).
39. Qi, Yunyun. 2016. The National Interests of the United States and Russia on the Syrian Issue and their Game. *Arab Studies* 02: 58–73 ((in Chinese)).
40. Hettena, Seth. 2017. Trump v. Putin: What to Expect From the Meeting in Helsinki <https://www.rollingstone.com/politics/politics-news/trump-putin-helsinki-summit-preview-698547/>. Accessed.
41. Yu, Guoqing. 2013. Israel's Security Environment: Changes and Challenges. *West Asia and Africa* 06: 52–63 ((in Chinese)).

Chapter 8
Construction of the China-GCC Energy Community of Interests Under the BRI

Dehua Wang

Chairman Xi Jinping proposed the initiative of constructing "Silk Road Economic Belt" when visiting Central Asian countries and attending SCO summit in September, 2013 and the initiative of constructing "twenty-first Century Maritime Silk Road" when visiting ASEAN in October, both are known collectively as "Belt and Road". The Belt and Road initiative is considered an important layout of our neighboring diplomacy during the new era which plays a leading role in cooperation between China and B&R countries. On 14 May, 2017, leaders of 29 countries and thousands of guests from all circles were invited to attend the B&R summit forum on international cooperation in Beijing, summarizing achievements of the BRI in the past four years and indicating the direction of further deepening cooperation. With a wide coverage and rich connotation, the BRI brings new development opportunities to Chinese energy diplomacy since planning for Chinese energy diplomacy highly coincides with the BRI. Vigorously promoting energy cooperation between China and the B&R countries through energy diplomacy can not only guarantee Chinese energy safety but also realize joint development of regional countries. In May, 2018, Chairman Xi Jinping pointed out in the first meeting of NPC Overseas Chinese Committee "making great efforts to implement achievements of the first B&R summit forum on international cooperation, reaching a consensus among all parties, planning the cooperation vision, opening wider to the outside world, strengthening inter-connectivity, communication and cooperation among the B&R countries, promote comprehensive, practical and stable Belt and Road construction and bringing more benefits to people all around the world". He also emphasized that, "the Belt and Road construction is an important practice platform to promote the construction of a community with shared future for humanity".

D. Wang (✉)
Institute of South and Central Asia Studies, Shanghai Municipal Center for International Studies, Shanghai, China
e-mail: dehuawangz@126.com

© Shanghai Jiao Tong University Press 2021
T. Zhang and D. Wang (eds.), *China-Gulf Oil Cooperation Under the Belt and Road Initiative*, https://doi.org/10.1007/978-981-15-9283-6_8

As energy suppliers along the B&R, the GCC countries are crucial for Chinese energy safety assurance. China has always kept on good terms with the GCC countries and they are in trade complementarities in energy and other fields. With further cooperation between China and the GCC countries, their appeals to protecting common interests and coping with challenges increase. So it's necessary to treat foreign cooperation between China and the GCC from a new perspective. Chairman Xi Jinping elevates international cooperation to the level of reciprocity and mutual benefit during external contacts. When delivering a keynote speech in the opening ceremony of Boao Forum for Asia on 28 March 2015, Chairman Xi Jinping mentioned "the Community of Shared Future" 25 times and stressed that "Asia belongs to the world. To march towards the Community of Shared Future and open up a new future, Asia must advance with advance of the world and develop with the development of the world". Later on, when visiting Russia and African countries and even in many occasions such as UN and Internet Conference, he mentioned "the Community of Shared Future". Obviously, Chinese diplomatic theory has developed from "Five Principles of Peaceful Coexistence" to "Peace and Development" and "the Community of Shared Future" and China has formed a more comprehensive theoretical system and organically combined national destiny and human's destiny. The BRI is feasible to realize joint development of all countries and "a community with shared future for humanity".

As to cooperation between China and Arab countries represented by the GCC countries, Chairman Xi Jinping also encouraged Arab countries to co-construct the Belt and Road and build a "1 + 2 + 3" Sino-Arab cooperation pattern. "1" takes energy cooperation as the main axis, deepens the cooperation of the entire industrial chain in the oil and gas field, maintains the safety of energy transportation channels, and builds a mutually beneficial, safe, reliable, and long-term China-Arab strategic cooperation relationship. "2" is based on infrastructure construction, trade and investment facilitation. Strengthen China-Arab cooperation on major development projects and iconic people's livelihood projects; "3" is a breakthrough in the three high-tech fields of nuclear energy, aerospace satellites, and new energy, and strive to enhance the level of practical cooperation between China and Arab. Xi Jinping suggested to design China-Arabic cooperation at a top level and make good planning for objective and direction. It is observed that energy cooperation is the main line running through China-Arabic cooperation; while the BRI enriches the connotation of China-Arabic energy cooperation and expands the cooperation scope and both have broad prospects for energy cooperation. However, geopolitical complexity of the Middle East brings uncertain risks and challenges to China-Arabic energy cooperation under the BRI. For years, China and the GCC have been in trade complementarities and deep contact in energy trade. If China could establish and deepen cooperation with the Middle East and Arab countries represented by the GCC based on common interests and build a community of shared interests in China-GCC energy cooperation, it will certainly a multi-win measure in favor of joint development of both parties, regional joint development and regional peace and stability.

8.1 Background of Constructing a Community for Shared Interests in China-GCC Energy Cooperation

China and the GCC have maintained steady development and in view of highly complementary economic, trade and energy relations, China-GCC relations can be deepened for a community of shared interests.

8.1.1 The BRI Helps Public Diplomacy of China Energy

Since the BRI was proposed, the rooting of many projects showed its charm and it has become a star initiative guiding bilateral and multilateral international cooperation. The BRI relates to development strategies of many countries and regions involved in the BRI such as "Juncker Plan" of Europe, "The Glory Way" of Kazakhstan, "Eurasian Economic Union" of Russia, "The Grassland Way" of Mongolia, "Global Ocean Fulcrum" of Indonesia, "Eurasia Initiative" of Korea and "Monsoon Plan" of India. For more than 6 years, the BRI has achieved satisfactory outcomes in policy coordination, infrastructure connectivity, unimpeded trade, financial integration and people-to-people bond.

As to policy coordination, China has continuously boosted political mutual trust with the B&R countries and heads of the B&R countries and Chinese leaders have exchanged visits frequently. By late July 2019, the Chinese government had concluded 195 intergovernmental cooperation agreements with 136 countries and 30 international organizations [1]. The scope of negotiation and conclusion has extended from Eurasia to African, Latin American, South Pacific and Western European countries. The broad international consensus on jointly building the BRI is reflected in the Belt and Road Forum for International Cooperation, So far, the forum was successfully held in Beijing for two consecutive sessions in 1 May 2017, and 2 April 2019 respectively. 38 heads and high-ranking government official attended to the 2019, with over 6000 foreign guests joined and 283 constructive outcomes in 6 categories achieved [1].

As to infrastructure connectivity, with the rooting of a group of land, sea, air and network facility projects, the interconnection level of aviation and railway within the B&R countries increased significantly. For example, the BRI promotes the construction of China-Lao Railway, China-Thailand Railway, Jakarta-Bandung High-speed Railway, Hungary-Serbia Railway and others, and these projects has been advanced steadily. The construction of Gwadar Port, Hambantota Port, Port of Piraeus, Khalifa Port and other ports have progressed smoothly as well. In addition, major progress has been made in the construction of six economic corridors. Take the China-Pakistan Economic Corridor for example, 19 projects under the framework of the corridor have been started or completed by late 2018, with a total investment of nearly 20 billion U.S. dollars. By late June 2019, nearly 17,000 China–Europe CR Express had been dispatched from 62 Chinese cities to 53 foreign cities in 16 countries. 99% of the dispatched trains have returned with a comprehensive load rate of 88%. Regarding the aviation, the construction of the Air Silk Road has been sped up, and China has concluded bilateral intergovernmental air transport agreements with 126 countries and regions [1].

As to unimpeded trade, the BRI has made outstanding achievements in trade cooperation and highlights the increase of export and import. By the end of 2017, the trade volume among countries and regions involved in the Belt and Road Initiative accounted for 13.4% of the global trade volume and 65% of the trade volume in the European Union [2]. The proportion of China's trade value with the B&R countries in China's total foreign trade value grew year by year from 25% in 2013 to 27.4% in 2018. China International Import Expo took place successfully in 2018 and 2019 respectively, and a large amount of deal was made. Besides, China has promoted the construction of overseas cooperative parks under the principle of marketization and legalization, to create new tax sources and employment channels for these countries [1]. According to growth of contract foreign projects, the contract value of contract works in three B&R countries increases faster than that in the world.

As to financial integration, financial cooperation and capacity cooperation between China and the B&R countries has been gradually deepened. With a focus on promoting the building of a long-standing, sustained and risk-controllable diversified financing system, Chinese financial institutions have provided adequate and secure financial support for Belt and Road construction projects by releasing the *Debt Sustainability Framework for Participating Countries of the Belt and Road Initiative*, establishing the Multilateral Cooperation Center for Development Finance, setting the Silk Road Fund and the AIIB, and driving banks and insurance institutions to provide financial support for Belt and Road construction projects. By late June 2019, China Export & Credit Insurance Cooperation had achieved and insured sum of 770.4 billion U.S. dollars in the Belt and Road countries, and paid insurance indemnities of some 2.87 billion U.S. dollars; the Silk Road Fund actually contributed a sum of nearly 10 billion U.S. dollars [1]. In addition, RMB internationalization is another import way to ensure the financial support of the BRI.

As to people-to-people bond, Chinese has strengthened contacts with the B&R countries through tourism, cultural and technical exchange, dispatching of overseas students, medical assistance, talent flow and non-governmental and party communication, which builds a bridge for people-to-people bond. For example, China has advanced the construction of The Belt and Road News Network, with its council comprising 40 mainstream media outlets from 25 countries [1]. With over 300 members, the Silk Road NGO Cooperation Network has become an important platform promoting non-governmental friendly cooperation [1]. Besides, technology innovation cooperation and foreign aid are also the key work to deepen the people-to-people exchanges and cooperation.

Energy cooperation is an important part of the BRI cooperation. The National Development and Reform Commission and National Energy Administration jointly issued *Visions and Actions on Energy Cooperation in Jointly Building Silk Road Economic Belt and twenty-first Century Maritime Silk Road* in Belt and Road Forum for International Cooperation in May, 2017 [3], which clarifies the cooperation concept of sticking to openness and inclusiveness, mutual benefit and win–win result and market operation, puts up with strengthening policy communication, freedom of trade, energy investment and cooperation, energy capacity cooperation and energy infrastructure interconnection, promote the B&R energy cooperation priorities of 7 fields such as sustainable energy for all and improvement of global energy management structure and indicates the direction of B&R energy cooperation. The cooperation in energy and resources communication facilities has been intensified so far, China-Russia Crude Oil Pipeline and China-Central Asia Gas Pipeline have operated steadily, while China-Myanmar Oil & Gas Pipeline has been fully operated. The B&R energy cooperation can not only guarantee Chinese energy supply safety, but also promote the construction and avail world economic growth.

First, the countries and regions involved in the BRI is the core of global energy supply pattern. From quantity of oil and gas resources, the B&R is the global oil & gas supply center rich in oil and gas resources. From known oil reserve, 6 of top 10 countries with the largest oil reserve in 2018 were distributed along the B&R. They were Saudi Arabia, Iran, Iraq, Russia, Kuwait and the UAE and their total oil reserve accounted for 52.4% of global known oil reserve [4]. From known natural gas reserve, 6 of top 10 countries with the largest gas reserve were distributed along the Belt and Road. They were Iran, Russia, Qatar, Turkmenistan, Saudi Arabia and the UAE and their total natural gas reserve accounted for 62.3% of global known natural gas reserve [4]. From quality of energy resources, most oil & gas resources in the B&R countries have good quality and are easy and inexpensive to explore. From transportation of energy resources, the B&R is connected to Eurasia and covers a wide area. Whether for marine transportation or land transportation of oil and gas resources, energy safety of the B&R is critical to transportation safety of global oil and gas and even energy safety of China.

Then, the reconstruction of global energy pattern brings opportunities to B&R energy construction and the success of Shale Gas Revolution rewrites the energy pattern. Benefited from it, the USA as the largest oil consuming country, lessens oil import from the Middle East so that democratization of the Middle East will no longer be confined to oil. From an unfavorable point of view, the USA may take a tougher and more radical attitude towards some key issues and even get involved by political pressure or military threat so as to add new variables to the international energy market. However, oil producing countries of the Middle East have to adjust oil export strategy due to the U.S.'s reduction of oil import. It was proved by facts in the past two years that Russia and the Middle East countries such as Saudi Arabia turned to emerging oil consuming markets in succession, which was beneficial to the implementation of the BRI. We can take this opportunity to further strengthen energy contact and cooperation with energy exporting countries along the B&R in order to promote the construction of the BRI and guarantee energy safety.

Third, energy cooperation under the BRI can facilitate to fulfill common prosperity of countries and regions involved in the BRI. The huge market demand of China, one of the largest energy consuming markets, can help the B&R countries with resource development, export and sale and promote local economic growth. The B&R countries are the most potential economic belts in the world. Since the reform and opening-up, China has made great achievements that amazed the world and become the world's second largest economy with comprehensive national strength greatly improved. Simultaneously, China also has accumulated rich experience, talents and strong infrastructure capacity of the energy industry and is able to transfer its capacity to the B&R countries and to overcome the bottleneck of energy infrastructure which restricts local economic growth. The B&R countries suit well with China in the energy industry and are quite willing to carry out long-term and stable cooperation with China on a certain basis. So far, the B&R energy cooperation has made a series of achievements in promoting cooperation in trade, investment and related industries.

Promoting economic growth through cooperation, eliminating barriers through interconnection, increasing cohesion through win–win and promoting development through popular support, the Belt and Road Initiative opens up a new mechanism for cooperative development and common prosperity over joint discussion, common construction and win–win between China and other countries.

8.1.2 Regional Organizational Features and GCC Energy Development Strategy

Located in a key strategic position, the significance of the GCC is self-evident. It is an important cradle of human culture, one of crossing points of eastern and western civilization, the cradle of Islam and a place to which Moslems pilgrimage worship. Plus abundant oil and gas resources, the GCC is honored as "oil depot of the world". Sharing common religious faith, language foundation, cultural identity, political and economic system and interest, such 6 gulf monarchies as Saudi Arabia, Kuwait, Bahrain, Qatar, the UAE and Oman founded the GCC in May, 1981 with the aim of "strengthening coordination, cooperation and integration of member countries in all fields, enhancing and making contacts and cooperation among people of member countries close, promoting the development of industry, agriculture and technology, establishing scientific research centers and joint projects and encouraging economic and trade cooperation among private enterprises."

Since its establishment, the GCC has play an active role in strengthening coordination and cooperation among the member countries in politics, economy, diplomacy, security and military, composing disputes between member countries and other countries, maintaining peace and stability of the Gulf region, promoting regional economic cooperation and accelerating the Middle East peace process and has made progress in the integration process. We can see that the GCC has been the most successful regional political and economic cooperation organization in the Arab world and the Gulf region till now. After 30 years of trials and hardships, the GCC has always advanced, made great achievements and played a unique role in international affairs regardless of difficulties in uniting as one for self-improvement and promoting integrated construction.

Except for monarchy, countries with oil as the economic pillar tie the GCC countries together. To stabilize national revenues, they develop energy development strategies accordingly. In the short run, the GCC countries aim to resist the slide of international oil prices using a series of policies and the plummet of oil prices in the second half of 2014 inflicted heavy losses on their oil revenues. Therefore, the OPEC and Russia cooperated in output reduction after repeated negotiations and consequently oil prices showed an uptrend while fluctuating in 2017. Although the GCC countries could not get rid of "the depression of oil prices", their financial deficit was eased to some extent. As a matter of fact, the OPEC countries have disputed about the slump of oil prices, but some oil producing countries thought that low oil prices would get overinvesting shale oil and gas producers out of the international market and the GCC countries would regain market shares and consolidate international standing. In the long run, economic restructuring is a long-term strategic target of the GCC countries and the fundamental of the GCC countries to get rid of oil-dependent economy. After decades of long-term efforts, the GCC countries have been aware of joint development of service industry and manufacturing industry instead of oil industry. Confined to political system and religion, the path of economic diversification of the GCC is full of thistles and thorns. In spite of this, the GCC countries still focus on development and upgrading of traditional petrochemical industry and related industries and seek cooperation with the OPEC countries and other countries in other fields during long-term development planning so as to lay a foundation for economic diversification.

8.1.3 Historical Background and Origin of China-GCC Energy Cooperation

China has cooperated with Gulf Arab states for years and their brotherly political friendship, long-standing historical communication, complementary needs and progressive economic and trade cooperation lay a solid foundation for energy cooperation between China and the GCC.

Dated from the history of contacts between China and Arab countries, Sino-Arabic contacts have become increasingly closer since Zhang Qian travelled to the Western Regions. Then, China transported silk, chinaware and paper, etc. to Arab states through the ancient Silk Road and Arab states transport medicinal materials and condiments, etc. to China. A great number of the Arabic merchants lived in Chang'an and Luoyang, etc. China imported oil from Arab States early before thousands of years and imported oil massively more than 3 decades ago. The Chinese Government started to strengthen contacts with Arab states after the founding of PRC. At that time, China and the most Arab countries were third world countries and they supported and understood each other for anti-imperialism, anti-colonization, national liberation movement in favor of national sovereignty and independence struggle. In line with the Five Principles of Peaceful Coexistence, China established sincere and mutually beneficial partnership with all Arab states including Egypt and Saudi Arabia from 1956 to 1990. In the end of the 1990s, with the reform and opening-up, China and the Arab states cooperated with each other in politics, economy, trade and technology and established increasing closer partnership. In the twenty-first century, Chinese energy need soared with rapid economic growth. Since 2004, above 40% of crude oil of China has been imported from Arab states. Presently, the partnership between China and the Arab states is deeper, the cooperation scope is wider and innumerable great achievements have been made.

With the China-Gulf cooperation as an example, the development history of China-Gulf relations can be divided into four stages. The first stage was from 1981 to 1990. After the 1970s, the China-Gulf relations turned from estrangement and suspicion to mutual understanding and support and China developed diplomatic relations with Kuwait and Oman successively. After the reform and opening-up, the China-Gulf relations developed rapidly with change of international situation and regulation of Chinese diplomatic policy. China has built a relationship with the Gulf States since it was founded in 1981 and built diplomatic relations with the UAE, Qatar and Bahrain. The second stage was from 1990 to 2004. China and Saudi Arabia announced to develop formal diplomatic relations in July, 1990, which injected a strong impetus to the China-Gulf relations. One of the main reasons for establishing diplomatic relations between China and Saudi Arabia was that the "leading" position of Saudi Arabia in the Gulf region facilitated to build a relationship between China and Gulf countries. Establishing diplomatic relations between China and Saudi Arabia enhanced the influence of China in the Gulf region and served as a model for other Gulf countries. The third stage was from 2004 to 2011. With signing and performance of several trade agreements, China established an increasingly closer partnership with the Gulf states centered on economic and trade cooperation and the Gulf countries including Saudi Arabia and Kuwait became main sources of Chinese crude oil. Besides, bilateral ties between heads became more active. When visiting Qatar in June, 2008, Vice-chairman Xi Jinping met with Secretary General of GCC Al-Attiyah and both sides exchanged opinions about consolidating China-GCC contacts and international and regional questions of common interest. In February, 2009, Chairman Hu Jintao met with Secretary General of GCC Al-Attiyah when visiting Saudi Arabia. Both sides conducted in-depth discussions on initiating the China-GCC strategic dialogue mechanism as soon as possible, building China-GCC FTA and strengthening exchange and cooperation in investment, finance and humanity and reached a new consensus. On June 4 2010, the first China-GCC strategic dialogue was held in Beijing and Vice-chairman Xi Jinping met with the GCC delegation. Both sides signed MOU of the strategic dialogue and published a press communiqué [5].

The last stage was from 2012 till now. Since the BRI was presented, China has kept closer contacts with the GCC countries. On 17 January, 2014, the third strategic dialogue of China-Gulf Arab states Cooperation Council was held in Beijing. Chairman Xi Jinping expressed that "we are willing to make concerted efforts with the GCC to promote the construction of the Silk Road Economic Belt and twenty-first Century Maritime Silk Road". GCC also expressed that "GCC countries are willing to take an active part in the construction of the Silk Road Economic

Belt and twenty-first Century Maritime Silk Road". On 13 March, 2014, Chairman Xi Jinping met with Salman, the Crown Prince, Vice-Premier and Defence Secretary of Saudi Arabia, in the Great Hall of People. Both sides exchanged opinions about cooperation fields, promoting the construction of the China-GCC FTA and hot issues of the Middle East. Chairman Xi Jinping visited Saudi Arabia at the beginning of 2016 and met with the Crown Prince of Saudi Arabia Mohammed Diaoyutai State Guesthouse on 31 August 2016. Xi Jinping pointed out that China was willing to strengthen cooperation with Saudi Arabia in infrastructure, manufacturing industry, finance, investment and energy. Saudi Arabia also hoped to further deepen political and economic relations with China through top-level joint committee, connect development strategy to the BRI and strengthen cooperation in economy and trade, logistics and finance. On 16 March 2017, Xi Jinping held talks with the King of Saudi Arabia Salman and both sides agreed to facilitate the comprehensive strategic partnership to make new achievements. Recently, the heads of China and the GCC countries are still keeping a good relationship.

Generally speaking, the integrated development of China-GCC relations will help strengthen the strategic position of China in the Middle East, provide China with a wider and more stable space for production and development and set up a demonstration role. On the contrary, China will be treated by the GCC countries as an example for reform and economic development and also sets up an example of self-independence for third world countries. With the implementation of the BRI, the GCC countries will expect more from cooperation with China and they can expand living space through enhancing the relationship with China so as to maintain their interests. In future, China and the GCC will take the BRI advantage to sustain safe, reliable, reciprocal, long-term and friendly energy cooperation and achieve the goal of national rejuvenation.

8.1.4 BRI Creates New Opportunities for China-GCC Energy Cooperation

The international and domestic situations underwent drastic change and adjustment in the first two decades of the twenty-first century. With the enhancement of national power and the implementation of the BRI, China slowly marched into the center world stage. The new situation creates new opportunities for China-GCC energy cooperation.

8.1.4.1 Change of Global Energy Pattern Creates New Opportunities for China-GCC Energy Cooperation

Presently, the global energy pattern changes drastically and has a marked impact on various countries. Upon energy transition, energy consuming countries concern most about safety and acquisition mode of traditional fossil energy. The Global Energy Structure Index published by WEF (World Economic Forum) in 2016 predicted the energy system of 126 countries based on safety and acquisition mode of energy and concluded top 10 countries with the best acquisition mode and the highest safety of energy, Norway, Denmark, the USA, Sweden, U.K., Switzerland, Canada, Netherlands and Austria, among which only Norway and Canada were energy exporting countries and others are energy importing countries. However, energy safety cannot be a sustaining competitive advantage. In the energy industry, it is a future challenge to fulfill effective cooperation among interested parties and help various countries satisfy their energy needs in a sustainable way. Moreover, the rebalancing of energy supply and demand is updating global energy safety and order. Particularly in recent two years, a lot of wealth flew from net oil exporters to oil importers due to constant decrease of oil prices. Meanwhile, non-traditional oil and gas resources developed continuously and economy of emerging markets such as China and India slowed down. As a result, oil prices were readjusted with change in energy supply structure. Change of geopolitics, redistribution of great powers and circulation of energy trade brought opportunities and challenges to energy safety of the new energy structure and energy cooperation between China, a major energy consumer, and the GCC countries, major oil & gas exporters, is an inevitable result of energy structure change.

8.1.4.2 Integration Between "Westward" of China and "Eastward" of GCC Countries

In 2002, General Secretary of CPC Jiang Zemin pointed in the report on the 16th National Congress of CPC that the first two decades of the twenty-first century was an important strategic opportunity which China must grasp and by which China can accomplish much. Asia is the geostrategic focus of China. When it was inconvenient to reach Central Asia and South Asia in the past, development strategy and economic interest of China focused on eastern coastal cities and the Pacific Rim. For more than a decade, the Chinese Government has carried out develop-the-west strategy in Tibet and Xinjiang, etc. China is initiating and participating in new economic development projects in India, Pakistan, Afghan, Central Asia and Caspian Sea more actively and terminates Europe via these areas. Particularly, the Belt and Road initiative proposed by Chairman Xi Jinping in 2013 covers Central Asia, South Asia, West Asia and even Central and Eastern Europe. Such "westward" strategy will inject brand new vigor to the B&R countries and more than half of world population will share the benefits from development. From the perspective of energy cooperation, "westward" strategy of China aims to diversify energy supply and reduce risk of energy import. The Gulf region, as one of places rich in oil and gas resources, is the rear area of Chinese oil and gas supply, so China cries for maintaining energy cooperation with GCC countries.

The GCC countries were confronted with complex internal and external situations in recent years. On one hand, the GCC countries strived for more international energy market shares. The Middle East, called "the world oil valve", has always dominated the global energy export market. With the discovery of non-conventional oil and gas resources such as shale gas, the international crude oil market has initially shaped a situation of tripartite confrontation. In the short term, energy powers such as Russia, the USA and the Middle East will continue to engage in a tough competition for market share and consequently potential uncertain risks will be caused to the international energy market. From the energy supply and demand market, the Middle East, Central Asia, North America and Russia are important energy suppliers; while Europe and East Asia are the most active energy demanders. Thus, Arab countries such as the GCC countries with oil and other energy resources as the economic pillar hope to occupy more market shares in the energy consumer market. On the other hand, GCC countries want to get rid of dependence on America and strive for greater independence. America started the Iraq War and carried out "the greater Middle East initiative" in the Middle East after "9/11" and regulated Middle East policy after the upheaval of the Middle East, which seriously impacted the relations and exacerbates the rift between America and Arab countries. Furthermore, the USA and Arab countries began to have disagreements on oil interests. As the largest oil consuming country, the USA started to seek new energy importers after "9/11" so as to reduce oil dependence on the Middle East. With the success of Shale Gas Revolution, the USA pursued "energy independence", intensified oil exploitation and gradually reduced oil import from Gulf countries. From foreign policy, America made strategic adjustment, carried out strategic contraction to the Middle East and transferred the strategic focus to Asian-Pacific region. These policies deepened the rift between America and Gulf Arab states. Being in the dock, Gulf Arab states realized that they cannot just depend on the USA.

To get rid of the predicament, the Gulf countries diversify the economic structure and actively seek new partners. In recent years, they saw a huge cooperative potential with China from the rise of "made in China". China and the Gulf countries can complement each other's advantages of import and export. For example, China mainly imports crude oil products and liquefied petroleum gas from Gulf countries and mainly exports mechanical and electrical products, textile products and light industrial products to them. In order to further stabilize the position in the energy market, Gulf countries turned their eyes to East Asia and "eastward" became the theme of energy market expansion. "Eastward" means to look at developing countries such as China and India instead of looking at China only. In addition to consolidating and strengthening the relationship with East Asia energy consumers, "eastward" also refers to reaching a strategic balance and resisting western powers through strengthening the relationship with eastern countries. For instance, from the viewpoint of Arab countries represented by Gulf countries, China is the only country without political conflicts with any countries, without military bases in any countries and without colonies in any countries. Chinese culture is a kind of introverted and self-contained culture open to the world and a kind of interactive and mutually benefited culture.

Evidently, "westward" strategy and "eastward" strategy are intersected. With the implementation of the BRI and the landing of projects, the China-GCC energy cooperation will certainly be deepened, which will serve as a model for energy cooperation between China and other Arab countries.

8.1.4.3 There Are Many Entry Points for China-GCC Energy Cooperation Under BRI

For one thing, the BRI suits the need of Arab countries for the construction of energy project. 6 strategic objectives have been developed for the BRI. For energy cooperation, focus on the construction of a group of oil & gas, thermal power, hydropower, nuclear power and mineral projects, gradually expand oil and gas import of the B&R countries involved in the BRI, enhance the level of energy safety and boost our strategic initiative and anti-risk capability. This strategic objective not only suits the need of the Gulf Arab states for promoting the construction of energy projects, but also adapts to energy development trends such as rational resource allocation and optimization of industry chain. Many energy experts from the Middle East countries said that it is a wise choice for the Arab countries to participate in the B&R construction, especially deepening energy cooperation, to realize win–win cooperation in economy, politics, diplomacy and social field.

For another, cooperation in new energy other than traditional fossil energy will be a new engine for deepening energy cooperation between China and Gulf Arab states. Affected by global warming, global oil price fluctuation and financial crisis exacerbation, the Middle East oil producing countries such as Saudi Arabia began to develop alternative energy sources in recent years. Enjoying exceptional geographical conditions, the Middle East is rich in solar energy, wind energy and other energy resources. It's estimated that in the case of the GCC countries, power demand can be satisfied by only 0.2% of total land area if solar energy is developed. But in fact, the Middle East especially the GCC countries take the lead in utilizing solar energy and other new energy resources. However, solar energy is far underdeveloped mainly because of immature technology and high maintenance cost. Saudi Arabia and UAE invested a lot in construction of solar power station and R&D in recent years, but they still face great challenges regardless of a certain success. The Chinese solar energy industry has unique advantages and Chinese solar energy enterprises represented by Ruineng, Jingke and CZAlmaden march into the Middle East market. As China-GCC cooperation is further deepened in future, such new energy resources as solar energy will be an important part of bilateral energy cooperation.

8.2 Policy Recommendations for the Construction of China-GCC Energy Community for Shared Destiny

In view of common interest appeal of China and Gulf countries, the China-GCC cooperation is bound to be deepened, of which energy cooperation can be deepened based on the Energy Community for Shared Destiny. To build a China-GCC Energy Community for Shared Destiny, we need to make an overall survey and develop a series of feasible policies according to our own characteristics.

8.2.1 Closer Attention of State Leaders Paid to Building an Energy-Focused, All-Round Strategic Partnership

Abundant oil and gas resources in the Gulf region is very attractive for such a country like China with limited oil and gas output, so she hopes to increase her direct investment in the Gulf region. Meanwhile, China's huge market potential also attracts the oil producing countries in the Gulf region. As such, the complementary demands between China and the GCC countries lay a solid foundation for the mutual investment and trades. The close connection between China and the GCC countries facilitates the mutual investment and trades; in turn, based on mutual investment and trades, the two parties will witness more integration of interests. This will lay the groundwork for all-round strategic partnership between China and the GCC countries. Closer attention paid by state leaders will be a guarantee for the energy-focused, all-round strategic partnership.

In the matter of Middle East affairs, the Chinese government has always upheld a fair, just and pragmatic attitude while supporting the efforts of the international community to solve the hot issues in the Middle East peacefully. Just for this reason, the Gulf Arab states speak highly of the attitudes of China towards international and regional issues, and the determination and practices of China for mutual development and world peace. Along with the increase of China's status and prestige in international community and the great achievements because of peaceful development and reform and opening–up, China impresses the Gulf Arab states greatly with its rapid development and enormous energy market potential. The Gulf Arab states seek to build a partnership with China in oil–gas exploration, refining and sales. The head of the secretariat of the Cooperation Council for the Arab States of the Gulf (GCC) once pointed out, close relations and commercial intercourses between China and the Gulf Arab states are mutually beneficial.

Heads of China and the GCC conducted frequent exchanges in recent years. In July, 2014, treasurer and secretary general of the Gulf countries visited China and concluded Cooperation Framework Agreement on Economy, Trade, Investment and Technology with the aim of deepening energy cooperation. An expert of Gulf issues suggested to build China-GCC FTA as soon as possible. Chinese scholars also pointed that [6] "the Middle East is still the core of world oil pattern, Strait of Hormuz and the Persian Gulf are the focus and the strategic target is to scramble for oil interest and power." which also an impetus for continuously deepening China-GCC energy cooperation. The energy group of China and the GCC had a dialogue in 2005 and again in 2008. In June, 2010, both sides had the first strategic dialogue in Beijing and signed an MOU on further strengthening energy cooperation and actively promoting negotiations about the construction of free trade area. On 17 January 2014, Sabeh, chairman of the GCC presidency and the first Vice-Premier and foreign secretary of Kuwait, expressed when visiting Beijing that the GCC countries attached great importance to the development of relations with China and they wished to establish friendly relations and cooperation in all fields. At the beginning of 2014, both sides had the third strategic dialogue in Beijing, in which they developed 2014–2017 action plan, reached a series of consensuses and agreed to accelerate negotiations about free trade zone and further deepen pragmatic cooperation in all fields. Both sides also put up with jointly developing the BRI, boosting friendly relations and cooperation and achieving mutual benefit and win–win result. On 5 June 2014, the 6th ministerial conference of China-Arab States Cooperation Forum was held in Beijing. Chairman Xi Jinping proposed in the opening ceremony that to co-construct the BRI to build a "1 + 2 + 3" cooperation framework "with energy cooperation as the core, with infrastructure construction and facilitation of trade and investment as two wings, and with nuclear energy, space satellite and new energy as a new breakthrough". In Abu Dhabi Sustainability Week in 2016, Arab states attached great importance to deepening energy cooperation with China and wished to be based on existing cooperation achievements further strengthen cooperation with China in oil and gas exploitation, technical exchange, energy investment and new energy and to make great contributions to enrich the connotation of strategic partnership. Chairman Xi Jinping paid the first visit to Saudi Arabia, Egypt and Iran at the beginning of 2016 and published a signed article in Saudi media titled "both sides should scale up bilateral trade and build and long-term and stable energy cooperation community". This was a new strategy for foreign energy cooperation of China during the new period which was proposed just in the opening year of "the 13th Five-Year Plan" and in the critical node of China's economic transformation.

Nowadays, the Arab states attach increasing importance to establishing all-around strategic partnership with China based on energy, so do the Gulf countries. The proposal of Chairman Xi to build an Energy Community of Shared Destiny with Saudi Arabia accords with common interests of both countries and common interests between China and most oil producers in the Gulf region. Heads of both sides value it and agree that it is an important foundation and guideline for China-GCC Energy Community of Shared Destiny.

8.2.2 Seek Common Points While Reserving Difference and Build a Multilevel Cooperation System Using Multilateral Framework

To build a China-GCC Energy Community of Shared Destiny, we need to seek common points while shelving difference, develop new cooperation rules based on existing bilateral and multilateral cooperation framework and form new cooperation modes.

First, make use of international cooperation framework of the UN. China has always persisted in an independent foreign policy of peace, actively engaged in diplomatic work and strengthened exchange and cooperation with other countries. It not only plays a constructive role in international affairs but also creates a good international environment for building a well-off society in an all-around way, which is inseparable from the role and effect of the UN. As the most common, representative and authoritative inter-governmental organization, UN is the best place to practice multilateralism and an effective platform to collectively cope with threats and challenges. China has stood by the multilateralism in the UN, the most authoritative unique inter-governmental organization, while abiding by the United Nations Charter. In the Gulf region, under the framework of the UN, China has made concerted efforts and contributions to multilateral diplomacy such as the appointment of Special Envoy for the Middle East and participation in negotiation and mediation of related hot issues. After the Gulf War, it expressed active support for the Middle East peace conference in Madrid of Spain, and took an active part in the multilateral conference of the third stage. Besides, China upheld justice in the Gulf War and condemned the Iraq invasion and stood for addressing the crisis peacefully in the United Nations Security Council. China should continue promoting peaceful and stable development with the Gulf region under the UN framework.

Second, make use of international multilateral cooperation organization of the Group 20 (G20). As an emerging developing country, China is a founder of the G20. The state leaders of China repeatedly declared the standpoint and measures for global economic governance, which showed the responsibility of a great power for international affairs such as international financial crisis. Saudi Arabia is a G20 member country and a major member country dominating the GCC decisions. China can use G20 to strengthen cooperation with Saudi Arabia and set up an example for energy cooperation between China and Saudi Arabia. Being an important energy supplier, Saudi Arabia also needs to play a role and has the speaking right in international community especially in global governance just like China. The G20 can provide certain opportunities for political cooperation between China and the GCC and both sides can use it to enhance the speaking right of international and regional affairs.

Third, make use of China-Arab States Cooperation Forum to deepen the China-GCC energy cooperation. The China-Arab States Cooperation Forum was founded in January, 2014 to strengthen dialogue and cooperation and promote peace and development. Since its founding, both sides have conducted frequent exchanges and made many cooperation achievements. The 7th ministerial conference of China-Arab

States Cooperation Forum was held on 12 May 2016 in Doha of Qatar. Both sides praised the 6th ministerial conference and its positive results as well as Chairman Xi Jinping's BRI while hoping to establish all-around strategic partnership in order to solidify international and regional safety and stability and co-BRI construction. After the conference, the "Declaration of 2016–2018 Action on China-Arab States Belt and Road Cooperation" in oil & gas, renewable energy sources, electric power, energy efficiency and nuclear energy was adopted. Since the UAE, Bahrain, Saudi Arabia, Oman, Qatar and Kuwait are both GCC countries and Arab League countries, it's visible that GCC countries also take an active part in activities of China-Arab States Cooperation Forum. Expanding China-Arab strategic partnership under the framework of China-Arab States Cooperation Forum cannot be separated from regionally influential GCC.

Besides, we should give play to related domestic organizations and promote communication with related international organizations so as to deepen the dialogue with the Gulf countries. For example, the National People's Congress (NPC), an organ of supreme power, makes praiseworthy achievements in "parliamentary diplomacy" with related countries. With wide external contacts, the NPC can enrich the development of national relations. As for foreign contacts, the NPC conducts exchanges with senior leaders, senators, special committees, friendly groups, administrative bodies, assistants and local legislative institutions while it forms relatively perfect communication system; conducts righteous confrontations and negotiations, engages in quiet work and communication and exerts a subtle influence; conducts routine work exchange and consultation, accumulates personal feelings and enjoys popular support; conducts official interviews and talks and convenes seminars and recreational and sports activities in different forms; exchanges experience in ruling state and dealing with politics, gives top priority to promoting economic and trade cooperation and acts as a pimp in economic cooperation among enterprises and regional economic cooperation; "goes out" and introduces China to parliaments and politicians in various countries, "invites" more foreign senators to witness the growth of China so as to let them to have an objective understanding of China, and actively evaluates China to promote the development of national relations. Again, official and civil organizations with obvious Chinese characteristics such as the International Liaison Department, Chinese People's Association for Friendship with Foreign Countries and Chinese People's Institute of Foreign Affairs can assist diplomatic services in acting as a special channel in exchange and cooperation between the GCC and its member countries. Above all, such extensive and diversified external contacts just can cope with the GCC and its member countries whose political system, state system and political party system differ greatly from ours and under the guidance of NPC, local NPCs at all levels and other organizations can carry out various activities and promote political cooperation with the GCC.

8.2.3 Surpass Complementarities and Deepen Mutual Contacts Through Economic Cooperation

China and the GCC are highly complementary in economic and trade cooperation and adopt almost all economic cooperation modes such as import and export, bilateral investment, engineering contract and labor and technical cooperation since the reform and opening-up. With rapid development of Chinese market economy and change of international situation, economic and trade cooperation between China and the GCC countries entered an all-around, multipath new era led by energy cooperation and based on merchandise trade. The GCC has become the 8th trade partner of China and it is an emerging market which we are striving to explore. The GCC has invested in oil refining industry, petrochemical industry and even upstream offshore oil exploration of China; in turn, China has invested in oil exploration and production of the GCC. Therefore, a close upstream and downstream investment relationship is good for building interdependency between China and the GCC, which can help China to obtain stable energy supply and cooperate with the GCC in other fields.

In spite of steady economic contacts and cooperative partners between China and the GCC, closeness and priority of economic contacts remain to be further improved. In future, China-GCC economic cooperation will be deepened in the following aspects:

First, to improve the concept of contact. The economic and trade exchanges between China and the GCC member countries for more than three decades, whether at a governmental or non-governmental level, have clear limitations. For instance, governmental planning and guidance considers the advantages of infrastructure construction, but it lacks long-term and systematic follow-up measures. As a result, projects are fragmentized and unsustainable. Similarly, non-governmental economic and trade exchange and activities are immature for a poor understanding of local customs and shortsightedness. Not only is it difficult for related industries and projects to become bigger and stronger for lack of long-term continuous investments, but also they have bad influence on environmental protection and abidance of customs. In future, we must value and abide by the relevant laws, customs and rules during economic and trade exchanges with the GCC countries. First, we should deal with the relationship with royal families, governments and chambers of commerce. Then, we must respect local customs and keep close contact with local residents. Again, through the convening of the seminar and the extension of relevant mechanisms, the Chinese and Arab governments and well-known experts and scholars from various circles have made many positive suggestions on consolidating and strengthening cooperation in various fields, especially in the fields of culture, education, and news. Received fruitful results, for example, the two sides agreed to have established a China-Arab mutual cultural festival mechanism, a China-Arab media cooperation forum, a Sino-Arab higher education cooperation committee, a Sino-Arab language and cultural exchange seminar, and a Confucius Institute.

Second, strengthen cultural and educational exchanges. In the first place, we should respect the diversity of civilizations. The Islamic civilization and Chinese civilization are treasures of human civilization while they have made indelible contributions to progress and development of the human society. Dialogue and exchange between the two have a very long history. Chinese civilization contains great ideas such as "harmony and peacefulness are prized", "harmony in diversity" and "don't do to others what you don't want others to do to you"; while Islamic civilization contains the ideas of upholding peace and inclusiveness. Dialogue and exchange between the two develop with times and meet the need for the progress of humanity. Thus, the Chinese government encourages exchanging with Arab countries in education, culture, tourism and other fields, while she encourages more youthful students to study in Arab countries and welcome the Arabic young students to study in China. The cultural communication not only helps both sides to deepen the understanding of historical and present situations, improve friendly and consolidate the social foundation of China-Arab friendship, but also promotes construction and extension of dialogue among civilizations. The "China-Arab Seminar Dialogue among Civilizations" mechanism established under the framework of China-Arab States Cooperation Forum, which has opened up a new channel for China-Arab dialogue and exchange among civilizations. Through the establishment of the mechanism and the extension of related mechanisms, both sides and famous specialists and scholars of all circles offer positive suggestions on consolidating and strengthening China-Arab cooperation especially in culture, education and media so as to make fruitful achievements. For example, both sides establish cultural festival mechanism, China-Arab media cooperation forum, China-Arab higher education cooperation committee, China-Arab language culture exchange seminar and Confucius Institute. The GCC and its member countries, key members of the Arab world, play their important roles in dialogue among civilizations.

Third, to seek an early free trade agreement (FTA) with the Gulf Cooperation Council (GCC). The China-GCC FTA is the second largest free trade zone in progress of China and heads of both sides attach great importance to it. China and the GCC has strong economic complementarities and huge cooperative potentials. Deepening the reform and opening up in an all-around way during the new era is essential for promoting the construction of China-GCC FTA, is crucial for implementing the B&R cooperation strategy in the Gulf region and is of overall significance for comprehensively elevating the level of economic and trade cooperation between China and the GCC countries while seeking an early free trade agreement (FTA) with the GCC. In other words, the economic cooperation between China and the GCC is more than supplementary based on the construction of China-GCC FTA. Through more than 10 years of negotiation and after its suspension, the China-GCC FTA finally made substantial progress at the beginning of 2016. Re-initiating negotiation of China-GCC FTA is a requirement for economic growth of China and the GCC countries, a need for strengthening Chinese energy import and guaranteeing export safety of the GCC countries, a strong guarantee for constructing China-GCC Energy Community for Shared Destiny, which is an inevitable option under the BRI framework.

8.2.4 Consolidate the Backup Force and Guarantee Cooperation Using Energy Finance

Financial support is an indispensable and important condition for economic construction, and the development of energy cannot be separated from financial support. Energy finance is the mutual penetration and integration of both the international energy and financial markets. It also emerged with the evolution of the energy strategy of the United States and other western developed countries. Since its development, energy finance has covered all aspects of the energy industry (mining, transportation, processing, sales, use, etc.) and all levels of the international financial system [10]. Among them, energy prices are the core of energy finance, and oil has become the most important one of the financial instruments. It is based on this core that the world's major energy suppliers and energy consumers will compete for the pricing power of energy commodities such as oil.

For China, the current status of China's energy security is mainly reflected in the relatively concentrated sources of oil and gas imports, the ease of oil and gas transportation channels in other countries, the lack of free ocean transportation capabilities, the need to strengthen financial support systems, and the need to improve energy reserve systems. To this end, China urgently needs to ensure the security of energy supply and improve its ability to respond to international market fluctuations and emergencies. In recent years, China has recognized the importance of financial instruments such as oil and increased investment in this area to enhance China's right to speak in the international market and its ability to obtain investment returns. For example, China has participated in the trading and investment of some major resource commodities in the international market, covering products such as oil, iron ore and gold. As China does not yet have a high investment profitability in these commodity trades, it is mostly based on passive acceptance of pricing. Finance and energy have always been the two most direct causes of major economic crises. However, China's current investment in energy finance is still insufficient. Therefore, specific plans for the development of energy finance need to be made strategically.

Along the "Belt and Road" involves nearly 70 countries where constitutes the region with the fastest economic growth. The region is highly dependent on energy and at the same time has strong demand for finance, currency and capital. The energy cooperation is an important topic of the "B & R" initiative, and specific implementation projects need energy finance as support. Therefore, combining energy and finance is one of the keys to the success of the BRI. At present, the promotion of the BRI mainly relies on the Asian Infrastructure Investment Bank (AIIB) and the Silk Road Fund as the main platforms for investment and financing. Compared with other well-known banks and financial institutions in the world and Asia, the Asian Infrastructure Investment Bank and the Silk Road Fund have their advantages in terms of capital scale, participating members, and cash flow. Some experts pointed out that the "Belt and Road" is not only an open and inclusive concept of common development, but its financing mechanism should also be diversified. As of 13 May 2017, the AIIB has joined a total of 77 official member countries, and cumulative loans have been issued to support nine infrastructure projects in Pakistan, Bangladesh, Tajikistan, Indonesia, Myanmar, Azerbaijan, and Oman. However, the "Belt and Road" initiative still faces difficulties in financing, such as a large funding gap, a unified demand for currency settlement, and urgent need for innovation in financial services. Subsequent "Belt and Road" financial support needs to be promoted from the perspective of the overall system design, the construction of a three-party cooperative investment and financing platform for banking, securities, and insurance, and financial innovation.

Likewise, energy finance is essential for the construction of China-GCC Energy Community for Shared Destiny. Cooperation with large banks, public departments, private departments and financial institutions of the Gulf countries can facilitate to apply multilateral development mechanism of related countries to BRI projects and to land BRI projects in the Gulf countries and countries and regions along the Belt and Road. In accordance with five development ideas of "innovative, harmonious, green, open and sharing" of "the 19th National Congress", the energy finance innovation system of China-GCC energy community should be built from the following four aspects. First, establish an RMB transaction linked pricing mechanism for China-GCC energy cooperation and set up a fund for international energy industry of China and the GCC countries. The purpose is to facilitate China-GCC energy trade and encourage the GCC countries to invest in the B&R energy projects together with China. The fund also can provide long-term, stable and diversified financial support to regional energy development and infrastructure construction. The second is to innovate the industry-finance integration strategy in the integration of China-GCC energy finance. The "Belt and Road" industry involves many industries, covering energy resources, transportation, hydropower, telecommunications, chemicals, high-tech and other fields. China and the GCC countries are highly complementary in trade. The integration of energy industry and financial capital can further promote the integration of trade between the two sides in other fields. The third is to establish a consultation and communication mechanism for the infrastructure construction of China-GCC energy finance. Financial infrastructure includes complex hardware facilities and institutional arrangements such as payment systems, accounting standards, credit environment, legal environment, and financial supervision. The primary task of constructing China-GCC energy finance infrastructure is to build a unified and convenient payment system. The construction of energy financial infrastructure requires China and the GCC to establish a consultation and communication mechanism, and to conduct full communication and negotiation under this platform to reach consensus. The fourth is to jointly organize a China-GCC Energy Finance Cooperation Forum to build a bridge for humanities and science and technology.

In short, through the joint energy and finance cooperation between China and the GCC, the shortage of funds can be effectively solved, which is conducive to the in-depth promotion of energy projects, and thus provides the most important foundation for the realization of the China-GCC energy community of shared destiny.

References

1. Six Years of "Belt and Road"! 2019. https://eng.yidaiyilu.gov.cn/qwyw/rdxw/105854.htm. Accessed Oct 11 2019.
2. BRI economies contributing 13.4% of global trade volume. 2019. https://eng.yidaiyilu.gov.cn/qwyw/rdxw/89501.htm. Accessed 9 May 2019.
3. Vision and Actions on Energy Cooperation in Jointly Building Silk Road Economic Belt and 21st-Century Maritime Silk Road. 2017. https://eng.yidaiyilu.gov.cn/zchj/qwfb/13754.htm. Accessed May 16 2017.
4. BP. 2019. *BP Statistical Review of World Energy 2019*. London: BP.
5. Jiang, Yingmei. 2009. Emergence of the Gulf Cooperation Council (GCC) and its economic and trade cooperation with China. *International Petroleum Economics* (03): 8–11+85. (in Chinese).
6. Wu, Lei. 2012. The world oil's new order and the Middle Eastern oil. *West Asia and Africa* 06: 23–36 ((in Chinese)).